EROS
AND CIVILIZATION

A Philosophical Inquiry into Freud

HERBERT MARCUSE

With a New Preface by the Author

BEACON PRESS   BOSTON

Copyright 1955, © 1966 by The Beacon Press
Library of Congress catalog card number: 66–3219
International Standard Book Numbers: 0–8070–1554–7
0–8070–1555–5 (pbk.)
First published as a Beacon Paperback in 1974
Beacon Press books are published under the auspices
of the Unitarian Universalist Association

10 9 8 7 6 5

Contents

Part II: BEYOND THE REALITY PRINCIPLE

*   *   *

Political Preface 1966

Eros and Civilization: the title expressed an optimistic, euphemistic, even positive thought, namely, that the achievements of advanced industrial society would enable man to reverse the direction of progress, to break the fatal union of productivity and destruction, liberty and repression — in other words, to learn the gay science (*gaya sciencia*) of how to use the social wealth for shaping man's world in accordance with his Life Instincts, in the concerted struggle against the purveyors of Death. This optimism was based on the assumption that the rationale for the continued acceptance of domination no longer prevailed, that scarcity and the need for toil were only "artificially" perpetuated — in the interest of preserving the system of domination. I neglected or minimized the fact that this "obsolescent" rationale had been vastly strengthened (if not replaced) by even more efficient forms of social control. The very forces which rendered society capable of pacifying the struggle for existence served to repress in the individuals the need for such a liberation. Where the high standard of living does not suffice for reconciling the people with their life and their rulers, the "social engineering" of the soul and the "science of human relations" provide the necessary libidinal cathexis. In the affluent society, the authorities are hardly forced to justify their dominion. They deliver the goods; they satisfy the sexual and the aggressive energy of their subjects. Like the unconscious, the destructive power of which they so successfully represent, they are this side of good and evil, and the principle of contradiction has no place in their logic.

As the affluence of society depends increasingly on the uninterrupted production and consumption of waste, gadgets, planned obsolescence, and means of destruction, the individuals have to be adapted to these requirements in more than the traditional ways. The " economic whip," even in its most refined forms, seems no longer adequate to insure the continuation of the struggle for existence in today's outdated organization, nor do the laws and patriotism seem adequate to insure active popular support for the ever more dangerous expansion of the system. Scientific management of instinctual needs has long since become a vital factor in the reproduction of the system: merchandise which has to be bought and used is made into objects of the libido; and the national Enemy who has to be fought and hated is distorted and inflated to such an extent that he can activate and satisfy aggressiveness in the depth dimension of the unconscious. Mass democracy provides the political paraphernalia for effectuating this introjection of the Reality Principle; it not only permits the people (up to a point) to chose their own masters and to participate (up to a point) in the government which governs them — it also allows the masters to disappear behind the technological veil of the productive and destructive apparatus which they control, and it conceals the human (and material) costs of the benefits and comforts which it bestows upon those who collaborate. The people, efficiently manipulated and organized, are free; ignorance and impotence, introjected heteronomy is the price of their freedom.

It makes no sense to talk about liberation to free men — and we are free if we do not belong to the oppressed minority. And it makes no sense to talk about surplus repression when men and women enjoy more sexual liberty than ever before. But the truth is that this freedom and satisfaction are transforming the earth into hell. The inferno is still concentrated in certain far away places: Vietnam, the Congo, South Africa, and in the ghettos of the " affluent society ": in Mississippi and Alabama, in Harlem. These infernal places illuminate the whole. It is easy and sensible to see in them only pockets of poverty and misery in a growing society capable of eliminating them gradually and without a catastrophe. This interpretation may even be realistic and correct. The question is: eliminated at what cost — not in dollars and cents, but in human lives and in human freedom?

I hesitate to use the word — freedom — because it is precisely in the name of freedom that crimes against humanity are being perpetrated. This situation is certainly not new in history: poverty and exploitation were products of economic freedom; time and again, people were liberated all over the globe by their lords and masters, and their new liberty turned out to be submission, not to the rule of law but to the rule of the law of the others. What started as subjection by force soon became " voluntary servitude," collaboration in reproducing a society which made servitude increasingly rewarding and palatable. The reproduction, bigger and better, of the same ways of life came to mean, ever more clearly and consciously, the closing of those other possible ways of life which could do away with the serfs and the masters, with the productivity of repression.

Today, this union of freedom and servitude has become "natural" and a vehicle of progress. Prosperity appears more and more as the prerequisite and by-product of a self-propelling productivity ever seeking new outlets for consumption and for destruction, in outer and inner space, while being restrained from "overflowing" into the areas of misery — at home and abroad. As against this amalgam of liberty and aggression, production and destruction, the image of human freedom is dislocated: it becomes the project of the *subversion of this sort of progress*. Liberation of the instinctual needs for peace and quiet, of the "asocial" autonomous Eros presupposes liberation from repressive affluence: a reversal in the direction of progress.

It was the thesis of *Eros and Civilization*, more fully developed in my *One-Dimensional Man*, that man could avoid the fate of a Welfare-Through-Warfare State only by achieving a new starting point where he could reconstruct the productive apparatus without that "innerworldly asceticism" which provided the mental basis for domination and exploration. This image of man was the determinate negation of Nietzsche's superman: man intelligent enough and healthy enough to dispense with all heros and heroic virtues, man without the impulse to live dangerously, to meet the challenge; man with the good conscience to make life an end-in-itself, to live in joy a life without fear.

"Polymorphous sexuality" was the term which I used to indicate that the new direction of progress would depend completely on the opportunity to activate repressed or arrested *organic*, biological needs: to make the human body an instrument of pleasure rather than labor. The old formula, the development of prevailing needs and faculties, seemed to be inadequate; the emergence of new, qualitatively different needs and faculties seemed to be the prerequisite, the content of liberation.

The idea of such a new Reality Principle was based on the assumption that the material (technical) preconditions for its development were either established, or could be established in the advanced industrial societies of our time. It was self-understood that the translation of technical capabilities into reality would mean a revolution. But the very scope and effectiveness of the democratic introjection have suppressed the historical subject, the agent of revolution: free people are not in need of liberation, and the oppressed are not strong enough to liberate themselves. These conditions redefine the concept of Utopia: liberation is the most realistic, the most concrete of all historical possibilities and at the same time the most rationally and effectively repressed — the most abstract and remote possibility. No philosophy, no theory can undo the democratic introjection of the masters into their subjects. When, in the more or less affluent societies, productivity has reached a level at which the masses participate in its benefits, and at which the opposition is effectively and democratically "contained," then the conflict between master and slave is also effectively contained. Or rather it has changed its social location. It exists, and explodes, in the revolt of the backward countries against the intolerable heritage of colonialism and its prolongation by neo-colonialism. The Marxian concept stipulated that only those who were free from the blessings of capitalism could possibly change it into a free society: those whose existence was the very negation of capitalist property could become the historical agents of liberation. In the international arena, the Marxian concept regains its full validity. To the degree to which the exploitative societies have become global powers, to the degree to which the new independent nations have become the battlefield of their interests, the " external " forces of rebellion have ceased to be extraneous forces: they are the enemy within the system. This does not make these rebels the messengers of humanity. By themselves, they are not (as little as the Marxian proletariat was) the representatives of freedom. Here too, the Marxian concept applies according to which the international proletariat would get its intellectual armor from outside: the " lightning of thought " would strike the *"naiven Volksboden."* Grandiose ideas about the union of theory and practice do injustice to the feeble beginnings of such a union. Yet the revolt in the backward countries has found a response in the advanced countries where youth is in protest against repression in affluence and war abroad.

Revolt against the false fathers, teachers, and heroes — solidarity with the wretched of the earth: is there any " organic " connection between the two facets of the protest? There seems to be an all but instinctual solidarity. The revolt at home against home seems largely impulsive, its targets hard to define: nausea caused by " the way of life," revolt as a matter of physical and mental hygiene. The body against " the machine " — not against the mechanism constructed to make life safer and milder, to attenuate the cruelty of nature, but against the machine which has taken over the mechanism: the political machine, the corporate machine, the cultural and educational machine which has welded blessing and curse into one rational whole. The whole has become too big, its cohesion too strong, its functioning too efficient — does the power of the negative concentrate in still partly unconquered, primitive, elemental forces? The body against the machine: men, women, and children fighting, with the most primitive tools, the most brutal and destructive machine of all times and keeping it in check — does guerilla warfare define the revolution of our time?

Historical backwardness may again become the historical chance of turning the wheel of progress to another direction. Technical and scientific overdevelopment stands refuted when the radar-equipped bombers, the chemicals, and the " special forces " of the affluent society are let loose on the poorest of the earth, on their shacks, hospitals, and rice fields. The " accidents " reveal the substance: they tear the technological veil behind which the real powers are hiding. The capability to overkill and to overburn, and the mental behavior that goes with it are by-products of the development of the productive forces within a system of exploitation and repression; they seem to become more productive the more comfortable the system becomes to its privileged subjects. The affluent society has now demonstrated that it is a society at war; if its citizens have not noticed it, its victims certainly have.

The historical advantage of the late-comer, of technical backwardness, may be that of skipping the stage of the affluent society. Backward peoples by their poverty and weakness may be forced to forego the aggressive and wasteful use of science and technology, to keep the productive apparatus *à la mesure de l'homme,* under his control, for the satisfaction and development of vital individual and collective needs.

For the overdeveloped countries, this chance would be tantamount to the abolition of the conditions under which man's labor perpetuates, as self-propelling power, his subordination to the productive apparatus, and, with it, the obsolete forms of the struggle for existence. The abolition of these forms is, just as it has always been, the task of political action, but there is a decisive difference in the present situation. Whereas previous revolutions brought about a larger and more rational development of the productive forces, in the overdeveloped societies of today, revolution would mean reversal of this trend: elimination of overdevelopment, and of its repressive rationality. The rejection of affluent productivity, far from being a commitment to purity, simplicity, and "nature," might be the token (and weapon) of a higher stage of human development, based on the achievements of the technological society. As the production of wasteful and destructive goods is discontinued (a stage which would mean the end of capitalism in all its forms) — the somatic and mental mutilations inflicted on man by this production may be undone. In other

words, the shaping of the environment, the transformation
of nature, may be propelled by the liberated rather than
the repressed Life Instincts, and aggression would be subjected to their demands.

The historical chance of the backward countries is in the
absence of conditions which make for repressive exploitative
technology and industrialization for aggressive productivity.
The very fact that the affluent warfare state unleashes its an-
nihilating power on the backward countries illuminates the
magnitude of the threat. In the revolt of the backward
peoples, the rich societies meet, in an elemental and brutal
form, not only a social revolt in the traditional sense, but
also an instinctual revolt — biological hatred. The spread
of guerilla warfare at the height of the technological century
is a symbolic event: the energy of the human body rebels
against intolerable repression and throws itself against the
engines of repression. Perhaps the rebels know nothing
about the ways of organizing a society, of constructing a
socialist society; perhaps they are terrorized by their own
leaders who know something about it, but the rebels' frightful existence is in total need of liberation, and their freedom
is the contradiction to the overdeveloped societies.

Western civilization has always glorified the hero, the
sacrifice of life for the city, the state, the nation; it has
rarely asked the question of whether the established city,
state, nation were worth the sacrifice. The taboo on the
unquestionable prerogative of the whole has always been
maintained and enforced, and it has been maintained and
enforced the more brutally the more the whole was supposed to consist of free individuals. The question is now

being asked — asked from without — and it is taken up by those who refuse to play the game of the affluents — the question of whether the abolition of this whole is not the precondition for the emergence of a truly human city, state, nation.

The odds are overwhelmingly on the side of the powers that be. What is romantic is not the positive evaluation of the liberation movements in the backward countries, but the positive evaluation of their prospects. There is no reason why science, technology, and money should not again do the job of destruction, and then the job of reconstruction in their own image. The price of progress is frightfully high, but we shall overcome. Not only the deceived victims but also their chief of state have said so. And yet there are photographs that show a row of half naked corpses laid out for the victors in Vietnam: they resemble in all details the pictures of the starved, emasculated corpses of Auschwitz and Buchenwald. Nothing and nobody can ever overcome these deeds, nor the sense of guilt which reacts in further aggression. But aggression can be turned against the aggressor. The strange myth according to which the unhealing wound can only be healed by the weapon that afflicted the wound has not yet been validated in history: the violence which breaks the chain of violence may start a new chain. And yet, in and against this continuum, the fight will continue. It is not the struggle of Eros against Thanatos, because the established society too has its Eros: it protects, perpetuates, and enlarges life. And it is not a bad life for those who comply and repress. But in the balance, the general presumption is that aggressiveness in defense of life is less detrimental to the Life Instincts than aggressiveness in aggression.

In defense of life: the phrase has explosive meaning in the affluent society. It involves not only the protest against neo-colonial war and slaughter, the burning of draft cards at the risk of prison, the fight for civil rights, but also the refusal to speak the dead language of affluence, to wear the clean clothes, to enjoy the gadgets of affluence, to go through the education for affluence. The new bohème, the beatniks and hipsters, the peace creeps — all these " decadents " now have become what decadence probably always was: poor refuge of defamed humanity.

Can we speak of a juncture between the erotic and political dimension?

In and against the deadly efficient organization of the affluent society, not only radical protest, but even the attempt to formulate, to articulate, to give word to protest assume a childlike, ridiculous immaturity. Thus it is ridiculous and perhaps "logical" that the Free Spech Movement at Berkeley terminated in the row caused by the appearance of a sign with the four-letter word. It is perhaps equally ridiculous and right to see deeper significance in the buttons worn by some of the demonstrators (among them infants) against the slaughter in Vietnam: MAKE LOVE, NOT WAR. On the other side, against the new youth who refuse and rebel, are the representatives of the old order who can no longer protect its life without sacrificing it in the work of destruction and waste and pollution. They now include the representatives of organized labor — correctly so to the extent to which employment within the capitalist prosperity depends on the continued defense of the established social system.

Can the outcome, for the near future, be in doubt? The people, the majority of the people in the affluent society, are on the side of that which is — not that which can and ought to be. And the established order is strong enough and efficient enough to justify this adherence and to assure its continuation. However, the very strength and efficiency of this order may become factors of disintegration. Perpetuation of the obsolescent need for full-time labor (even in a very reduced form) will require the increasing waste of resources, the creation of ever more unnecessary jobs and services, and the growth of the military or destructive sector. Escalated wars, permanent preparation for war, and total administration may well suffice to keep the people under control, but at the cost of altering the morality on which the society still depends. Technical progress, itself a necessity for the maintenance of the established society, fosters needs and faculties which are antagonistic to the social organization of labor on which the system is built. In the course of automation, the value of the social product is to an increasingly smaller degree determined by the labor time necessary for its production. Consequently, the real social need for productive labor declines, and the vacuum must be filled with unproductive activities. An ever larger amount of the work actually performed becomes superfluous, expendable, meaningless. Although these activities can be sustained and even multiplied under total administration, there seems to exist an upper limit to their augmentation.

This limit would be reached when the surplus value created by productive labor no longer suffices to pay for non-production work. A progressive reduction of labor seems to be inevitable, and for this eventuality, the system has to provide for occupation without work; it has to develop needs which transcend the market economy and may even be incompatible with it.

The affluent society is in its own way preparing for this eventuality by organizing "the desire for beauty and the hunger for community," the renewal of the "contact with nature," the enrichment of the mind, and honors for "creation for its own sake." The false ring of such proclamations is indicative of the fact that, within the established system, these aspirations are translated into administered cultural activities, sponsored by the government and the big corporations — an extension of their executive arm into the soul of the masses. It is all but impossible to recognize in the aspirations thus defined those of Eros and its autonomous transformation of a repressive environment and a repressive existence. If these goals are to be satisfied without an irreconcilable conflict with the requirements of the market economy, they must be satisfied within the framework of commerce and profit. But this sort of satisfaction would be tantamount to denial, for the erotic energy of the Life Instincts cannot be freed under the dehumanizing conditions of profitable affluence. To be sure, the conflict between the necessary development of noneconomic needs which would validate the idea of the abolition of labor (life as an end in itself) on the one hand, and the necessity for maintaining the need for earning a living on the other is quite manageable (especially as long as the Enemy within and without can serve as propelling force behind the defense of the status quo). However, the conflict may become explosive if it is accompanied and aggravated by the prospective changes at the very base of advanced industrial society, namely, the gradual undermining of capitalist enterprise in the course of automation.

In the meantime, there are things to be done. The system has its weakest point where it shows its most brutal strength: in the escalation of its military potential (which seems to press for periodic actualization with ever shorter interruptions of peace and preparedness). This tendency seems reversible only under strongest pressure, and its reversal would open the danger spots in the social structure: its conversion into a "normal" capitalist system is hardly imaginable without a serious crisis and sweeping economic and political changes. Today, the opposition to war and military intervention strikes at the roots: it rebels against those whose economic and political dominion depends on the continued (and enlarged) reproduction of the military establishment, its "multipliers," and the policies which necessitate this reproduction. These interests are not hard to identify, and the war against them does not require missiles, bombs, and napalm. But it does require something that is much harder to produce — the spread of uncensored and unmanipulated knowledge, consciousness, and above all, the organized refusal to continue work on the material and *intellectual* instruments which are now being used against man — for the defense of the liberty and prosperity of those who dominate the rest.

To the degree to which organized labor operates in defense of the status quo, and to the degree to which the share of labor in the material process of production declines, *intellectual* skills and capabilities become social and political factors. Today, the organized refusal to cooperate of the scientists, mathematicians, technicians, industrial psychologists and public opinion pollsters may well accomplish what a strike, even a large-scale strike, can no longer accomplish but once accomplished, namely, the beginning of the reversal, the preparation of the ground for political action. That the idea appears utterly unrealistic does not reduce the political responsibility involved in the position and function of the intellectual in contemporary industrial society. The intellectual refusal may find support in another catalyst, the instinctual refusal among the youth in protest. It is their lives which are at stake, and if not their lives, their mental health and their capacity to function as unmutilated humans. Their protest will continue because it is a biological necessity. "By nature," the young are in the forefront of those who live and fight for Eros against Death, and against a civilization which strives to shorten the "detour to death" while controlling the means for lengthening the detour. But in the administered society, the biological necessity does not immediately issue in action; organization demands counter-organization. Today the fight for life, the fight for Eros, is the *political* fight.

Preface to First Edition

This essay employs psychological categories because they have become political categories. The traditional border-lines between psychology on the one side and political and social philosophy on the other have been made obsolete by the condition of man in the present era: formerly autono-mous and identifiable psychical processes are being absorbed by the function of the individual in the state — by his pub-lic existence. Psychological problems therefore turn into political problems: private disorder reflects more directly than before the disorder of the whole, and the cure of per-sonal disorder depends more directly than before on the cure of the general disorder. The era tends to be totali-tarian even where it has not produced totalitarian states. Psychology could be elaborated and practiced as a special discipline as long as the psyche could sustain itself against the public power, as long as privacy was real, really desired, and self-shaped; if the individual has neither the ability nor the possibility to be for himself, the terms of psychology be-come the terms of the societal forces which define the psy-che. Under these circumstances, applying psychology in the analysis of social and political events means taking an approach which has been vitiated by these very events. The task is rather the opposite: to develop the political and sociological substance of the psychological notions.

I have tried to reformulate certain basic questions and to follow them in a direction not yet fully explored. I am aware of the tentative character of this inquiry and hope to discuss some of the problems, especially those of an aesthetic theory, more adequately in the near future.

The ideas developed in this book were first presented in a series of lectures at the Washington School of Psychiatry in 1950–51. I wish to thank Mr. Joseph Borkin of Washington, who encouraged me to write this book. I am deeply grateful to Professors Clyde Kluckhohn and Barrington Moore, Jr., of Harvard University, and to Doctors Henry and Yela Loewenfeld of New York, who have read the manuscript and offered valuable suggestions and criticism. For the content of this essay, I take the sole responsibility. As to my theoretical position, I am indebted to my friend Professor Max Horkheimer and to his collaborators at the Institute of Social Research, now in Frankfurt.

H. M.

Introduction

Sigmund Freud's proposition that civilization is based on the permanent subjugation of the human instincts has been taken for granted. His question whether the suffering thereby inflicted upon individuals has been worth the benefits of culture has not been taken too seriously — the less so since Freud himself considered the process to be inevitable and irreversible. Free gratification of man's instinctual needs is incompatible with civilized society: renunciation and delay in satisfaction are the prerequisites of progress. "Happiness," said Freud, "is no cultural value." Happiness must be subordinated to the discipline of work as full-time occupation, to the discipline of monogamic reproduction, to the established system of law and order. The methodical sacrifice of libido, its rigidly enforced deflection to socially useful activities and expressions, *is* culture.

The sacrifice has paid off well: in the technically advanced areas of civilization, the conquest of nature is practically complete, and more needs of a greater number of people are fulfilled than ever before. Neither the mechanization and standardization of life, nor the mental impoverishment, nor the growing destructiveness of present-day progress provides sufficient ground for questioning the "principle" which has governed the progress of Western civilization. The continual increase of productivity makes constantly more realistic the promise of an even better life for all.

However, intensified progress seems to be bound up with intensified unfreedom. Throughout the world of industrial civilization, the domination of man by man is growing in scope and efficiency. Nor does this trend appear as an incidental, transitory regression on the road to progress. Concentration camps, mass exterminations, world wars, and atom bombs are no " relapse into barbarism," but the unrepressed implementation of the achievements of modern science, technology, and domination. And the most effective subjugation and destruction of man by man takes place at the height of civilization, when the material and intellectual attainments of mankind seem to allow the creation of a truly free world.

These negative aspects of present-day culture may well indicate the obsolescence of established institutions and the emergence of new forms of civilization: repressiveness is perhaps the more vigorously maintained the more unnecessary it becomes. If it must indeed belong to the essence of civilization as such, then Freud's question as to the price of civilization would be meaningless — for there would be no alternative.

But Freud's own theory provides reasons for rejecting his identification of civilization with repression. On the ground of his own theoretical achievements, the discussion of the problem must be reopened. Does the interrelation between freedom and repression, productivity and destruction, domination and progress, really constitute the principle of civilization? Or does this interrelation result only from a specific historical organization of human existence? In Freudian terms, is the conflict between pleasure principle and reality principle irreconcilable to such a degree that it necessitates the repressive transformation of man's instinctual structure? Or does it allow the concept of a non-repressive civilization, based on a fundamentally different experience of being, a fundamentally different relation between man and nature, and fundamentally different existential relations?

The notion of a non-repressive civilization will be discussed not as an abstract and utopian speculation. We believe that the discussion is justified on two concrete and realistic grounds: first, Freud's theoretical conception itself seems to refute his consistent denial of the historical possibility of a non-repressive civilization, and, second, the very achievements of repressive civilization seem to create the preconditions for the gradual abolition of repression. To elucidate these grounds, we shall try to reinterpret Freud's theoretical conception in terms of its own socio-historical content.

This procedure implies opposition to the revisionist Neo-Freudian schools. In contrast to the revisionists, I believe that Freud's theory is in its very substance " sociological," [1] and that no new cultural or sociological orientation is needed to reveal this substance. Freud's " biologism " is

[1] For a discussion of the sociological character of psychoanalytic concepts, see Heinz Hartmann, " The Application of Psychoanalytic Concepts to Social Science," in *Psychoanalytic Quarterly*, Vol. XIX, No. 3 (1950). Clyde Kluckhohn, *Mirror for Man* (New York: McGraw-Hill, 1949); and Heinz Hartmann, Ernst Kris, and Rudolph M. Lowenstein, " Some Psychoanalytic Comments on ' Culture and Personality,' " in *Psychoanalysis and Culture: Essays in Honor of Géza Róheim* (New York: International Universities Press, 1951).

social theory in a depth dimension that has been consistently flattened out by the Neo-Freudian schools. In shifting the emphasis from the unconscious to the conscious, from the biological to the cultural factors, they cut off the roots of society in the instincts and instead take society at the level on which it confronts the individual as his ready-made " environment," without questioning its origin and legitimacy. The Neo-Freudian analysis of this environment thus succumbs to the mystification of societal relations, and their critique moves only within the firmly sanctioned and well-protected sphere of established institutions. Consequently, the Neo-Freudian critique remains in a strict sense ideological: it has no conceptual basis outside the established system; most of its critical ideas and values are those provided by the system. Idealistic morality and religion celebrate their happy resurrection: the fact that they are embellished with the vocabulary of the very psychology that originally refuted their claim ill conceals their identity with officially desired and advertised attitudes.[2] Moreover, we believe that the most concrete insights into the historical structure of civilization are contained precisely in the concepts that the revisionists reject. Almost the entire Freudian metapsychology, his late theory of the instincts, his reconstruction of the prehistory of mankind belong to these concepts. Freud himself treated them as mere working hypotheses, helpful in elucidating certain obscurities, in establishing tentative links between theoretically unconnected

[2] For a more specific discussion of Neo-Freudian revisionism, see the Epilogue below.

insights — always open to correction, and to be discarded if they no longer facilitated the progress of psychoanalytic theory and practice. In the post-Freudian development of psychoanalysis, this metapsychology has been almost entirely eliminated. As psychoanalysis has become socially and scientifically respectable, it has freed itself from compromising speculations. Compromising they were, indeed, in more than one sense: not only did they transcend the realm of clinical observation and therapeutic usefulness, but also they interpreted man in terms far more offensive to social taboos than Freud's earlier " pan-sexualism " — terms that revealed the explosive basis of civilization. The subsequent discussion will try to apply the tabooed insights of psychoanalysis (tabooed even in psychoanalysis itself) to an interpretation of the basic trends of civilization.

The purpose of this essay is to contribute to the *philosophy* of psychoanalysis — not to psychoanalysis itself. It moves exclusively in the field of theory, and it keeps outside the technical discipline which psychoanalysis has become. Freud developed a theory of man, a " psycho-logy " in the strict sense. With this theory, Freud placed himself in the great tradition of philosophy and under philosophical criteria. Our concern is not with a corrected or improved interpretation of Freudian concepts but with their philosophical and sociological implications. Freud conscientiously distinguished his philosophy from his science; the Neo-Freudians have denied most of the former. On therapeutic grounds, such a denial may be perfectly justified. However, no therapeutic argument should hamper the development of a theoretical construction which aims, not at curing individual sickness, but at diagnosing the general disorder.

A few preliminary explanations of terms are necessary:

" Civilization " is used interchangeably with " culture " — as in Freud's *Civilization and Its Discontents*.

"Repression," and "repressive" are used in the non-technical sense to designate both conscious and unconscious, external and internal processes of restraint, constraint, and suppression.

"Instinct," in accordance with Freud's notion of *Trieb*, refers to primary "drives" of the human organism which are subject to *historical* modification; they find mental as well as somatic representation.

PART ONE

UNDER THE RULE OF THE REALITY PRINCIPLE

CHAPTER ONE

The Hidden Trend in Psychoanalysis

The concept of man that emerges from Freudian theory is the most irrefutable indictment of Western civilization — and at the same time the most unshakable defense of this civilization. According to Freud, the history of man is the history of his repression. Culture constrains not only his societal but also his biological existence, not only parts of the human being but his instinctual structure itself. However, such constraint is the very precondition of progress. Left free to pursue their natural objectives, the basic instincts of man would be incompatible with all lasting association and preservation: they would destroy even where they unite. The uncontrolled Eros is just as fatal as his deadly counterpart, the death instinct. Their destructive force derives from the fact that they strive for a gratification which culture cannot grant: gratification as such and as an end in itself, at any moment. The instincts must therefore be deflected from their goal, inhibited in their aim. Civilization begins when the primary objective — namely, integral satisfaction of needs — is effectively renounced.

The vicissitudes of the instincts are the vicissitudes of the mental apparatus in civilization. The animal drives become human instincts under the influence of the external reality. Their original "location" in the organism and their basic direction remain the same, but their objectives and their manifestations are subject to change. All psycho-analytic concepts (sublimation, identification, projection, repression, introjection) connote the mutability of the instincts. But the reality which shapes the instincts as well as their needs and satisfaction is a socio-historical world. The animal man becomes a human being only through a fundamental transformation of his nature, affecting not only the instinctual aims but also the instinctual "values" — that is, the principles that govern the attainment of the aims. The change in the governing value system may be tentatively defined as follows:

from:	to:
immediate satisfaction	delayed satisfaction
pleasure	restraint of pleasure
joy (play)	toil (work)
receptiveness	productiveness
absence of repression	security

Freud described this change as the transformation of the *pleasure principle* into the *reality principle*. The interpretation of the "mental apparatus" in terms of these two principles is basic to Freud's theory and remains so in spite of all modifications of the dualistic conception. It corresponds largely (but not entirely) to the distinction between unconscious and conscious processes. The individual exists, as it were, in two different dimensions, characterized by different mental processes and principles. The difference between these two dimensions is a genetic-historical as well as a structural one: the unconscious, ruled by the pleasure principle, comprises " the older, primary processes, the residues of a phase of development in which they were the only kind of mental processes." They strive for nothing but for " gaining pleasure; from any operation which might arouse unpleasantness ('pain') mental activity draws back."[1] But the unrestrained pleasure principle comes into conflict with the natural and human environment. The individual comes to the traumatic realization that full and painless gratification of his needs is impossible. And after this experience of disappointment, a new principle of mental functioning gains ascendancy. The reality principle supersedes the pleasure principle: man learns to give up momentary, uncertain, and destructive pleasure for delayed, restrained, but " assured " pleasure.[2] Because of this lasting gain through renunciation and restraint, according to Freud, the reality principle " safeguards " rather than " dethrones," " modifies " rather than denies, the pleasure principle.

However, the psychoanalytic interpretation reveals that the reality principle enforces a change not only in the form and timing of pleasure but in its very substance. The adjustment of pleasure to the reality principle implies the subjugation and diversion of the destructive force of instinctual gratification, of its incompatibility with the established societal norms and relations, and, by that token, implies the transubstantiation of pleasure itself.

[1] " Formulations Regarding the Two Principles in Mental Functioning," in *Collected Papers* (London: Hogarth Press, 1950), IV, 14. Quotations are used by permission of the publisher.
[2] *Ibid.*, p. 18.

With the establishment of the reality principle, the human being which, under the pleasure principle, has been hardly more than a bundle of animal drives, has become an organized ego. It strives for "what is useful" and what can be obtained without damage to itself and to its vital environment. Under the reality principle, the human being develops the function of *reason:* it learns to "test" the reality, to distinguish between good and bad, true and false, useful and harmful. Man acquires the faculties of attention, memory, and judgment. He becomes a conscious, thinking *subject,* geared to a rationality which is imposed upon him from outside. Only one mode of thought-activity is "split off" from the new organization of the mental apparatus and remains free from the rule of the reality principle: *phantasy* is "protected from cultural alterations" and stays committed to the pleasure principle. Otherwise, the mental apparatus is effectively subordinated to the reality principle. The function of "motor discharge," which, under the supremacy of the pleasure principle, had "served to unburden the mental apparatus of accretions of stimuli," is now employed in the "appropriate alteration of reality": it is converted into *action.*[3]

The scope of man's desires and the instrumentalities for their gratification are thus immeasurably increased, and his ability to alter reality consciously in accordance with "what is useful" seems to promise a gradual removal of extraneous barriers to his gratification. However, neither his desires nor his alteration of reality are henceforth his own: they are now "organized" by his society. And this "organization"

[3] *Ibid.,* p. 16.

represses and transubstantiates his original instinctual needs. If absence from repression is the archetype of freedom, then civilization is the struggle against this freedom.

The replacement of the pleasure principle by the reality principle is the great traumatic event in the development of man — in the development of the genus (phylogenesis) as well as of the individual (ontogenesis). According to Freud, this event is not unique but recurs throughout the history of mankind and of every individual. Phylogenetically, it occurs first in the *primal horde*, when the *primal father* monopolizes power and pleasure and enforces renunciation on the part of the sons. Ontogenetically, it occurs during the period of early childhood, and submission to the reality principle is enforced by the parents and other educators. But, both on the generic and on the individual level, submission is continuously reproduced. The rule of the primal father is followed, after the first rebellion, by the rule of the sons, and the brother clan develops into institutionalized social and political domination. The reality principle materializes in a system of institutions. And the individual, growing up within such a system, learns the requirements of the reality principle as those of law and order, and transmits them to the next generation.

The fact that the reality principle has to be re-established continually in the development of man indicates that its triumph over the pleasure principle is never complete and never secure. In the Freudian conception, civilization does not once and for all terminate a " state of nature." What civilization masters and represses — the claim of the pleasure principle — continues to exist in civilization itself. The unconscious retains the objectives of the defeated pleasure principle. Turned back by the external reality or even unable to reach it, the full force of the pleasure principle not only survives in the unconscious but also affects in manifold ways the very reality which has superseded the pleasure principle. The *return of the repressed* makes up the tabooed and subterranean history of civilization. And the exploration of this history reveals not only the secret of the individual but also that of civilization. Freud's individual psychology is in its very essence social psychology. Repression is a historical phenomenon. The effective subjugation of the instincts to repressive controls is imposed not by nature but by man. The primal father, as the archetype of domination, initiates the chain reaction of enslavement, rebellion, and reinforced domination which marks the history of civilization. But ever since the first, prehistoric restoration of domination following the first rebellion, repression from without has been supported by repression from within: the unfree individual introjects his masters and their commands into his own mental apparatus. The struggle against freedom reproduces itself in the psyche of man, as the self-repression of the repressed individual, and his self-repression in turn sustains his masters and their institutions. It is this mental dynamic which Freud unfolds as the dynamic of civilization.

According to Freud, the repressive modification of the instincts under the reality principle is enforced and sustained by the " eternal primordial struggle for existence, . . . persisting to the present day." Scarcity (*Lebensnot*, Ananke) teaches men that they cannot freely gratify their instinctual impulses, that they cannot live under the pleasure principle. Society's motive in enforcing the decisive modification of the instinctual structure is thus " economic; since it has not means enough to support life for its members without work on their part, it must see to it that the number of these members is restricted and their energies directed away from sexual activities on to their work." [4]

This conception is as old as civilization and has always provided the most effective rationalization for repression. To a considerable extent, Freud's theory partakes of this rationalization: Freud considers the " primordial struggle for existence " as " eternal " and therefore believes that the pleasure principle and the reality principle are " eternally " antagonistic. The notion that a non-repressive civilization is impossible is a cornerstone of Freudian theory. However, his theory contains elements that break through this rationalization; they shatter the predominant tradition of Western thought and even suggest its reversal. His work is characterized by an uncompromising insistence on showing up the repressive content of the highest values and achievements of culture. In so far as he does this, he denies the equation of reason with repression on which the ideology of culture is built. Freud's metapsychology is an ever-renewed attempt to uncover, and to question, the terrible necessity of the inner connection between civilization and barbarism, progress and suffering, freedom and unhappiness — a connection which reveals itself ultimately as that between Eros and Thanatos. Freud questions culture not from a roman-

[4] A *General Introduction to Psychoanalysis* (New York: Garden City Publishing Co., 1943), p. 273.

ticist or utopian point of view, but on the ground of the
suffering and misery which its implementation involves.
Cultural freedom thus appears in the light of unfreedom,
and cultural progress in the light of constraint. Culture is
not thereby refuted: unfreedom and constraint are the price
that must be paid.

But as Freud exposes their scope and their depth, he up-
holds the tabooed aspirations of humanity: the claim for a
state where freedom and necessity coincide. Whatever liberty exists in the realm of the developed consciousness, and
in the world it has created, is only derivative, compromised
freedom, gained at the expense of the full satisfaction of
needs. And in so far as the full satisfaction of needs is happiness, freedom in civilization is essentially antagonistic to
happiness: it involves the repressive modification (*sublimation*) of happiness. Conversely, the unconscious, the deepest and oldest layer of the mental personality, *is* the drive
for integral gratification, which is absence of want and repression. As such it is the immediate identity of necessity
and freedom. According to Freud's conception the equation of freedom and happiness tabooed by the conscious is
upheld by the unconscious. Its truth, although repelled by
consciousness, continues to haunt the mind; it preserves the
memory of past stages of individual development at which
integral gratification is obtained. And the past continues to
claim the future: it generates the wish that the paradise be
re-created on the basis of the achievements of civilization.

If memory moves into the center of psychoanalysis as a
decisive mode of *cognition*, this is far more than a therapeutic device; the therapeutic role of memory derives from
the *truth value* of memory. Its truth value lies in the spe-

cific function of memory to preserve promises and potentialities which are betrayed and even outlawed by the mature, civilized individual, but which had once been fulfilled in his dim past and which are never entirely forgotten. The reality principle restrains the cognitive function of memory — its commitment to the past experience of happiness which spurns the desire for its conscious re-creation. The psychoanalytic liberation of memory explodes the rationality of the repressed individual. As cognition gives way to re-cognition, the forbidden images and impulses of childhood begin to tell the truth that reason denies. Regression assumes a progressive function. The rediscovered past yields critical standards which are tabooed by the present. Moreover, the restoration of memory is accompanied by the restoration of the cognitive content of phantasy. Psychoanalytic theory removes these mental faculties from the noncommittal sphere of daydreaming and fiction and recaptures their strict truths. The weight of these discoveries must eventually shatter the framework in which they were made and confined. The liberation of the past does not end in its reconciliation with the present. Against the self-imposed restraint of the discoverer, the orientation on the past tends toward an orientation on the future. The *recherche du temps perdu* becomes the vehicle of future liberation.[5]

[5] See Chapter 11 below. Ernest G. Schachtel's paper "On Memory and Childhood Amnesia" gives the only adequate psychoanalytic interpretation of the function of memory at the individual as well as societal level. The paper is entirely focused on the explosive force of memory, and its control and "conventionalization" by society. It is, in my view, one of the few real contributions to the philosophy of psychoanalysis. Schachtel's paper is in *A Study of Interpersonal Relations*, edited by Patrick Mullahy (New York: Hermitage Press, 1950), pp. 3–49.

The subsequent discussion will be focused on this hidden trend in psychoanalysis.

Freud's analysis of the development of the repressive mental apparatus proceeds on two levels:

(a) Ontogenetic: the growth of the repressed individual from early infancy to his conscious societal existence.

(b) Phylogenetic: the growth of repressive civilization from the primal horde to the fully constituted civilized state.

The two levels are continually interrelated. This interrelation is epitomized in Freud's notion of the return of the repressed in history: the individual re-experiences and re-enacts the great traumatic events in the development of the genus, and the instinctual dynamic reflects throughout the conflict between individual and genus (between particular and universal) as well as the various solutions of this conflict.

We shall first follow the ontogenetic development to the mature state of the civilized individual. We shall then return to the phylogenetic origins and extend the Freudian conception to the mature state of the civilized genus. The constant interrelation between the two levels means that recurrent cross-references, anticipations, and repetitions are unavoidable.

CHAPTER TWO

The Origin of the Repressed Individual (Ontogenesis)

Freud traces the development of repression in the instinctual structure of the individual. The fate of human freedom and happiness is fought out and decided in the struggle of the instincts — literally a struggle of life and death — in which soma and psyche, nature and civilization participate. This biological and at the same time sociological dynamic is the center of Freud's metapsychology. He unfolded these decisive hypotheses with constant hesitations and qualifications — and then left them in abeyance. The final theory of instincts, in whose context they emerged after 1920, was preceded by at least two different conceptions of the anatomy of the mental personality. There is no need here to review the history of the psychoanalytic theory of instincts; [1] a brief summary of some of its features may suffice to prepare for our discussion.

Throughout the various stages of Freud's theory, the

---

[1] In addition to Freud's own survey (especially in the *New Introductory Lectures*), see Siegfried Bernfeld, " Ueber die Einteilung der Triebe," in *Imago*, Vol. XXI (1935); Ernest Jones, "Psychoanalysis and the Instincts," in *British Journal of Psychology*, Vol. XXVI (1936); and Edward Bibring, " The Development and Problems of the Theory of the Instincts," in *International Journal of Psychoanalysis*, Vol. XXI (1941).

mental apparatus appears as a dynamic union of opposites
of the unconscious and the conscious structures; of primary
and secondary processes; of inherited, " constitutionally
fixed " and acquired forces; of soma-psyche and the external
reality. This dualistic construction continues to prevail
even in the later tripartite topology of id, ego, and superego; the intermediary and " overlapping " elements tend
toward the two poles. They find their most striking expression in the two ultimate principles which govern the mental apparatus: pleasure principle and reality principle.

At the earliest stage of its development, Freud's theory is
built around the antagonism between sex (libidinous) and
ego (self-preservation) instincts; at the latest stage, it is
centered on the conflict between the *life instincts* (*Eros*)
and the *death instinct*. During a brief intermediary period,
the dualistic conception was replaced by the assumption
of one all-pervasive (narcissistic) libido. Throughout all
these modifications of Freud's theory, sexuality retains its
predominant place in the instinctual structure. The predominant role of sexuality is rooted in the very nature of
the mental apparatus as Freud conceived it: if the primary
mental processes are governed by the pleasure principle,
then that instinct which, in operating under this principle,
sustains life itself must be *the* life instinct.

But Freud's early concept of sexuality is still far remote
from that of Eros as life instinct. The sexual instinct is
first only one specific instinct (or, rather, group of instincts)
side by side with the ego (or self-preservation) instincts,
and is defined by its specific genesis, aim, and object. Far
from being " pan-sexualism," Freud's theory is, at least until

his introduction of narcissism in 1914, characterized by a restriction of the scope of sexuality — a restriction which is maintained in spite of the persistent difficulty in verifying the independent existence of non-sexual self-preservation instincts.   It is still a long way to the hypothesis that the latter are merely component instincts " whose function it is to assure that the organism shall follow its own path to death, and to ward off any possible ways of returning to inorganic existence other than those which are immanent in the organism itself," [2] or — which might be another way of saying the same thing — that they are themselves of a libidinal nature, part of Eros.   However, the discovery of infantile sexuality and of the all but unlimited erotogenic zones of the body anticipates the subsequent recognition of the libidinal components of the self-preservation instincts and prepares the ground for the final reinterpretation of sexuality in terms of the life instinct (Eros).

In the final formulation of the theory of instincts, the self-preservation instincts — the cherished sanctuary of the individual and his justification in the " struggle for existence " — are dissolved: their work now appears as that of the generic sex instincts or, in so far as self-preservation is achieved through socially useful aggression, as the work of the destruction instincts.   Eros and the death instinct are now the two basic instincts.   But it is of the greatest importance to notice that, in introducing the new conception, Freud is driven to emphasize time and again the common nature of the instincts prior to their differentiation.   The

---

[2] *Beyond the Pleasure Principle* (New York: Liveright Publishing Corp., 1950), p. 51.

outstanding and frightening event is the discovery of the
fundamental *regressive* or "conservative" tendency in all
instinctual life. Freud cannot escape the suspicion that
he has come upon a hitherto unnoticed "universal attrib-
ute of the instincts and perhaps of organic life in general,"
namely, "a compulsion inherent in organic life to restore
an earlier state of things which the living entity has been
obliged to abandon under the pressure of external disturbing forces" — a kind of "organic elasticity" or "inertia
inherent in organic life."[3] This would be the ultimate
content or substance of those "primary processes" which
Freud from the beginning recognized as operating in the
unconscious. They were first designated as the striving
for "the free outflow of the quantities of excitation"
caused by the impact of external reality on the organism;[4]
the entirely free outflow would be the complete gratification. Now, twenty years later, Freud still starts from this
assumption:

> The pleasure principle, then, is a tendency operating in the serv-
> ice of a function whose business it is to free the mental apparatus
> entirely from excitation or to keep the amount of excitation in it
> constant or to keep it as low as possible. We cannot yet decide
> with certainty in favour of any of these ways of putting it.[5]

But more and more the inner logic of the conception asserts
itself. Constant freedom from excitation has been finally
abandoned at the birth of life; the instinctual tendency to-

[3] *Ibid.*, p. 47. See also *New Introductory Lectures on Psychoanalysis*
(New York: W. W. Norton, 1933), pp. 145–146.
[4] *The Interpretation of Dreams*, in *The Basic Writings of Sigmund
Freud* (New York: Modern Library, 1938), p. 534.
[5] *Beyond the Pleasure Principle*, p. 86.

ward equilibrium thus is ultimately regression behind life itself. The primary processes of the mental apparatus, in their striving for integral gratification, seem to be fatally bound to the " most universal endeavour of all living substance — namely to return to the quiescence of the inorganic world." [6] The instincts are drawn into the orbit of death. " If it is true that life is governed by Fechner's principle of constant equilibrium, it consists of a continuous descent toward death." [7] The *Nirvana principle* now emerges as the " dominating tendency of mental life, and perhaps of nervous life in general." And the pleasure principle appears in the light of the Nirvana principle — as an " expression " of the Nirvana principle:

. . . the effort to reduce, to keep constant or to remove internal tension due to stimuli (the " Nirvana Principle " . . .) . . . finds expression in the pleasure principle; and our recognition of this fact is one of our strongest reasons for believing in the existence of death instincts. [8]

However, the primacy of the Nirvana principle, the terrifying convergence of pleasure and death, is dissolved as soon as it is established. No matter how universal the regressive inertia of organic life, the instincts strive to attain their objective in fundamentally different modes. The difference is tantamount to that of sustaining and destroying life. Out of the common nature of instinctual life develop two antagonistic instincts. The life instincts (Eros) gain ascendency over the death instincts. They continuously

---

[6] *Ibid.*
[7] *The Ego and the Id* (London: Hogarth Press, 1950), p. 66. Quotations are used by permission of the publisher.
[8] *Beyond the Pleasure Principle*, p. 76.

counteract and delay the " descent toward death ": " fresh tensions are introduced by the claims of Eros, of the sexual instincts, as expressed in instinctual needs." [9] They begin their life-reproducing function with the separation of the germ cells from the organism and the coalescence of two such cell bodies,[10] proceeding to the establishment and preservation of " ever greater unities " of life.[11] They thus win, against death, the " potential immortality " of the living substance.[12] The dynamic dualism of instinctual life seems assured. However, Freud at once harks back to the original common nature of the instincts. The life instincts " are conservative in the same sense as the other instincts in that they bring back earlier states of the living substance " — although they are conservative " to a higher degree." [13] Sexuality would thus ultimately obey the same principle as the death instinct. Later, Freud, in order to illustrate the regressive character of sexuality, recalls Plato's " fantastic hypothesis " that " living substance at the time of its coming to life was torn apart into small particles, which have ever since endeavoured to reunite through the sexual instincts." [14] Does Eros, in spite of all the evidence, in the last analysis work in the service of the death instinct, and is life really only one long " detour to death "? [15] But the evidence is strong enough, and the detour is long

[9] The Ego and the Id, p. 66.
[10] Beyond the Pleasure Principle, pp. 52–53.
[11] An Outline of Psychoanalysis (New York: W. W. Norton, 1949), p. 20.
[12] Beyond the Pleasure Principle, p. 53.
[13] Ibid.
[14] Ibid., p. 80.
[15] Ibid., pp. 50–51.

enough to warrant the opposite assumption. Eros is defined as the great unifying force that preserves all life.[16]
The ultimate relation between Eros and Thanatos remains
obscure.

If Eros and Thanatos thus emerge as the two basic instincts whose ubiquitous presence and continuous fusion
(and de-fusion) characterize the life process, then this
theory of instincts is far more than a reformulation of the
preceding Freudian concepts. Psychoanalysts have correctly emphasized that Freud's last metapsychology is based
on an essentially new concept of instinct: the instincts are
defined no longer in terms of their origin and their organic
function, but in terms of a determining force which gives
the life processes a definite " direction " (Richtung), in
terms of " life-principles." The notions instinct, principle,
regulation are being assimilated.   " The rigid opposition
between a mental apparatus regulated by certain principles
on the one side, and instincts penetrating into the apparatus
from the outside on the other, could no longer be maintained." [17] Moreover, the dualistic conception of the instincts, which had become questionable ever since the introduction of narcissism, now seems to be threatened from
quite a different direction.   With the recognition of the
libidinal components of the ego instincts, it became

[16] The Ego and the Id, p. 88; Civilization and Its Discontents (London: Hogarth Press, 1949), p. 102.   Subsequent quotations are used by
permission of the publisher.
[17] Edward Bibring, " The Development and Problems of the Theory
of the Instincts " loc. cit.   See also Heinz Hartmann, " Comments on the
Psychoanalytic Theory of Instinctual Drives," in Psychoanalytic Quarterly,
Vol. XVII, No. 3 (1948).

practically impossible "to point to any instincts other than the libidinal ones," [18] to find any instinctual impulses which do not "disclose themselves as derivatives of Eros." [19]

This inability to discover in the primary instinctual structure anything that is not Eros, the monism of sexuality — an inability which, as we shall see, is the very token of the truth — now seems to turn into its opposite: into a monism of death. To be sure, the analysis of the repetition and regression-compulsion, and "ultimately" the sadistic constituents of Eros, restores the shaken dualistic conception: the death instinct becomes Eros' partner in its own right in the primary instinctual structure, and the perpetual struggle between the two constitutes the primary dynamic. However, the discovery of the common "conservative nature" of the instincts militates against the dualistic conception and keeps Freud's late metapsychology in that state of suspense and depth which makes it one of the great intellectual ventures in the science of man. The *quest for the common origin* of the two basic instincts can no longer be silenced. Fenichel pointed out [20] that Freud himself made a decisive step in this direction by assuming a "displaceable energy, which is in itself neutral, but is able to join forces either with an erotic or with a destructive impulse" — with the life or the death instinct. Never before has death been so consistently taken into the essence of life;

[18] *Beyond the Pleasure Principle*, p. 73.
[19] *The Ego and the Id*, p. 66.
[20] "Zur Kritik des Todestriebes," in *Imago*, XXI (1935), 463. This paper is translated as "A Critique of the Death Instinct," in *Collected Papers* (New York: W. W. Norton, 1953), pp. 363–372.

but never before also has death come so close to Eros. Fenichel raises the decisive question whether the antithesis of Eros and death instinct is not the " differentiation of an originally common root." He suggests that the phenomena grouped together as the death instinct may be taken as expression of a principle " valid for all instincts," a principle which, in the course of development, " might have been modified . . . by external influences." [21] Moreover, if the " regression-compulsion " in all organic life is striving for integral quiescence, if the Nirvana principle is the ground of the pleasure principle, then the necessity of death appears in an entirely new light. The death instinct is destructiveness not for its own sake, but for the relief of tension. The descent toward death is an unconscious flight from pain and want. It is an expression of the eternal struggle against suffering and repression. And the death instinct itself seems to be affected by the historical changes which affect this struggle. Further explanation of the historical character of the instincts requires placing them in the *new concept of the person* which corresponds to the last version of Freud's theory of instincts.

The main " layers " of the mental structure are now designated as *id*, *ego*, and *superego*. The fundamental, oldest, and largest layer is the *id*, the domain of the unconscious, of the primary instincts. The id is free from the forms and principles which constitute the conscious, social individual. It is neither affected by time nor troubled by contradictions; it knows " no values, no good and evil, no morality." [22] It

[21] *The Psychoanalytic Theory of Neurosis* (New York: W. W. Norton, 1945), p. 59.
[22] *New Introductory Lectures*, p. 105.

does not aim at self-preservation: [23] all it strives for is satisfaction of its instinctual needs, in accordance with the pleasure principle.[24]

Under the influence of the external world (the environment), a part of the id, which is equipped with the organs for the reception of and the protection from stimuli, gradually developed into the *ego*. It is the " mediator " between the id and the external world. Perception and consciousness are only the smallest and " most superficial " part of the ego, the part topographically closest to the external world; but by virtue of these instrumentalities (the " perceptual-conscious system ") the ego preserves its existence, observing and testing the reality, taking and preserving a " true picture " of it, adjusting itself to the reality, and altering the latter in its own interest. Thus the ego has the task of " representing the external world for the id, and so of saving it; for the id, blindly striving to gratify its instincts in complete disregard of the superior strength of outside forces, could not otherwise escape annihilation." [25] In fulfilling this task, the chief function of the ego is that of co-ordinating, altering, organizing, and controlling the instinctual impulses of the id so as to minimize conflicts with the reality: to repress impulses that are incompatible with the reality, to " reconcile " others with the reality by changing their object, delaying or diverting their gratification, transforming their mode of gratification, amalgamating them with other impulses, and so on. In this way, the ego " dethrones the pleasure-principle, which exerts undisputed

[23] *An Outline of Psychoanalysis*, p. 19.
[24] *New Introductory Lectures*, p. 104.
[25] *New Introductory Lectures*, p. 106.

sway over the processes in the id, and substitutes for it the reality-principle, which promises greater security and greater success."

In spite of its all-important functions, which secure instinctual gratification to an organism that would otherwise almost certainly be destroyed or destroy itself, the ego retains its birthmark as an " outgrowth " of the id. In relation to the id, the processes of the ego remain *secondary processes*. Nothing elucidates more strikingly the dependent function of the ego than Freud's early formulation that all thinking " is merely a detour from the memory of gratification . . . to the identical cathexis of the same memory, which is to be reached once more by the path of motor experiences." [26] The memory of gratification is at the origin of all thinking, and the impulse to recapture past gratification is the hidden driving power behind the process of thought. Because the reality principle makes this process an unending series of " detours," the ego experiences reality as predominantly hostile, and the ego's attitude is predominantly one of " defense." But, on the other hand, since reality, via these detours, provides gratification (although only " modified " gratification), the ego has to reject those impulses which would, if gratified, destroy its life. The ego's defense is thus a two-front struggle.

In the course of the development of the ego another mental "entity" arises: the *superego*. It originates from the long dependency of the infant on his parents; the pa-

---

[26] *The Interpretation of Dreams*, p. 535. In the later development of psychoanalysis, the role of the ego has been viewed as more " positive," with emphasis on its " synthetic " and " integrating " functions. For the significance of this shift in emphasis, see the Epilogue below.

rental influence remains the core of the superego. Subsequently, a number of societal and cultural influences are taken in by the superego until it coagulates into the powerful representative of established morality and " what people call the ' higher ' things in human life." Now the " external restrictions " which first the parents and then other societal agencies have imposed upon the individual are " introjected " into the ego and become its " conscience "; henceforth, the sense of guilt — the need for punishment generated by the transgressions or by the wish to transgress these restrictions (especially in the Oedipus situation) — permeates the mental life. " As a rule the ego carries out repressions in the service and at the behest of its superego." [27] However, the repressions soon become unconscious, automatic as it were, and a " great part " of the sense of guilt remains unconscious.

Franz Alexander speaks of the " transformation of conscious condemnation, which depends upon perception (and judgment), into an unconscious process of repression "; he assumes a tendency toward a decrease of mobile psychic energy to a " tonic form " — *corporealization of the psyche*.[28] This development, by which originally conscious struggles with the demands of reality (the parents and their successors in the formation of the superego) are transformed into unconscious automatic reactions, is of the utmost importance for the course of civilization. The reality principle asserts itself through a shrinking of the conscious ego in a significant direction: the autonomous

[27] *The Ego and the Id*, p. 75.
[28] Franz Alexander, *The Psychoanalysis of the Total Personality* (New York: Nervous and Mental Disease Monograph No. 52, 1929), p. 14.

development of the instincts is frozen, and their pattern is fixed at the childhood level. Adherence to a *status quo ante* is implanted in the instinctual structure. The individual becomes instinctually re-actionary — in the literal as well as the figurative sense. It exercises against itself, unconsciously, a severity which once was appropriate to an infantile stage of its development but which has long since become obsolete in the light of the rational potentialities of (individual and social) maturity.[29] The individual punishes itself (and then is punished) for deeds which are undone or which are no longer incompatible with civilized reality, with civilized man.

The superego thus enforces not only the demands of reality but also those of a *past* reality. By virtue of these unconscious mechanisms, the mental development lags behind the real development, or (since the former is itself a factor in the latter) retards the real development, denies its potentialities in the name of the past. The past reveals its twofold function in the shaping of the individual — and of his society. Recalling the dominion of the primal pleasure principle, where freedom from want was a necessity, the id carries the memory traces of this state forward into every present future: it projects the past into the future. However, the superego, also unconscious, rejects this instinctual claim on the future, in the name of a past no longer one of integral satisfaction but one of bitter adjustment to a punitive present. Phylogenetically and ontogenetically, with the progress of civilization and with the

[29] *Ibid.*, pp 23–25. For the further differentiation in the origin and structure of the superego, see pages 94–95 below.

growth of the individual, the memory traces of the unity between freedom and necessity become submerged in the acceptance of the necessity of unfreedom; rational and rationalized, memory itself bows to the reality principle.

The reality principle sustains the organism in the external world. In the case of the human organism, this is an *historical* world. The external world faced by the growing ego is at any stage a specific socio-historical organization of reality, affecting the mental structure through specific societal agencies or agents. It has been argued that Freud's concept *reality principle* obliterates this fact by making historical contingencies into biological necessities: his analysis of the repressive transformation of the instincts under the impact of the reality principle generalizes from a specific historical form of reality to reality pure and simple. This criticism is valid, but its validity does not vitiate the truth in Freud's generalization, namely, that a repressive organization of the instincts underlies *all* historical forms of the reality principle in civilization. If he justifies the repressive organization of the instincts by the irreconcilability between the primary pleasure principle and the reality principle, he expresses the historical fact that civilization has progressed as organized *domination*. This awareness guides his entire phylogenetic construction, which derives civilization from the replacement of the patriarchal despotism of the primal horde by the internalized despotism of the brother clan. Precisely because all civilization has been organized domination, the historical development assumes the dignity and necessity of a universal biological development. The " unhistorical " character of the Freudian concepts thus contains the elements of its opposite: their historical substance must be recaptured, not by adding some sociological factors (as do the "cultural" Neo-Freudian schools), but by unfolding their own content. In this sense, our subsequent discussion is an "extrapolation," which derives from Freud's theory notions and propositions implied in it only in a reified form, in which historical processes appear as natural (biological) processes.

Terminologically, this extrapolation calls for a duplication of concepts: the Freudian terms, which do not adequately differentiate between the biological *and* the socio-historical vicissitudes of the instincts, must be paired with corresponding terms denoting the specific socio-historical component. Presently we shall introduce two such terms:

(a) *Surplus-repression:* the restrictions necessitated by social domination. This is distinguished from (basic) *repression:* the "modifications" of the instincts necessary for the perpetuation of the human race in civilization.

(b) *Performance principle:* the prevailing historical form of the *reality principle.*

Behind the reality principle lies the fundamental fact of Ananke or scarcity (*Lebensnot*), which means that the struggle for existence takes place in a world too poor for the satisfaction of human needs without constant restraint, renunciation, delay. In other words, whatever satisfaction is possible necessitates *work*, more or less painful arrangements and undertakings for the procurement of the means for satisfying needs. For the duration of work, which occupies practically the entire existence of the mature individual, pleasure is "suspended" and pain prevails. And since the basic instincts strive for the prevalence of pleasure and for the absence of pain, the pleasure principle is incompatible with reality, and the instincts have to undergo a repressive regimentation.

However, this argument, which looms large in Freud's metapsychology, is fallacious in so far as it applies to the brute *fact* of scarcity what actually is the consequence of a specific *organization* of scarcity, and of a specific existential attitude enforced by this organization. The prevalent scarcity has, throughout civilization (although in very different modes), been organized in such a way that it has not been distributed collectively in accordance with individual needs, nor has the procurement of goods for the satisfaction of needs been organized with the objective of best satisfying the developing needs of the individuals. Instead, the *distribution* of scarcity as well as the effort of overcoming it, the mode of work, have been *imposed* upon individuals — first by mere violence, subsequently by a more rational utilization of power. However, no matter how useful this rationality was for the progress of the whole, it remained the rationality of *domination*, and the gradual conquest of scarcity was inextricably bound up with and shaped by the interest of domination. Domination differs from rational exercise of authority. The latter, which is inherent in any societal division of labor, is derived from knowledge and confined to the administration of functions and arrangements necessary for the advancement of the whole. In contrast, domination is exercised by a particular group or individual in order to sustain and enhance itself in a privileged position. Such domination does not exclude technical, material, and intellectual progress, but only as an unavoidable by-product while preserving irrational scarcity, want, and constraint.

The various modes of domination (of man and nature) result in various historical forms of the reality principle. For example, a society in which all members normally work for a living requires other modes of repression than a society in which labor is the exclusive province of one specific group. Similarly, repression will be different in scope and degree according to whether social production is oriented on individual consumption or on profit; whether a market economy prevails or a planned economy; whether private or collective property. These differences affect the very content of the reality principle, for every form of the reality principle must be embodied in a system of societal institutions and relations, laws and values which transmit and enforce the required " modification " of the instincts. This " body " of the reality principle is different at the different stages of civilization. Moreover, while any form of the reality principle demands a considerable degree and scope of repressive control over the instincts, the specific historical institutions of the reality principle and the specific interests of domination introduce *additional* controls over and above those indispensable for civilized human association. These additional controls arising from the specific institutions of domination are what we denote as *surplus-repression*.

For example, the modifications and deflections of instinctual energy necessitated by the perpetuation of the monogamic-patriarchal family, or by a hierarchical division of labor, or by public control over the individual's private existence are instances of surplus-repression pertaining to the institutions of a *particular* reality principle. They are added to the basic (phylogenetic) restrictions of the instincts which mark the development of man from the human animal to the *animal sapiens*. The power to restrain and guide instinctual drives, to make biological necessities into individual needs and desires, increases rather than reduces gratification: the "mediatization" of nature, the breaking of its compulsion, is the human form of the pleasure principle. Such restrictions of the instincts may first have been enforced by scarcity and by the protracted dependence of the human animal, but they have become the privilege and distinction of man which enabled him to transform the blind necessity of the fulfillment of want into desired gratification.[30]

The "containment" of the partial sexual impulses, the progress to genitality belong to this basic layer of repression which makes possible intensified pleasure: the maturation of the organism involves normal and natural maturation of pleasure. However, the mastery of instinctual drives may also be used *against* gratification; in the history of civilization, basic repression and surplus-repression have been inextricably intertwined, and the normal progress to genitality has been organized in such a way that the partial impulses and their "zones" were all but desexualized in order to conform to the requirements of a specific social organization of the human existence. The vicissitudes of the "proximity senses" (smell and taste) provide a good example for the interrelation between basic repression and

[30] See Chapter 11 below.

surplus-repression. Freud thought that "the coprophilic elements in the instinct have proved incompatible with our aesthetic ideas, probably since the time when man developed an upright posture and so removed his organ of smell from the ground." [31] There is, however, another aspect to the subduing of the proximity senses in civilization: they succumb to the rigidly enforced taboos on too intense bodily pleasure. The pleasure of smell and taste is "much more of a bodily, physical one, hence also more akin to sexual pleasure, than is the more sublime pleasure aroused by sound and the least bodily of all pleasures, the sight of something beautiful." [32] Smell and taste give, as it were, unsublimated pleasure *per se* (and unrepressed disgust). They relate (and separate) individuals immediately, without the generalized and conventionalized forms of consciousness, morality, aesthetics. Such immediacy is incompatible with the effectiveness of organized *domination*, with a society which "tends to isolate people, to put distance between them, and to prevent spontaneous relationships and the 'natural' animal-like expressions of such relations." [33] The pleasure of the proximity senses plays on the erotogenic zones of the body — and does so only for the sake of pleasure. Their unrepressed development would eroticize the organism to such an extent that it would counteract the desexualization of the organism required by its social utilization as an instrument of labor.

[31] "The Most Prevalent Form of Degradation in Erotic Life," in *Collected Papers* (London: Hogarth Press, 1950), IV, 215.

[32] Ernest Schachtel, "On Memory and Childhood Amnesia," in *A Study of Interpersonal Relations*, ed. Patrick Mullahy (New York: Hermitage Press, 1950), p. 24.

[33] *Ibid.*, p. 26.

Throughout the recorded history of civilization, the instinctual constraint enforced by scarcity has been intensified by constraints enforced by the hierarchical distribution of scarcity and labor; the interest of domination added surplus-repression to the organization of the instincts under the reality principle. The pleasure principle was dethroned not only because it militated against progress in civilization but also because it militated against a civilization whose progress perpetuates domination and toil. Freud seems to acknowledge this fact when he compares the attitude of civilization toward sexuality with that of a tribe or a section of the population "which has gained the upper hand and is exploiting the rest to its own advantage. Fear of a revolt among the oppressed then becomes a motive for even stricter regulations." [34]

The modification of the instincts under the reality principle affects the life instinct as well as the death instinct; but the development of the latter becomes fully understandable only in the light of the development of the life instinct, i.e., of the repressive *organization of sexuality*. The sex instincts bear the brunt of the reality principle. Their organization culminates in the subjection of the partial sex instincts to the primacy of genitality, and in their subjugation under the function of procreation. The process involves the diversion of libido from one's own body toward an alien object of the opposite sex (the mastery of primary and secondary narcissism). The gratification of the partial instincts and of non-procreative genitality are, according to the degree of their independence, tabooed as perversions,

[34] *Civilization and Its Discontents*, p. 74.

sublimated, or transformed into subsidiaries of procreative sexuality. Moreover, the latter is in most civilizations channeled into monogamic institutions. This organization results in a quantitative and qualitative restriction of sexuality: the unification of the partial instincts and their subjugation under the procreative function alter the very nature of sexuality: from an autonomous " principle " governing the entire organism it is turned into a specialized temporary function, into a means for an end. In terms of the pleasure principle governing the " unorganized " sex instincts, reproduction is merely a " by-product." The primary content of sexuality is the " function of obtaining pleasure from zones of the body "; this function is only " subsequently brought into the service of that of reproduction." [35] Freud emphasizes time and again that without its organization for such " service " sexuality would preclude all non-sexual and therefore all civilized societal relations — even at the stage of mature heterosexual genitality:

. . . The conflict between civilization and sexuality is caused by the circumstance that sexual love is a relationship between two people, in which a third can only be superfluous or disturbing, whereas civilization is founded on relations between larger groups of persons. When a love relationship is at its height no room is left for any interest in the surrounding world; the pair of lovers are sufficient unto themselves, do not even need the child they have in common to make them happy.[36]

And earlier, in arguing the distinction between sexual and self-preservation instincts, he points up the fatal implications of sexuality:

[35] *An Outline of Psychoanalysis*, p. 26.
[36] *Civilization and Its Discontents*, pp. 79–80.

It is undeniable that the exercise of this function does not always bring advantage to the individual, as do his other activities, but that for the sake of an exceptionally high degree of pleasure he is involved by this function in dangers which jeopardize his life and often enough exact it.[37]

But how does this interpretation of sexuality as an essentially explosive force in " conflict " with civilization justify the definition of Eros as the effort " to combine organic substances into ever larger unities," [38] to " establish ever greater unities and to preserve them thus — in short, to bind together "? [39]   How can sexuality become the probable " substitute " for the " instinct towards perfection," [40] the power that " holds together everything in the world "? [41] How does the notion of the asocial character of sexuality jibe with the " supposition that love relationships (or, to use a more neutral expression, emotional ties) also constitute the essence of the group mind? " [42]   The apparent contradiction is not solved by attributing the explosive connotations to the earlier concept of sexuality and the constructive ones to Eros — for the latter includes both.   In *Civilization and Its Discontents*, immediately following the passage quoted above, Freud joins the two aspects: " In no other case does Eros so plainly betray the core of his being, his aim of making one out of many; but when he has achieved it in the proverbial way through the love of two human beings, he is not willing to go further."   Nor can

[37] *A General Introduction to Psychoanalysis* (New York: Garden City Publishing Co., 1943), p. 358.
[38] *Beyond the Pleasure Principle*, p. 57.
[39] *An Outline of Psychoanalysis*, p. 20.
[40] *Beyond the Pleasure Principle*, p. 57.
[41] *Group Psychology and the Analysis of the Ego* (New York: Liveright Publishing Corp., 1949), p. 40.
[42] *Ibid.*

the contradiction be eliminated by locating the constructive cultural force of Eros only in the sublimated modes of
sexuality: according to Freud, the drive toward ever larger
unities belongs to the biological-organic nature of Eros
itself.

At this stage of our interpretation, rather than trying to
reconcile the two contradictory aspects of sexuality, we suggest that they reflect the inner unreconciled tension in
Freud's theory: against his notion of the inevitable " biological" conflict between pleasure principle and reality
principle, between sexuality and civilization, militates the
idea of the unifying and gratifying power of Eros, chained
and worn out in a sick civilization. This idea would imply that the *free* Eros does not preclude lasting civilized
societal relationships — that it repels only the supra-repres-
sive organization of societal relationships under a principle
which is the negation of the pleasure principle. Freud
allows himself the image of a civilization consisting of pairs
of individuals " libidinally satisfied in each other, and linked
to all the others by work and common interest." [43] But he
adds that such a " desirable " state does not exist and never
has existed, that culture " exacts a heavy toll of aim-inhibited libido, and heavy restrictions upon sexual life are unavoidable." He finds the reason for culture's " antagonism
to sexuality " in the aggressive instincts deeply fused with
sexuality: they threaten time and again to destroy civilization, and they force culture " to call up every possible re-
inforcement " against them. " Hence its system of methods

[43] *Civilization and Its Discontents*, p. 80. See also *The Future of
an Illusion* (New York: Liveright Publishing Corp., 1949), pp. 10–11.

by which mankind is to be driven to identifications and aim-inhibited love-relationships; hence the restrictions on sexual life." [44] But, again, Freud shows that this repressive system does not really solve the conflict. Civilization plunges into a destructive dialectic: the perpetual restrictions on Eros ultimately weaken the life instincts and thus strengthen and release the very forces against which they were " called up " — those of destruction. This dialectic, which constitutes the still unexplored and even tabooed core of Freud's metapsychology, will be explored later on; here, we shall use Freud's antagonistic conception of Eros for elucidating the specific historical mode of repressiveness imposed by the established reality principle.

In introducing the term *surplus-repression* we have focused the discussion on the institutions and relations that constitute the social " body " of the reality principle. These do not just represent the changing external manifestations of one and the same reality principle but actually change the reality principle itself. Consequently, in our attempt to elucidate the scope and the limits of the prevalent repressiveness in contemporary civilization, we shall have to describe it in terms of the specific reality principle that has governed the origins and the growth of this civilization. We designate it as *performance principle* in order to emphasize that under its rule society is stratified according to the competitive economic performances of its members. It is clearly not the only historical reality principle: other modes of societal organization not merely prevailed

[44] *Civilization and Its Discontents*, pp. 86–87.

in primitive cultures but also survived into the modern period.

The performance principle, which is that of an acquisitive and antagonistic society in the process of constant expansion, presupposes a long development during which domination has been increasingly rationalized: control over social labor now reproduces society on an enlarged scale and under improving conditions. For a long way, the interests of domination and the interests of the whole coincide: the profitable utilization of the productive apparatus fulfills the needs and faculties of the individuals. For the vast majority of the population, the scope and mode of satisfaction are determined by their own labor; but their labor is work for an apparatus which they do not control, which operates as an independent power to which individuals must submit if they want to live. And it becomes the more alien the more specialized the division of labor becomes. Men do not live their own lives but perform pre-established functions. While they work, they do not fulfill their own needs and faculties but work in *alienation*. Work has now become *general*, and so have the restrictions placed upon the libido: labor time, which is the largest part of the individual's life time, is painful time, for alienated labor is absence of gratification, negation of the pleasure principle. Libido is diverted for socially useful performances in which the individual works for himself only in so far as he works for the apparatus, engaged in activities that mostly do not coincide with his own faculties and desires.

However — and this point is decisive — the instinctual

energy thus withdrawn does not accrue to the (unsublimated) aggressive instincts because its social utilization (in labor) sustains and even enriches the life of the individual. The restrictions imposed upon the libido appear as the more rational, the more universal they become, the more they permeate the whole of society. They operate on the individual as external objective laws and as an internalized force: the societal authority is absorbed into the " conscience " and into the unconscious of the individual and works as his own desire, morality, and fulfillment. In the " normal " development, the individual lives his repression " freely " as his own life: he desires what he is supposed to desire; his gratifications are profitable to him and to others; he is reasonably and often even exuberantly happy. This happiness, which takes place part-time during the few hours of leisure between the working days or working nights, but sometimes also during work, enables him to continue his performance, which in turn perpetuates his labor and that of the others. His erotic performance is brought in line with his societal performance. Repression disappears in the grand objective order of things which rewards more or less adequately the complying individuals and, in doing so, reproduces more or less adequately society as a whole.

The conflict between sexuality and civilization unfolds with this development of domination. Under the rule of the performance principle, body and mind are made into instruments of alienated labor; they can function as such instruments only if they renounce the freedom of the libidinal subject-object which the human organism primarily is and desires. The distribution of *time* plays a fundamental role in this transformation. Man exists only *part-time*, during the working days, as an instrument of alienated performance; the rest of the time he is free for himself. (If the average working day, including preparation and travel to and from work, amounts to ten hours, and if the biological needs for sleep and nourishment require another ten hours, the free time would be four out of each twenty-four hours throughout the greater part of the individual's life.) This free time would be potentially available for pleasure. But the pleasure principle which governs the id is " timeless " also in the sense that it militates against the temporal dismemberment of pleasure, against its distribution in small separated doses. A society governed by the performance principle must of necessity impose such distribution because the organism must be trained for its alienation at its very roots — the *pleasure ego*.[45] It must learn to forget the claim for timeless and useless gratification, for the " eternity of pleasure." Moreover, from the working day, alienation and regimentation spread into the free time. Such co-ordination does not have to be, and normally is not, enforced from without by the agencies of society. The basic control of leisure is achieved by the length of the working day itself, by the tiresome and mechanical routine of alienated

---

[45] To be sure, every form of society, every civilization has to exact labor time for the procurement of the necessities and luxuries of life. But not every kind and mode of labor is essentially irreconcilable with the pleasure principle. The human relations connected with work may " provide for a very considerable discharge of libidinal component impulses, narcissistic, aggressive, and even erotic." (*Civilization and Its Discontents*, p. 34 note.) The irreconcilable conflict is not between work (reality principle) and Eros (pleasure principle), but between *alienated* labor (performance principle) and Eros. The notion of non-alienated, libidinal work will be discussed below.

labor; these require that leisure be a passive relaxation and a re-creation of energy for work. Not until the late stage of industrial civilization, when the growth of productivity threatens to overflow the limits set by repressive domination, has the technique of mass manipulation developed an entertainment industry which directly controls leisure time, or has the state directly taken over the enforcement of such controls.[46] The individual is not to be left alone. For left to itself, and supported by a free intelligence aware of the potentialities of liberation from the reality of repression, the libidinal energy generated by the id would thrust against its ever more extraneous limitations and strive to engulf an ever larger field of existential relations, thereby exploding the reality ego and its repressive performances.

The organization of sexuality reflects the basic features of the performance principle and its organization of society. Freud emphasizes the aspect of centralization. It is especially operative in the " unification " of the various objects of the partial instincts into one libidinal object of the opposite sex, and in the establishment of genital supremacy. In both cases, the unifying process is repressive — that is to say, the partial instincts do not develop freely into a " higher " stage of gratification which preserves their objectives, but are cut off and reduced to subservient functions. This process achieves the socially necessary desexualization of the body: the libido becomes concentrated in one part of the body, leaving most of the rest free for use as the instrument of labor. The temporal reduction of the libido is thus supplemented by its spatial reduction.

[46] See Chapter 4 below.

Originally, the sex instinct has no extraneous temporal and spatial limitations on its subject and object; sexuality is by nature " polymorphous-perverse." The societal organization of the sex instinct taboos as *perversions* practically all its manifestations which do not serve or prepare for the procreative function. Without the most severe restrictions, they would counteract the sublimation on which the growth of culture depends. According to Fenichel, " pregenital strivings are the object of sublimation," and genital primacy is its prerequisite.[47] Freud questioned why the taboo on the perversions is sustained with such an extraordinary rigidity. He concluded that no one can forget that the perversions are not merely detestable but also something monstrous and terrifying — " as if they exerted a seductive influence; as if at bottom a secret envy of those who enjoy them had to be strangled.[48] The perversions seem to give a *promesse de bonheur* greater than that of " normal " sexuality. What is the source of their promise? Freud emphasized the " exclusive " character of the deviations from normality, their rejection of the procreative sex act. The perversions thus express rebellion against the subjugation of sexuality under the order of procreation, and against the institutions which guarantee this order. Psychoanalytic theory sees in the practices that exclude or prevent procreation an opposition against continuing the chain of reproduction and thereby of paternal domination — an attempt to prevent the " reappearance of the father." [49] The

[47] *The Psychoanalytic Theory of Neurosis*, p. 142.
[48] A *General Introduction to Psychoanalysis*, p. 282.
[49] G. Barag, " Zur Psychoanalyse der Prostitution," in *Imago*, Vol. XXIII, No. 3 (1937), p. 345.

perversions seem to reject the entire enslavement of the
pleasure ego by the reality ego. Claiming instinctual freedom in a world of repression, they are often characterized
by a strong rejection of that feeling of guilt which accompanies sexual repression.[50]

By virtue of their revolt against the performance principle
in the name of the pleasure principle, the perversions show
a deep affinity to phantasy as that mental activity which
"was kept free from reality-testing and remained subordinated to the pleasure principle alone." [51] Phantasy not only
plays a constitutive role in the perverse manifestations of
sexuality; [52] as artistic imagination, it also links the perversions with the images of integral freedom and gratification.
In a repressive order, which enforces the equation between
normal, socially useful, and good, the manifestations of
pleasure for its own sake must appear as *fleurs du mal*.
Against a society which employs sexuality as means for a
useful end, the perversions uphold sexuality as an end in
itself; they thus place themselves outside the dominion of
the performance principle and challenge its very foundation. They establish libidinal relationships which society
must ostracize because they threaten to reverse the process
of civilization which turned the organism into an instrument of work. They are a symbol of what had to be suppressed so that suppression could prevail and organize the
ever more efficient domination of man and nature — a

---

[50] Otto Rank, *Sexualität und Schuldgefühl* (Leipzig, Vienna, Zurich:
Internationaler Psychoanalytischer Verlag, 1926), p. 103.
[51] Freud, ". . . Two Principles in Mental Functioning," in *Collected
Papers*, IV, 16–17.
[52] Rank, *Sexualität und Schuldgefühl*, pp. 14–15.

symbol of the destructive identity between freedom and happiness. Moreover, license in the practice of perversions would endanger the orderly reproduction not only of labor power but perhaps even of mankind itself. The fusion of Eros and death instinct, precarious even in the normal human existence, here seems to be loosened beyond the danger point. And the loosening of this fusion makes manifest the erotic component in the death instinct and the fatal component in the sex instinct. The perversions suggest the ultimate identity of Eros and death instinct, or the submission of Eros to the death instinct. The cultural task (the life task?) of the libido — namely, to make the "destructive instinct harmless " [53] — here comes to naught: the instinctual drive in search of ultimate and integral fulfillment regresses from the pleasure principle to the Nirvana principle. Civilization has acknowledged and sanctioned this supreme danger: it admires the convergence of death instinct and Eros in the highly sublimated and (monogamic) creations of the *Liebestod*, while outlawing the less complete but more realistic expressions of Eros as an end in itself.

There is no societal organization of the death instinct paralleling that of Eros: the very depth at which the instinct operates protects it from such a systematic and methodical organization; only some of its derivative manifestations are susceptible to control. As a component of sado-masochistic gratification, it falls under the strict taboo on perversions. Still, the entire progress of civilization is rendered possible

[53] Freud, "The Economic Problem in Masochism," in *Collected Papers*, II, 260.

only by the transformation and utilization of the death instinct or its derivatives. The diversion of primary destructiveness from the ego to the external world feeds technological progress, and the use of the death instinct for the formation of the superego achieves the punitive submission of the pleasure ego to the reality principle and assures civilized morality. In this transformation, the death instinct is brought into the service of Eros; the aggressive impulses provide energy for the continuous alteration, mastery, and exploitation of nature to the advantage of mankind. In attacking, splitting, changing, pulverizing things and animals (and, periodically, also men), man extends his dominion over the world and advances to ever richer stages of civilization. But civilization preserves throughout the mark of its deadly component:

. . . we seem almost forced to accept the dreadful hypothesis that in the very structure and substance of all human constructive social efforts there is embodied a principle of death, that there is no progressive impulse but must become fatigued, that the intellect can provide no permanent defence against a vigorous barbarism.[54]

The socially channeled destructiveness reveals time and again its origin in a drive which defies all usefulness. Beneath the manifold rational and rationalized motives for war against national and group enemies, for the destructive conquest of time, space, and man, the deadly partner of Eros becomes manifest in the persistent approval and participation of the victims.[55]

[54] Wilfred Trotter, *Instincts of the Herd in Peace and War* (London: Oxford University Press, 1953), pp. 196–197.
[55] See Freud, "Why War?" in *Collected Papers*, V, 273ff.

" In the construction of the personality the destruction instinct manifests itself most clearly in the formation of the super-ego." [56]   To be sure, by its defensive role against the "unrealistic" impulses of the id, by its function in the lasting conquest of the Oedipus complex, the super-ego builds up and protects the unity of the ego, secures its development under the reality principle, and thus works in the service of Eros.   However, the superego attains these objectives by directing the ego against its id, turning part of the destruction instincts against a part of the personality — by destroying, "splitting" the unity of the personality as a whole; thus it works in the service of the antagonist of the life instinct.   This inner-directed destructiveness, moreover, constitutes the moral core of the mature personality.   Conscience, the most cherished moral agency of the civilized individual, emerges as permeated with the death instinct; the categorical imperative that the superego enforces remains an imperative of self-destruction while it constructs the social existence of the personality.   The work of repression pertains to the death instinct as well as the life instinct.   Normally, their fusion is a healthy one, but the sustained severity of the superego constantly threatens this healthy balance.   " The more a man checks his aggressive tendencies toward others the more tyrannical, that is aggressive, he becomes in his ego-ideal . . . the more intense become the aggressive tendencies of his ego-ideal against his ego." [57]   Driven to the extreme, in melancholia, " a pure culture of the death instinct " may hold sway in the super-

[56] Franz Alexander, *The Psychoanalysis of the Total Personality*, p. 159.
[57] *The Ego and the Id*, pp. 79, 80.

ego: it may become a "kind of gathering place for the death instincts." [58]   But this extreme danger has its roots in the *normal* situation of the ego.   Since the ego's work results in a

. . . liberation of the aggressive instincts in the super-ego, its struggle against the libido exposes it to the danger of maltreatment and death.   In suffering under the attacks of the super-ego or perhaps even succumbing to them, the ego is meeting with a fate like that of the protozoa which are destroyed by the products of disintegration that they themselves have created.[59]

And Freud adds that "from the [mental] economic point of view the morality that functions in the super-ego seems to be a similar product of disintegration."

It is in this context that Freud's metapsychology comes face to face with the fatal dialectic of civilization: the very progress of civilization leads to the release of increasingly destructive forces. In order to elucidate the connection between Freud's individual psychology and the theory of civilization, it will be necessary to resume the interpretation of the instinctual dynamic at a different level — namely, the phylogenetic one.

[58] *Ibid.*, pp. 77, 79.   [59] *Ibid.*, p. 84.

CHAPTER THREE

The Origin of Repressive Civilization (Phylogenesis)

The quest for the origin of repression leads back to the origin of instinctual repression, which occurs during early childhood. The superego is the heir of the Oedipus complex, and the repressive organization of sexuality is chiefly directed against its pregenital and perverse manifestations. Moreover, the " trauma of birth " releases the first expressions of the death instinct — the impulse to return to the Nirvana of the womb — and necessitates the subsequent controls of this impulse. It is in the child that the reality principle completes its work, with such thoroughness and severity that the mature individual's behavior is hardly more than a repetitive pattern of childhood experiences and reactions. But the childhood experiences which become traumatic under the impact of reality are *pre*-individual, *generic*: with individual variations, the protracted dependence of the human infant, the Oedipus situation, and pregenital sexuality all belong to the *genus* man. Moreover, the unreasonable severity of the superego of the neurotic personality, the unconscious sense of guilt and the unconscious need for punishment, seem to be out of proportion with the actual " sinful " impulses of the individual; the perpetua-

tion and (as we shall see) intensification of the sense of
guilt throughout maturity, the excessively repressive organization of sexuality, cannot be adequately explained in
terms of the still acute danger of individual impulses. Nor
can the individual reactions to early traumata be adequately
explained by "what the individual himself has experienced"; they deviate from individual experiences "in a
way that would accord much better with their being reactions to genetic events," and in general they can be explained only "through such an influence."[1] The analysis
of the mental structure of the personality is thus forced to
regress behind early childhood, from the prehistory of the
individual to that of the genus. In the personality, according to Otto Rank, there operates a "biological sense of
guilt" which stands for the demands of the species. The
moral principles "which the child imbibes from the persons responsible for its upbringing during the first years of
its life" reflect "certain phylogenetic echoes of primitive
man."[2] Civilization is still determined by its *archaic heritage*, and this heritage, so Freud asserts, includes "not only
dispositions, but also ideational contents, memory traces of
the experiences of former generations." Individual psychology is thus *in itself* group psychology in so far as the
individual itself still is in archaic identity with the species.
This archaic heritage bridges the "gap between individual
and mass psychology."[3]

---

[1] Freud, *Moses and Monotheism* (New York: Alfred A. Knopf, 1949),
p. 157.
[2] Alexander, *The Psychoanalysis of the Total Personality* (New York:
Nervous and Mental Disease Monograph No. 52, 1929), p. 7.
[3] Freud, *Moses and Monotheism*, p. 158.

This conception has far-reaching implications for the method and substance of social science. As psychology tears the ideological veil and traces the construction of the personality, it is led to dissolve the individual: his autonomous personality appears as the *frozen* manifestation of the general repression of mankind. Self-consciousness and reason, which have conquered and shaped the historical world, have done so in the image of repression, internal and external. They have worked as the agents of domination; the liberties which they have brought (and these are considerable) grew in the soil of enslavement and have retained the mark of their birth. These are the disturbing implications of Freud's theory of the personality. By "dissolving" the idea of the ego-personality into its primary components, psychology now bares the sub-individual and pre-individual factors which (largely unconscious to the ego) actually *make* the individual: it reveals the power of the universal in and over the individuals.

This disclosure undermines one of the strongest ideological fortifications of modern culture — namely, the notion of the autonomous individual. Freud's theory here joins the great critical efforts to dissolve ossified sociological concepts into their historical content. His psychology does not focus on the concrete and complete personality as it exists in its private and public environment, because this existence conceals rather than reveals the essence and nature of the personality. It is the end result of long historical processes which are congealed in the network of human and institutional entities making up society, and these processes define the personality and its relationships. Consequently, to understand them for what they really are, psychology must *unfreeze* them by tracing their hidden origins. In doing so, psychology discovers that the determining childhood experiences are linked with the experiences of the species — that the individual lives the universal fate of mankind. The past defines the present because mankind has not yet mastered its own history. To Freud, the universal fate is in the instinctual drives, but they are themselves subject to historical " modifications." At their beginning is the experience of domination, symbolized by the primal father — the extreme Oedipus situation. It is never entirely overcome: the mature ego of the civilized personality still preserves the archaic heritage of man.

If this dependency of the ego is not kept in mind, the increased emphasis in Freud's later writings on the autonomy of the mature ego might be abused as justification for abandoning the most advanced conceptions of psychoanalysis — a retreat undertaken by the cultural and interpersonal schools. In one of his last papers,[4] Freud proposes that not all modifications of the ego are " acquired during the defensive conflicts of early childhood "; he suggests that " each individual ego is endowed from the beginning with its own peculiar dispositions and tendencies," that there exist " primary congenital variations in the ego." However, this new autonomy of the ego seems to turn into its opposite: far from retracting the notion of the ego's essential dependency on pre-individual, generic constellations, Freud strengthens the role of these constellations in the develop-

---

[4] " Analysis Terminable and Interminable," in *Collected Papers* (London: Hogarth Press, 1950), V, 343.

ment of the ego. For he interprets the congenital variations of the ego in terms of " our ' archaic heritage,' " and he thinks that " *even before the ego exists,* its subsequent lines of development, tendencies and reactions are already determined." [5] Indeed, the apparent renaissance of the ego is accompanied by the accentuation of the " deposits from primitive human development present in our archaic heritage." When Freud concludes from the congenital structure of the ego that the "topographical differentiation between ego and id loses much of its value for our investigation," then this assimilation of ego and id seems to alter the balance between the two mental forces in favor of the id rather than the ego, the generic rather than the individual processes.[6]

No part of Freud's theory has been more strongly rejected than the idea of the survival of the archaic heritage — his reconstruction of the prehistory of mankind from the primal horde through patricide to civilization. The difficulties in scientific verification and even in logical consistency are obvious and perhaps insurmountable. Moreover, they are reinforced by the taboos which the Freudian hypothesis so effectively violates: it does not lead back to the image of a paradise which man has forfeited by his sin against God but to the domination of man by man, estab-

---

[5] *Ibid.*, pp. 343–344. Italics added.

[6] In his paper on the " Mutual Influences in the Development of Ego and Id," Heinz Hartmann stresses the phylogenetic aspect: the " differentiation of ego and id, developed by whatever process of evolution through hundreds of thousands of years, is in the form of a disposition, in part an innate character of man." However, he assumes a " primary autonomy in ego development." Hartmann's paper is in *The Psychoanalytic Study of the Child,* Vol. VII (New York: International Universities Press, 1952).

lished by a very earthly father-despot and perpetuated by the unsuccessful or uncompleted rebellion against him. The " original sin " was against man — and it was no sin because it was committed against one who was himself guilty. And this phylogenctic hypothesis reveals that mature civilization is still conditioned by archaic mental immaturity. The memory of prehistoric impulses and deeds continues to haunt civilization: the repressed material returns, and the individual is still punished for impulses long since mastered and deeds long since undone.

If Freud's hypothesis is not corroborated by any anthropological evidence, it would have to be discarded altogether except for the fact that it telescopes, in a sequence of catastrophic events, the historical dialectic of domination and thereby elucidates aspects of civilization hitherto unexplained. We use Freud's anthropological speculation only in this sense: for its *symbolic* value. The archaic events that the hypothesis stipulates may forever be beyond the realm of anthropological verification; the alleged consequences of these events are historical facts, and their interpretation in the light of Freud's hypothesis lends them a neglected significance which points to the historical future. If the hypothesis defies common sense, it claims, in its defiance, a truth which common sense has been trained to forget.

In Freud's construction, the first human group was established and sustained by the enforced rule of one individual over all others. At one time in the life of the genus man, life was organized by *domination*. And the man who succeeded in dominating the others was the *father* — that is to say, the man who possessed the desired women and who had, with them, produced and kept alive the sons and daughters. The father monopolized for himself the woman (the supreme pleasure) and subjugated the other members of the horde to his power. Did he succeed in establishing his dominion *because* he succeeded in excluding them from supreme pleasure? In any case, for the group as a whole, the monopolization of pleasure meant an unequal distribution of pain: ". . . the fate of the sons was a hard one; if they excited the father's jealousy they were killed or castrated or driven out. They were forced to live in small communities and to provide themselves with wives by stealing them from others." [7] The burden of whatever work had to be done in the primal horde would have been placed on the sons who, by their exclusion from the pleasure reserved for the father, had now become "free" for the channeling of instinctual energy into unpleasurable but necessary activities. The constraint on the gratification of instinctual needs imposed by the father, the suppression of pleasure, thus not only was the result of domination but also created the mental preconditions for the *continued functioning* of domination.

In this organization of the primal horde, rationality and irrationality, biological and sociological factors, the common and the particular interest are inextricably intertwined. The primal horde is a temporarily functioning group, which sustains itself in some sort of order; it may therefore be assumed that the patriarchal despotism which established this order was "rational" to the extent to which it created and

[7] *Moses and Monotheism*, p. 128.

preserved the group — thereby the reproduction of the whole and the common interest. Setting the model for the subsequent development of civilization, the primal father prepared the ground for progress through enforced constraint on pleasure and enforced abstinence; he thus created the first preconditions for the disciplined "labor force" of the future. Moreover, this hierarchical division of pleasure was "justified" by protection, security, and even love: because the despot was the father, the hatred with which his subjects regarded him must from the beginning have been accompanied by a biological affection — ambivalent emotions which were expressed in the wish to replace and to imitate the father, to identify oneself with him, with his pleasure as well as with his power. The father establishes domination in his own interest, but in doing so he is justified by his age, by his biological function, and (most of all) by his success: he creates that "order" without which the group would immediately dissolve. In this role, the primal father foreshadows the subsequent domineering father-images under which civilization progressed. In his person and function, he incorporates the inner logic and necessity of the reality principle itself. He has "historical rights." [8]

The reproductive order of the horde survived the primal father:

> . . . one or the other son might succeed in attaining a situation similar to that of the father in the original horde. One favoured position came about in a natural way: it was that of the youngest son, who, protected by his mother's love, could profit by his father's advancing years and replace him after his death.[9]

[8] *Ibid.*, p. 135.   [9] *Ibid.*, p. 128.

Primal patriarchal despotism thus became an "effective" order. But the effectiveness of the superimposed organization of the horde must have been very precarious, and consequently the hatred against patriarchal suppression very strong. In Freud's construction, this hatred culminates in the rebellion of the exiled sons, the collective killing and devouring of the father, and the establishment of the brother clan, which in turn deifies the assassinated father and introduces those taboos and restraints which, according to Freud, generate social morality. Freud's hypothetical history of the primal horde treats the rebellion of the brothers as a rebellion against the father's taboo on the women of the horde; no "social" protest against the unequal division of pleasure is involved. Consequently, in a strict sense, civilization begins only in the brother clan, when the taboos, now self-imposed by the ruling brothers, implement repression in the *common interest* of preserving the group as a whole. And the decisive psychological event which separates the brother clan from the primal horde is the development of *guilt feeling*. Progress beyond the primal horde — i.e., civilization — presupposes guilt feeling: it introjects into the individuals, and thus sustains, the principal prohibitions, constraints, and delays in gratification on which civilization depends.

It is a reasonable surmise that after the killing of the father a time followed when the brothers quarrelled among themselves for the succession, which each of them wanted to obtain for himself alone. They came to see that these fights were as dangerous as they were futile. This hard-won understanding — as well as the memory of the deed of liberation they had achieved together and the attachment that had grown up among them during the time of their exile — led at last to a union among them, a sort of social contract. Thus there came into being the first form of a social organization accompanied by a renunciation of instinctual gratification; recognition of mutual obligations; institutions declared sacred, which could not be broken — in short, the beginnings of morality and law.[10]

The rebellion against the father is rebellion against biologically justified authority; his assassination destroys the order which has preserved the life of the group. The rebels have committed a crime against the whole and thereby also against themselves. They are guilty before the others and before themselves, and they must repent. The assassination of the father is the supreme crime because the father established the order of reproductive sexuality and thus *is*, in his person, the genus which creates and preserves all individuals. The patriarch, father and tyrant in one, unites sex and order, pleasure and reality; he evokes love and hatred; he guarantees the biological and sociological basis on which the history of mankind depends. The annihilation of his person threatens to annihilate lasting group life itself and to restore the prehistoric and subhistoric destructive force of the pleasure principle. But the sons want the same thing as the father: they want lasting satisfaction of their needs. They can attain this objective only by repeating, in a new form, the order of domination which had controlled pleasure and thereby preserved the group. The father survives as the god in whose adoration the sinners repent so that they can continue to sin, while the new fathers secure those suppressions of pleasure which are necessary for preserving their rule and their organization of the group.

[10] *Ibid.*, p. 129.

The progress from domination by one to domination by several involves a " social spread " of pleasure and makes repression self-imposed in the ruling group itself: *all* its members have to obey the taboos if they want to maintain their rule. Repression now permeates the life of the oppressors themselves, and part of their instinctual energy becomes available for sublimation in " work."

At the same time, the taboo on the women of the clan leads to expansion and amalgamation with other hordes; organized sexuality begins that formation of larger units which Freud regarded as the function of Eros in civilization. The role of the women gains increasing importance. "A good part of the power which had become vacant through the father's death passed to the women; the time of the matriarchate followed." [11] It seems essential for Freud's hypothesis that in the sequence of the development toward civilization the matriarchal period is *preceded* by primal patriarchal despotism: the low degree of repressive domination, the extent of erotic freedom, which are traditionally associated with matriarchy appear, in Freud's hypothesis, as consequences of the overthrow of patriarchal despotism rather than as primary " natural " conditions. In the development of civilization, freedom becomes possible only as *liberation*. Liberty *follows* domination — and leads to the reaffirmation of domination. Matriarchy is replaced by a patriarchal counter-revolution, and the latter is stabilized by the institutionalization of religion.

During that time a great social revolution had taken place. Matriarchy was followed by a restitution of the patriarchal order.

[11] *Ibid.*, pp. 129–130.

The new fathers, it is true, never succeeded to the omnipotence of
the primeval father. There were too many of them and they lived
in larger communities than the original horde had been; they had
to get on with one another and were restricted by social institutions.[12]

Male gods at first appear as sons by the side of the great
mother-deities, but gradually they assume the features of
the father; polytheism cedes to monotheism, and then returns the "one and only father deity whose power is unlimited."[13] .Sublime and sublimated, original domination
becomes eternal, cosmic, and good, and in this form guards
the process of civilization. The "historical rights" of the
primal father are restored.[14]

The sense of guilt, which, in Freud's hypothesis, is intrinsic to the brother clan and its subsequent consolidation
into the first "society," is primarily guilt feeling about the
perpetration of the supreme crime, patricide. Anxiety
arises over the consequences of the crime. However, these
consequences are twofold: they threaten to destroy the life
of the group by the removal of the authority which (although in terror) had preserved the group; and, at the same
time, this removal promises a society without the father —
that is, without suppression and domination. Must it not
be assumed that the sense of guilt reflects this twofold structure and its ambivalence? The rebellious parricides act
only to forestall the *first* consequence, the threat: they re-
establish domination by substituting many fathers for
one, and then by deifying and internalizing the one father. But in doing so they betray the promise of their
own deed — the promise of liberty. The despot-patriarch

---

[12] *Ibid.*, pp. 131–132.   [13] *Ibid.*   [14] *Ibid.*, pp. 135–136.

has succeeded in implanting his reality principle in the rebellious sons. Their revolt has, for a short span of time,
broken the chain of domination; then the new freedom is
again suppressed — this time by their own authority and
action. Must not their sense of guilt include guilt about
the betrayal and denial of their deed? Are they not guilty
of restoring the repressive father, guilty of self-imposed perpetuation of domination? The question suggests itself if
Freud's phylogenetic hypothesis is confronted with his notion of the instinctual dynamic. As the reality principle
takes root, even in its most primitive and most brutally enforced form, the pleasure principle becomes something
frightful and terrifying; the impulses for free gratification
meet with anxiety, and this anxiety calls for protection
against them. The individuals have to defend themselves
against the specter of their integral liberation from want
and pain, against integral gratification. And the latter is
represented by the woman who, as mother, has once, for
the first and last time, provided such gratification. These
are the instinctual factors which reproduce the rhythm of
liberation and domination.

Through her sexual power, woman is dangerous to the community, the social structure of which rests on the fear displaced to
the father. The king is slain by the people, not in order that they
may be free, but that they may take upon themselves a heavier
yoke, one that will protect them more surely from the mother.[15]

The king-father is slain not only because he imposes intolerable restraints but also because the restraints, imposed
by an individual person, are not effective enough a " barrier

[15] Otto Rank, *The Trauma of Birth* (New York: Harcourt, Brace,
1929), p. 93.

to incest," not effective enough to cope with the desire to return to the mother.[16]   Liberation is therefore followed by ever " better " domination:

The development of the paternal domination into an increasingly powerful state system administered by man is thus a continuance of the primal repression, which has as its purpose the ever wider exclusion of woman.[17]

The overthrow of the king-father is a crime, but so is his restoration — and both are necessary for the progress of civilization. The crime against the reality principle is redeemed by the crime against the pleasure principle: redemption thus cancels itself. The sense of guilt is sustained in spite of repeated and intensified redemption: anxiety persists because the crime against the pleasure principle is not redeemed. There is guilt over a deed that has not been accomplished: liberation. Some of Freud's formulations seem to indicate this: the sense of guilt was " the consequence of uncommitted aggression "; and

. . . it is not really a decisive matter whether one has killed one's father or abstained from the deed; one must feel guilty in either case, for guilt is the expression of the conflict of ambivalence, the eternal struggle between Eros and the destructive or death instinct.[18]

Much earlier Freud spoke of a pre-existing sense of guilt, which seems to be " lurking " in the individual, ready and waiting to " assimilate " an accusation made against him.[19] This notion seems to correspond to the idea of a " floating

[16] *Ibid.*, p. 92.
[17] *Ibid.*, p. 94.
[18] *Civilization and Its Discontents* (London: Hogarth Press, 1949), pp. 128, 121.
[19] " Psychoanalysis and the Ascertaining of Truth in Courts of Law," in *Collected Papers*, II, 23.

anxiety" which has subterranean roots even beneath the *individual* unconscious.

Freud assumes that the primal crime, and the sense of guilt attached to it, are reproduced, in modified forms, throughout history. The crime is re-enacted in the conflict of the old and new generation, in revolt and rebellion against established authority — and in subsequent repentance: in the restoration and glorification of authority. In explaining this strange perpetual recurrence, Freud suggested the hypothesis of the *return of the repressed*, which he illustrated by the psychology of religion. Freud thought that he had found traces of the patricide and of its "return" and redemption in the history of Judaism, which begins with the killing of Moses. The concrete implications of Freud's hypothesis become clearer in his interpretation of anti-Semitism. He believed that anti-Semitism had deep roots in the unconscious: jealousy over the Jewish claim of being the "first-born, favorite child of God the Father"; dread of circumcision, associated with the threat of castration; and, perhaps most important, "grudge against the new religion" (Christianity) which was forced on many modern peoples "only in relatively recent times." This grudge was "projected" onto the source from which Christianity came, namely, Judaism.[20]

If we follow this train of thought beyond Freud, and connect it with the twofold origin of the sense of guilt, the life and death of Christ would appear as a struggle against the father — and as a triumph over the father.[21] The message

[20] *Moses and Monotheism*, pp. 144f.
[21] See Erich Fromm, *Die Entwicklung des Christusdogmas* (Vienna: Internationaler Psychoanalytischer Verlag, 1931).

of the Son was the message of liberation: the overthrow of the Law (which is domination) by Agape (which is Eros). This would fit in with the heretical image of Jesus as the Redeemer in the flesh, the Messiah who came to save man here on earth. Then the subsequent transubstantiation of the Messiah, the deification of the Son beside the Father, would be a betrayal of his message by his own disciples — the denial of the liberation in the flesh, the revenge on the redeemer. Christianity would then have surrendered the gospel of Agape-Eros again to the Law; the father-rule would be restored and strengthened. In Freudian terms, the primal crime could have been expiated, according to the message of the Son, in an order of peace and love on earth. It was not; it was rather superseded by another crime — that against the Son. With his transubstantiation, his gospel too was transubstantiated; his deification removed his message from this world. Suffering and repression were perpetuated.

This interpretation would lend added significance to Freud's statement that the Christian peoples are "badly christened," that "under the thin veneer of Christianity they have remained what their ancestors were, barbarically polytheistic." [22] They are "badly christened" in so far as they accept and obey the liberating gospel only in a highly sublimated form — which leaves the reality unfree as it was before. Repression (in the technical Freudian sense) played only a minor role in the institutionalization of Christianity. The transformation of the original content, the deflection from the original objective, took place in

[22] *Moses and Monotheism*, p. 145.

broad daylight, consciously, with public argumentation and justification. Equally open was the armed struggle of institutionalized Christianity against the heretics, who tried or allegedly tried to rescue the unsublimated content and the unsublimated objective. There were good rational motives behind the bloody wars against the Christian revolutions which filled the Christian era. However, the cruel and organized slaughter of Cathari, Albigensians, Anabaptists, of slaves, peasants, and paupers who revolted under the sign of the cross, the burning of witches and their defenders — this sadistic extermination of the weak suggests that unconscious instinctual forces broke through all the rationality and rationalization. The executioners and their bands fought the specter of a liberation which they desired but which they were compelled to reject. The crime against the Son must be forgotten in the killing of those whose practice recalls the crime. It took centuries of progress and domestication before the return of the repressed was mastered by the power and progress of industrial civilization. But at its late stage its rationality seems to explode in another return of the repressed. The image of liberation, which has become increasingly realistic, is persecuted the world over. Concentration and labor camps, the trials and tribulations of non-conformists release a hatred and fury which indicate the total mobilization against the return of the repressed.

If the development of religion contains the basic ambivalence — the image of domination *and* the image of liberation — then Freud's thesis in *The Future of an Illusion* must be re-evaluated. Freud there stressed the role of religion in the historical deflection of energy from the real improvement of the human condition to an imaginary world of eternal salvation. He thought that the disappearance of this illusion would greatly accelerate the material and intellectual progress of mankind, and he praised science and scientific reason as the great liberating antagonists of religion. Perhaps no other writing shows Freud closer to the great tradition of Enlightenment; but also no other shows him more clearly succumbing to the dialectic of Enlightenment. In the present period of civilization, the progressive ideas of rationalism can be recaptured only when they are reformulated. The function of science and of religion has changed — as has their interrelation. Within the total mobilization of man and nature which marks the period, science is one of the most destructive instruments — destructive of that freedom from fear which it once promised. As this promise evaporated into utopia, "scientific" becomes almost identical with denouncing the notion of an earthly paradise. The scientific attitude has long since ceased to be the militant antagonist of religion, which has equally effectively discarded its explosive elements and often accustomed man to a good conscience in the face of suffering and guilt. In the household of culture, the functions of science and religion tend to become complementary; through their present usage, they both deny the hopes which they once aroused and teach men to appreciate the facts in a world of alienation. In this sense, religion is no longer an illusion, and its academic promotion falls in line with the predominant positivistic trend.[23] Where

---

[23] See Max Horkheimer, "Der neueste Angriff auf die Metaphysik," in Zeitschrift für Sozialforschung, VI (1937), 4ff.

religion still preserves the uncompromised aspirations for peace and happiness, its " illusions " still have a higher truth value than science which works for their elimination. The repressed and transfigured content of religion cannot be liberated by surrendering it to the scientific attitude.

Freud applies the notion of the return of the repressed, which was elaborated in the analysis of the history of individual neuroses,[24] to the general history of mankind. This step from individual to group psychology introduces one of the most controversial problems: How can the historical return of the repressed be understood?

> In the course of thousands of centuries it certainly became forgotten that there was a primeval father . . . , and what fate he met. . . . In what sense, therefore, can there be any question of a tradition? [25]

Freud's answer, which assumes " an impression of the past in unconscious memory traces," has encountered widespread rejection. However, the assumption loses much of its fantastic character if it is confronted with the concrete and tangible factors which refresh the memory of every generation. In enumerating the conditions under which the repressed material may penetrate into consciousness, Freud mentions a strengthening of the instincts " attached to the repressed material," and events and experiences " which are so much like the repressed material that they have the power to awaken it." [26] As an example for the strengthening of the instincts he cites the " processes during puberty." Under the impact of the ripening genital sexuality, there reappear in the

---

[24] " Repression," in *Collected Papers*, IV, 93.
[25] *Moses and Monotheism*, p. 148.
[26] *Ibid.*, p. 150.

. . . phantasies of all persons the infantile tendencies . . . and among them one finds in regular frequency and in the first place, the sexual feeling of the child for the parents. Usually, this has already been differentiated by sexual attraction, namely, the attraction of the son for the mother, and of the daughter for the father. Simultaneously with the overcoming and rejection of these distinctly incestuous phantasies, there occurs one of the most important as well as one of the most painful psychic accomplishments of puberty; it is the breaking away from the parental authority, through which alone is formed that opposition between the new and old generation, which is so important for cultural progress.[27]

The events and experiences which may "awaken" the repressed material — even without a specific strengthening of the instincts attached to it — are, at the societal level, encountered in the institutions and ideologies which the individual faces daily and which reproduce, in their very structure, both domination and the impulse to overthrow it (family, school, workshop and office, the state, the law, the prevailing philosophy and morality). The decisive difference between the primal situation and its civilized historical return is, of course, that in the latter the ruler-father is normally no longer killed and eaten, and that domination is normally no longer personal. The ego, the superego, and the external reality have done their work — but "it is not really a decisive matter whether one has killed one's father or abstained from the deed," if the function of the conflict and its consequences are the same.

In the Oedipus situation, the primal situation recurs under circumstances which from the beginning assure the last-

<hr/>

[27] *Three Contributions to the Theory of Sex*, in *The Basic Writings of Sigmund Freud* (New York: Modern Library, 1938), pp. 617–618. See also Anna Freud, *The Ego and the Mechanisms of Defense* (London: Hogarth Press, 1937), Chaps. 11, 12.

ing triumph of the father. But they also assure the life of
the son and his future ability to take the father's place.
How did civilization achieve this compromise? The multitude of somatic, mental, and social processes which resulted
in this achievement are practically identical with the contents of Freud's psychology. Force, identification, repression, sublimation co-operate in the formation of the ego and
superego. The function of the father is gradually trans-
ferred from his individual person to his social position, to
his image in the son (conscience), to God, to the various
agencies and agents which teach the son to become a mature and restrained member of his society. *Ceteris paribus,*
the intensity of restraint and renunciation involved in this
process is probably not smaller than it was in the primal
horde. However, they are more rationally distributed between father and son and among society as a whole; and
the rewards, though not greater, are relatively secure. The
monogamic family, with its enforceable obligations for the
father, restricts his monopoly of pleasure; the institution of
inheritable private property, and the universalization of labor, give the son a justified expectancy of his own sanctioned pleasure in accordance with his socially useful performances. Within this framework of objective laws and
institutions, the processes of puberty lead to the liberation
from the father as a necessary and legitimate event. It is
nothing short of a mental catastrophe — but it is nothing
more. Then the son leaves the patriarchal family and sets
out to become a father and boss himself.

The transformation of the pleasure principle into the performance principle, which changes the despotic monopoly

of the father into restrained educational and economic authority, also changes the original object of the struggle: the mother. In the primal horde, the image of the desired woman, the mistress-wife of the father, was Eros and Thanatos in immediate, natural union. She was the aim of the sex instincts, and she was the mother in whom the son once had that integral peace which is the absence of all need and desire — the Nirvana before birth. Perhaps the taboo on incest was the first great protection against the death instinct: the taboo on Nirvana, on the regressive impulse for peace which stood in the way of progress, of Life itself. Mother and wife were separated, and the fatal identity of Eros and Thanatos was thus dissolved. With regard to the mother, sensual love becomes *aim-inhibited* and transformed into *affection* (tenderness). Sexuality and affection are divorced; only later they are to meet again in the love to the wife which is sensual as well as tender, aim-inhibited as well as aim-attaining.[28] Tenderness is created out of abstinence — abstinence first enforced by the primal father. Once created, it becomes the psychical basis not only for the family but also for the establishment of lasting group relations:

the primal father had prevented his sons from satisfying their directly sexual tendencies; he forced them into abstinence and consequently into the emotional ties with him and with one another which could arise out of those of their tendencies that were inhibited in their sexual aim. He forced them, so to speak, into group psychology.[29]

[28] *Three Contributions to the Theory of Sex*, pp. 599, 615; *Group Psychology and the Analysis of the Ego* (New York: Liveright Publishing Corp., 1949), pp. 117–118; *Civilization and Its Discontents*, p. 71.
[29] *Group Psychology and the Analysis of the Ego*, p. 94.

At this level of civilization, within the system of rewarded inhibitions, the father can be overcome without exploding the instinctual and social order: his image and his function now perpetuate themselves in every child — even if it does not know him. He merges with duly constituted authority. Domination has outgrown the sphere of personal relationships and created the institutions for the orderly satisfaction of human needs on an expanding scale. But it is precisely the development of these institutions which undermines the established basis of civilization. Its inner limits appear in the late industrial age.

CHAPTER FOUR

The Dialectic of Civilization

Freud attributes to the sense of guilt a decisive role in the development of civilization; moreover, he establishes a correlation between progress and *increasing* guilt feeling. He states his intention " to represent the sense of guilt as the most important problem in the evolution of culture, and to convey that the price of progress in civilization is paid in forfeiting happiness through the heightening of the sense of guilt." [1] Recurrently Freud emphasizes that, as civilization progresses, guilt feeling is " further reinforced," " intensified," is " ever-increasing." [2] The evidence adduced by Freud is twofold: first, he derives it analytically from the theory of instincts, and, second, he finds the theoretical analysis corroborated by the great diseases and discontents of contemporary civilization: an enlarged cycle of wars, ubiquitous persecution, anti-Semitism, genocide, bigotry, and the enforcement of " illusions," toil, sickness, and misery in the midst of growing wealth and knowledge.

We have briefly reviewed the prehistory of the sense of guilt; it has " its origin in the Oedipus complex and was acquired when the father was killed by the association of

[1] *Civilization and Its Discontents* (London: Hogarth Press, 1949), p. 123.
[2] *Ibid.*, pp. 120–122.

the brothers." [3] They satisfied their aggressive instinct; but
the love which they had for the father caused remorse,
created the superego by identification, and thus created the
"restrictions which should prevent a repetition of the
deed." [4] Subsequently, man abstains from the deed; but
from generation to generation the aggressive impulse revives, directed against the father and his successors, and
from generation to generation aggression has to be inhibited anew:

> Every renunciation then becomes a dynamic fount of conscience;
> every fresh abandonment of gratification increases its severity and
> intolerance . . . every impulse of aggression which we omit to
> gratify is taken over by the super-ego and goes to heighten its
> aggressiveness (against the ego). [5]

The excessive severity of the superego, which takes the wish
for the deed and punishes even suppressed aggression, is
now explained in terms of the eternal struggle between Eros
and the death instinct: the aggressive impulse against the
father (and his social successors) is a derivative of the death
instinct; in "separating" the child from the mother, the
father also inhibits the death instinct, the Nirvana impulse.
He thus does the work of Eros; love, too, operates in the
formation of the superego. The severe father, who as the
forbidding representative of Eros subdues the death instinct
in the Oedipus conflict, enforces the first "communal" (social) relations: his prohibitions create identification among
the sons, aim-inhibited love (affection), exogamy, sublimation. On the basis of renunciation, Eros begins its cultural
work of combining life into ever larger units. And as the

---

[3] *Ibid.*, p. 118.   [4] *Ibid.*, p. 120.   [5] *Ibid.*, p. 114.

father is multiplied, supplemented, and replaced by the authorities of society, as prohibitions and inhibitions spread, so do the aggressive impulse and its objects. And with it grows, on the part of society, the need for strengthening the defenses — the need for reinforcing the sense of guilt:

> Since culture obeys an inner erotic impulse which bids it bind mankind into a closely knit mass, it can achieve this aim only by means of its vigilance in fomenting an ever-increasing sense of guilt. That which began in relation to the father ends in relation to the community. If civilization is an inevitable course of development from the group of the family to the group of humanity as a whole, then an intensification of the sense of guilt — resulting from the innate conflict of ambivalence, from the eternal struggle between the love and the death trends — will be inextricably bound up with it, until perhaps the sense of guilt may swell to a magnitude that individuals can hardly support.[6]

In this quantitative analysis of the growth of the sense of guilt, the change in the *quality* of guiltiness, its growing irrationality, seems to disappear. Indeed, Freud's central sociological position prevented him from following this avenue. To him, there was no higher rationality against which the prevailing one could be measured. If the irrationality of guilt feeling is that of civilization itself, then it is rational; and if the abolition of domination destroys culture itself, then it remains the supreme crime, and no effective means for its prevention are irrational. However, Freud's own theory of instincts impelled him to go further and to unfold the entire fatality and futility of this dynamic. Strengthened defense against aggression is necessary; but in order to be effective the defense against enlarged aggression would have to strengthen the sex instincts, for only a strong Eros can effectively " bind " the destruc-

[6] *Ibid.*, pp. 121–122.

tive instincts. And this is precisely what the *developed civilization is incapable of doing* because it depends for its very existence on extended and intensified regimentation and control. The chain of inhibitions and deflections of instinctual aims cannot be broken. " Our civilization is, generally speaking, founded on the suppression of instincts." [7]

Civilization is first of all progress in *work* — that is, work for the procurement and augmentation of the necessities of life. This work is normally without satisfaction in itself; to Freud it is unpleasurable, painful. In Freud's metapsychology there is no room for an original " instinct of workmanship," " mastery instinct," etc.[8] The notion of the conservative nature of the instincts under the rule of the pleasure and Nirvana principles strictly precludes such assumptions. When Freud incidentally mentions the " natural human aversion to work," [9] he only draws the inference from his basic theoretical conception. The instinctual syndrome " unhappiness and work " recurs throughout Freud's writings,[10] and his interpretation of the Prometheus myth is centered on the connection between curbing of sexual passion and civilized work.[11] The basic work in civilization

----

[7] " ' Civilized ' Sexual Morality and Modern Nervousness," in *Collected Papers* (London: Hogarth Press, 1950), II, 82.

[8] Ives Hendrick, " Work and the Pleasure Principle," in *Psychoanalytic Quarterly*, XII (1943), 314. For a further discussion of this paper, see Chapter 10 below.

[9] *Civilization and Its Discontents*, p. 34 note.

[10] In a letter of April 16, 1896, he speaks of the " moderate misery necessary for intensive work." Ernest Jones, *The Life and Work of Sigmund Freud*, Vol. I (New York: Basic Books, 1953), p. 305.

[11] *Civilization and Its Discontents*, pp. 50–51 note; *Collected Papers*, V, 288ff. For Freud's apparently contradictory statement on the libidinal satisfaction provided by work (*Civilization and Its Discontents*, p. 34 note), see page 212 below.

is non-libidinal, is labor; labor is " unpleasantness," and such unpleasantness has to be enforced. " For what motive would induce man to put his sexual energy to other uses if by any disposal of it he could obtain fully satisfying pleasure? He would never let go of this pleasure and would make no further progress." [12] If there is no original " work instinct," then the energy required for (unpleasurable) work must be " withdrawn " from the primary instincts — from the sexual and from the destructive instincts. Since civilization is mainly the work of Eros, it is first of all withdrawal of libido: culture " obtains a great part of the mental energy it needs by subtracting it from sexuality." [13]

But not only the work impulses are thus fed by aim-inhibited sexuality. The specifically " social instincts " (such as the " affectionate relations between parents and children, . . . feelings of friendship, and the emotional ties in marriage ") contain impulses which are " held back by internal resistance " from attaining their aims; [14] only by virtue of such renunciation do they become sociable. Each individual contributes his renunciations (first under the impact of external compulsion, then internally), and from " these sources the common stock of the material and ideal wealth of civilization has been accumulated." [15] Although Freud remarks that these social instincts " need not be described as sublimated " (because they have not abandoned their sexual aims but rest content with " certain approxima-

[12] " The Most Prevalent Form of Degradation in Erotic Life," in *Collected Papers*, IV, 216.
[13] *Civilization and Its Discontents*, p. 74.
[14] " The Libido Theory," in *Collected Papers*, V, 134.
[15] " ' Civilized ' Sexual Morality . . . ," p. 82.

tions to satisfaction "), he calls them " closely related " to sublimation.[16] Thus the main sphere of civilization appears as a sphere of *sublimation*. But sublimation involves *desexualization*. Even if and where it draws on a reservoir of " neutral displaceable energy " in the ego and in the id, this neutral energy " proceeds from the narcissistic reservoir of libido," i.e., it is desexualized Eros.[17] The process of sublimation alters the balance in the instinctual structure. Life is the fusion of Eros and death instinct; in this fusion, Eros has subdued its hostile partner. However:

> After sublimation the erotic component no longer has the power to bind the whole of the destructive elements that were previously combined with it, and these are released in the form of inclinations to aggression and destruction.[18]

Culture demands continuous sublimation; it thereby weakens Eros, the builder of culture. And desexualization, by weakening Eros, unbinds the destructive impulses. Civilization is thus threatened by an instinctual de-fusion, in which the death instinct strives to gain ascendancy over the life instincts. Originating in renunciation and developing under progressive renunciation, civilization tends toward self-destruction.

This argument runs too smooth to be true. A number of objections arise. In the first place, not all work involves desexualization, and not all work is unpleasurable, is renunciation. Secondly, the inhibitions enforced by culture also affect — and perhaps even chiefly affect — the deriva-

[16] " The Libido Theory," p. 134.
[17] *The Ego and the Id* (London: Hogarth Press, 1950), pp. 38, 61–63. See Edward Glover, " Sublimation, Substitution, and Social Anxiety," in *International Journal of Psychoanalysis*, Vol. XII, No. 3 (1931), p. 264.
[18] *The Ego and the Id*, p. 80.

tives of the death instinct, aggressiveness and the destruction impulses. In this respect at least, cultural inhibition would accrue to the strength of Eros. Moreover, work in civilization is itself to a great extent *social utilization* of aggressive impulses and is thus work in the service of Eros. An adequate discussion of these problems presupposes that the theory of the instincts is freed from its exclusive orientation on the performance principle, that the image of a non-repressive civilization (which the very achievements of the performance principle suggest) is examined as to its substance. Such an attempt will be made in the last part of this study; here, some tentative clarifications must suffice.

The psychical sources and resources of work, and its relation to sublimation, constitute one of the most neglected areas of psychoanalytic theory. Perhaps nowhere else has psychoanalysis so consistently succumbed to the official ideology of the blessings of " productivity." [19] Small wonder then, that in the Neo-Freudian schools, where (as we shall see in the Epilogue) the ideological trends in psychoanalysis triumph over its theory, the tenor of work morality is all-pervasive. The " orthodox " discussion is almost in its entirety focused on " creative " work, especially art, while work in the realm of necessity — labor — is relegated to the background.

To be sure, there is a mode of work which offers a high degree of libidinal satisfaction, which is pleasurable in its execution. And artistic work, where it is genuine, seems to grow out of a non-repressive instinctual constellation and to envisage non-repressive aims — so much so that the term

[19] Ives Hendrick's article cited above is a striking example.

sublimation seems to require considerable modification if applied to this kind of work. But the bulk of the work relations on which civilization rests is of a very different kind. Freud notes that the " daily work of earning a livelihood affords particular satisfaction when it has been selected by free choice." [20] However, if " free choice " means more than a small selection between pre-established necessities, and if the inclinations and impulses used in work are other than those preshaped by a repressive reality principle, then satisfaction in daily work is only a rare privilege. The work that created and enlarged the material basis of civilization was chiefly labor, alienated labor, painful and miserable — and still is. The performance of such work hardly gratifies *individual* needs and inclinations. It was imposed upon man by brute necessity and brute force; if alienated labor has anything to do with Eros, it must be very indirectly, and with a considerably sublimated and weakened Eros.

But does not the civilized inhibition of *aggressive* impulses in work offset the weakening of Eros? Aggressive as well as libidinal impulses are supposed to be satisfied in work " by way of sublimation," and the culturally beneficial " sadistic character " of work has often been emphasized.[21] The development of technics and technological rationality absorbs to a great extent the " modified " destructive instincts:

The instinct of destruction, when tempered and harnessed (as it were, inhibited in its aim) and directed towards objects, is com-

[20] *Civilization and Its Discontents*, p. 34 note.
[21] See Alfred Winterstein, " Zur Psychologie der Arbeit," in *Imago*, XVIII (1932), 142.

pelled to provide the ego with satisfaction of its needs and with power over nature.[22]

Technics provide the very basis for progress; technological rationality sets the mental and behaviorist pattern for productive performance, and " power over nature " has become practically identical with civilization. Is the destructiveness sublimated in these activities sufficiently subdued and diverted to assure the work of Eros? It seems that socially useful destructiveness is less sublimated than socially useful libido. To be sure, the diversion of destructiveness from the ego to the external world secured the growth of civilization. However, extroverted destruction remains destruction: its objects are in most cases actually and violently assailed, deprived of their form, and reconstructed only after partial destruction; units are forcibly divided, and the component parts forcibly rearranged. Nature is literally " violated." Only in certain categories of sublimated aggressiveness (as in surgical practice) does such violation directly strengthen the life of its object. Destructiveness, in extent and intent, seems to be more directly satisfied in civilization than the libido.

However, while the destructive impulses are thus being satisfied, such satisfaction cannot stabilize their energy in the service of Eros. Their destructive force must drive them beyond this servitude and sublimation, for their aim is, not matter, not nature, not any object, but life itself. If they are the derivatives of the death instinct, then they cannot accept as final any " substitutes." Then, through constructive technological destruction, through the con-

[22] *Civilization and Its Discontents*, p. 101.

structive violation of nature, the instincts would still operate toward the annihilation of life. The radical hypothesis of *Beyond the Pleasure Principle* would stand: the instincts of self-preservation, self-assertion, and mastery, in so far as they have absorbed this destructiveness, would have the function of assuring the organism's " own path to death." Freud retracted this hypothesis as soon as he had advanced it, but his formulations in *Civilization and Its Discontents* seem to restore its essential content. And the fact that the destruction of life (human and animal) has progressed with the progress of civilization, that cruelty and hatred and the scientific extermination of men have increased in relation to the real possibility of the elimination of oppression — this feature of late industrial civilization would have instinctual roots which perpetuate destructiveness beyond all rationality. The growing mastery of nature then would, with the growing productivity of labor, develop and fulfill the human needs *only as a by-product*: increasing cultural wealth and knowledge would provide the material for progressive destruction and the need for increasing instinctual repression.

This thesis implies the existence of objective criteria for gauging the degree of instinctual repression at a given stage of civilization. However, repression is largely unconscious and automatic, while its degree is measureable only in the light of consciousness. The differential between (phylogenetically necessary) repression and surplus-repression [23] may provide the criteria. Within the total structure of the repressed personality, surplus-repression is that portion

[23] See page 37 above.

which is the result of specific societal conditions sustained
in the specific interest of domination. The extent of this
surplus-repression provides the standard of measurement:
the smaller it is, the less repressive is the stage of civilization. The distinction is equivalent to that between the
biological and the historical sources of human suffering. Of
the three " sources of human suffering" which Freud enu-
merates — namely, "the superior force of nature, the disposition to decay of our bodies, and the inadequacy of our
methods of regulating human relations in the family, the
community and the state" [24] — at least the first and the
last are in a strict sense *historical* sources; the superiority of
nature and the organization of societal relations have essentially changed in the development of civilization. Consequently, the necessity of repression, and of the suffering derived from it, varies with the maturity of civilization, with
the extent of the achieved rational mastery of nature and of
society. Objectively, the need for instinctual inhibition
and restraint depends on the need for toil and delayed
satisfaction. The same and even a reduced scope of instinctual regimentation would constitute a higher degree of
repression at a mature stage of civilization, when the need
for renunciation and toil is greatly reduced by material and
intellectual progress — when civilization could actually afford a considerable release of instinctual energy expended
for domination and toil. Scope and intensity of instinctual
repression obtain their full significance only in relation to
the historically possible extent of freedom. For Freud, is
progress in civilization progress in freedom?

[24] *Civilization and Its Discontents*, p. 43.

We have seen that Freud's theory is focused on the recurrent cycle " domination-rebellion-domination." But the second domination is not simply a repetition of the first one; the cyclical movement is *progress* in domination. From the primal father via the brother clan to the system of institutional authority characteristic of mature civilization, domination becomes increasingly impersonal, objective, universal, and also increasingly rational, effective, productive. At the end, under the rule of the fully developed performance principle, subordination appears as implemented through the social division of labor itself (although physical and personal force remains an indispensable instrumentality). Society emerges as a lasting and expanding system of useful performances; the hierarchy of functions and relations assumes the form of objective reason: law and order are identical with the life of society itself. In the same process, repression too is depersonalized: constraint and regimentation of pleasure now become a function (and " natural " result) of the social division of labor. To be sure, the father, as *paterfamilias*, still performs the basic regimentation of the instincts which prepares the child for the surplus-repression on the part of society during his adult life. But the father performs this function as the representative of the family's position in the social division of labor rather than as the " possessor " of the mother. Subsequently, the individual's instincts are controlled through the social utilization of his labor power. He has to work in order to live, and this work requires not only eight, ten, twelve daily hours of his time and therefore a corresponding diversion of energy, but also during these hours and the remaining ones a behavior in conformity with the standards and morals of the performance principle. Historically, the reduction of Eros to procreative-monogamic sexuality (which completes the subjection of the pleasure principle to the reality principle) is consummated only when the individual has become a subject-object of labor in the apparatus of his society; whereas, ontogenetically, the primary suppression of infantile sexuality remains the precondition for this accomplishment.

The development of a hierarchical system of social labor not only rationalizes domination but also " contains " the rebellion against domination. At the individual level, the primal revolt is contained within the framework of the normal Oedipus conflict. At the societal level, recurrent rebellions and revolutions have been followed by counter-revolutions and restorations. From the slave revolts in the ancient world to the socialist revolution, the struggle of the oppressed has ended in establishing a new, " better " system of domination; progress has taken place through an improving chain of control. Each revolution has been the conscious effort to replace one ruling group by another; but each revolution has also released forces that have " overshot the goal," that have striven for the abolition of domination and exploitation. The ease with which they have been defeated demands explanations. Neither the prevailing constellation of power, nor immaturity of the productive forces, nor absence of class consciousness provides an adequate answer. In every revolution, there seems to have been a historical moment when the struggle against domination might have been victorious — but the moment passed. An

element of *self-defeat* seems to be involved in this dynamic
(regardless of the validity of such reasons as the prematurity
and inequality of forces). In this sense, every revolution
has also been a betrayed revolution.

Freud's hypothesis on the origin and the perpetuation of
guilt feeling elucidates, in psychological terms, this sociological dynamic: it explains the " identification " of those
who revolt with the power against which they revolt. The
economic and political incorporation of the individuals into
the hierarchical system of labor is accompanied by an instinctual process in which the human objects of domination
reproduce their own repression. And the increasing rationalization of power seems to be reflected in an increasing rationalization of repression. In retaining the individuals as instruments of labor, forcing them into renunciation and toil, domination no longer merely or primarily sustains specific privileges but also sustains society as a whole
on an expanding scale. The guilt of rebellion is thereby
greatly intensified. The revolt against the primal father
eliminated an individual person who could be (and was)
replaced by other persons; but when the dominion of the
father has expanded into the dominion of society, no such
replacement seems possible, and the guilt becomes fatal.
Rationalization of guilt feeling has been completed. The
father, restrained in the family and in his individual biological authority, is resurrected, far more powerful, in the administration which preserves the life of society, and in the
laws which preserve the administration. These final and
most sublime incarnations of the father cannot be overcome
" symbolically," by emancipation: there is no freedom from

administration and its laws because they appear as the ultimate guarantors of liberty. The revolt against them would be the supreme crime again — this time not against the despot-animal who forbids gratification but against the wise order which secures the goods and services for the progressive satisfaction of human needs. Rebellion now appears as the crime against the whole of human society and therefore as beyond reward and beyond redemption.

However, the very progress of civilization tends to make this rationality a spurious one. The existing liberties and the existing gratifications are tied to the requirements of domination; they themselves become instruments of repression. The excuse of scarcity, which has justified institutionalized repression since its inception, weakens as man's knowledge and control over nature enhances the means for fulfilling human needs with a minimum of toil. The still prevailing impoverishment of vast areas of the world is no longer due chiefly to the poverty of human and natural resources but to the manner in which they are distributed and utilized. This difference may be irrelevant to politics and to politicians but it is of decisive importance to a theory of civilization which derives the need for repression from the " natural " and perpetual disproportion between human desires and the environment in which they must be satisfied. If such a " natural " condition, and not certain political and social institutions, provides the rationale for repression, then it has become irrational. The culture of industrial civilization has turned the human organism into an ever more sensitive, differentiated, exchangeable instrument, and has created a social wealth sufficiently great to transform this instrument into an end in itself. The available resources make for a *qualitative* change in the human needs. Rationalization and mechanization of labor tend to reduce the quantum of instinctual energy channeled into toil (alienated labor), thus freeing energy for the attainment of objectives set by the free play of individual faculties. Technology operates against the repressive utilization of energy in so far as it minimizes the time necessary for the production of the necessities of life, thus saving time for the development of needs *beyond* the realm of necessity and of necessary waste.

But the closer the real possibility of liberating the individual from the constraints once justified by scarcity and immaturity, the greater the need for maintaining and streamlining these constraints lest the established order of domination dissolve. Civilization has to defend itself against the specter of a world which could be free. If society cannot use its growing productivity for reducing repression (because such usage would upset the hierarchy of the *status quo*), productivity must be turned *against* the individuals; it becomes itself an instrument of universal control. Totalitarianism spreads over late industrial civilization wherever the interests of domination prevail upon productivity, arresting and diverting its potentialities. The people have to be kept in a state of permanent mobilization, internal and external. The rationality of domination has progressed to the point where it threatens to invalidate its foundations; therefore it must be reaffirmed more effectively than ever before. This time there shall be no killing of the father, not even a " symbolic " killing — because he may not find a successor.

The " automatization " of the superego [25] indicates the defense mechanisms by which society meets the threat. The defense consists chiefly in a strengthening of controls not so much over the instincts as over consciousness, which, if left free, might recognize the work of repression in the bigger and better satisfaction of needs. The manipulation of consciousness which has occurred throughout the orbit of contemporary industrial civilization has been described in the various interpretations of totalitarian and " popular cultures ": co-ordination of the private and public existence, of spontaneous and required reactions. The promotion of thoughtless leisure activities, the triumph of anti-intellectual ideologies, exemplify the trend. This extension of controls to formerly free regions of consciousness and leisure permits a relaxation of sexual taboos (previously more important because the over-all controls were less effective). Today compared with the Puritan and Victorian periods, sexual freedom has unquestionably increased (although a reaction against the 1920's is clearly noticeable). At the same time, however, the sexual relations themselves have become much more closely assimilated with social relations; sexual liberty is harmonized with profitable conformity. The fundamental antagonism between sex and social utility — itself the reflex of the conflict between pleasure principle and reality principle — is blurred by the progressive encroachment of the reality principal on the pleas-

[25] See pages 32–33 above.

ure principle. In a world of alienation, the liberation of Eros would necessarily operate as a destructive, fatal force — as the total negation of the principle which governs the repressive reality. It is not an accident that the great literature of Western civilization celebrates only the "unhappy love," that the Tristan myth has become its representative expression. The morbid romanticism of the myth is in a strict sense "realistic." In contrast to the destructiveness of the liberated Eros, the relaxed sexual morality within the firmly entrenched system of monopolistic controls itself serves the system. The negation is co-ordinated with "the positive": the night with the day, the dream world with the work world, phantasy with frustration. Then, the individuals who relax in this uniformly controlled reality recall, not the dream but the day, not the fairy tale but its denunciation. In their erotic relations, they "keep their appointments" — with charm, with romance, with their favorite commercials.

But, within the system of unified and intensified controls, decisive changes are taking place. They affect the structure of the superego and the content and manifestation of guilt feeling. Moreover, they tend toward a state in which the completely alienated world, expending its full power, seems to prepare the stuff and material for a new reality principle.

The superego is loosened from its origin, and the traumatic experience of the father is superseded by more exogenous images. As the family becomes less decisive in directing the adjustment of the individual to society, the father-son conflict no longer remains the model-conflict.

This change derives from the fundamental economic processes which have characterized, since the beginning of the century, the transformation of " free " into " organized " capitalism. The independent family enterprise and, subsequently, the independent personal enterprise cease to be the units of the social system; they are being absorbed into large-scale impersonal groupings and associations. At the same time, the social value of the individual is measured primarily in terms of standardized skills and qualities of adjustment rather than autonomous judgment and personal responsibility.

The technological abolition of the individual is reflected in the decline of the social function of the family.[26] It was formerly the family which, for good or bad, reared and educated the individual, and the dominant rules and values were transmitted personally and transformed through personal fate. To be sure, in the Oedipus situation, not individuals but " generations " (units of the genus) faced each other; but in the passing and inheritance of the Oedipus conflict they became individuals, and the conflict continued into an individual life history. Through the struggle with father and mother as personal targets of love and aggression, the younger generation entered societal life with impulses, ideas, and needs which were largely *their own*. Consequently, the formation of their superego, the repressive modification of their impulses, their renunciation and sublimation were very personal experiences. Precisely because of this, their adjustment left painful scars, and life

[26] For the analysis of these processes, see *Studien über Autorität und Familie*, ed. Max Horkheimer (Paris: Felix Alcan, 1936); Max Horkheimer, *Eclipse of Reason* (New York: Oxford University Press, 1946).

under the performance principle still retained a sphere of private non-conformity.

Now, however, under the rule of economic, political, and cultural monopolies, the formation of the mature superego seems to skip the stage of individualization: the generic atom becomes directly a social atom. The repressive organization of the instincts seems to be *collective*, and the ego seems to be prematurely socialized by a whole system of extra-familial agents and agencies. As early as the preschool level, gangs, radio, and television set the pattern for conformity and rebellion; deviations from the pattern are punished not so much within the family as outside and against the family. The experts of the mass media transmit the required values; they offer the perfect training in efficiency, toughness, personality, dream, and romance. With this education, the family can no longer compete. In the struggle between the generations, the sides seem to be shifted: the son knows better; he represents the mature reality principle against its obsolescent paternal forms. The father, the first object of aggression in the Oedipus situation, later appears as a rather inappropriate target of aggression. His authority as transmitter of wealth, skills, experiences is greatly reduced; he has less to offer, and therefore less to prohibit. The progressive father is a most unsuitable enemy and a most unsuitable " ideal " — but so is any father who no longer shapes the child's economic, emotional, and intellectual future. Still, the prohibitions continue to prevail, the repressive control of the instincts persists, and so does the aggressive impulse. Who are the father-substitutes against which it is primarily directed?

As domination congeals into a system of objective administration, the images that guide the development of the superego become depersonalized. Fomerly the superego was " fed " by the master, the chief, the principal. These represented the reality principle in their tangible personality: harsh and benevolent, cruel and rewarding, they provoked and punished the desire to revolt; the enforcement of conformity was their personal function and responsibility. Respect and fear could therefore be accompanied by hate of what they were and did as persons; they presented a living object for the impulses and for the conscious efforts to satisfy them. But these personal father-images have gradually disappeared behind the institutions. With the rationalization of the productive apparatus, with the multiplication of functions, all domination assumes the form of administration. At its peak, the concentration of economic power seems to turn into anonymity: everyone, even at the very top, appears to be powerless before the movements and laws of the apparatus itself. Control is normally administered by offices in which the controlled are the employers and the employed. The masters no longer perform an individual function. The sadistic principals, the capitalist exploiters, have been transformed into salaried members of a bureaucracy, whom their subjects meet as members of another bureaucracy. The pain, frustration, impotence of the individual derive from a highly productive and efficiently functioning system in which he makes a better living than ever before. Responsibility for the organization of his life lies with the whole, the " system," the sum total of the institutions that determine, satisfy, and control his needs.

The aggressive impulse plunges into a void — or rather the hate encounters smiling colleagues, busy competitors, obedient officials, helpful social workers who are all doing their duty and who are all innocent victims.

Thus repulsed, aggression is again introjected: not suppression but the suppressed is guilty. Guilty of what? Material and intellectual progress has weakened the force of religion below the point where it can sufficiently explain the sense of guilt. The aggressiveness turned against the ego threatens to become senseless: with his consciousness co-ordinated, his privacy abolished, his emotions integrated into conformity, the individual has no longer enough " mental space " for developing himself *against* his sense of guilt, for living with a conscience of his own. His ego has shrunk to such a degree that the multiform antagonistic processes between id, ego, and superego cannot unfold themselves in their classic form.

Still, the guilt is there; it seems to be a quality of the whole rather than of the individuals — collective guilt, the affliction of an institutional system which wastes and arrests the material and human resources at its disposal. The extent of these resources can be defined by the level of fulfilled human freedom attainable through truly rational use of the productive capacity. If this standard is applied, it appears that, in the centers of industrial civilization, man is kept in a state of impoverishment, both cultural and physical. Most of the clichés with which sociology describes the process of dehumanization in present-day mass culture are correct; but they seem to be slanted in the wrong direction. What is retrogressive is not mechanization and standardization but their containment, not the universal co-ordination but its concealment under spurious liberties, choices, and individualities. The high standard of living in the domain of the great corporations is *restrictive* in a concrete sociological sense: the goods and services that the individuals buy control their needs and petrify their faculties. In exchange for the commodities that enrich their life, the individuals sell not only their labor but also their free time. The better living is offset by the all-pervasive control over living. People dwell in apartment concentrations — and have private automobiles with which they can no longer escape into a different world. They have huge refrigerators filled with frozen foods. They have dozens of newspapers and magazines that espouse the same ideals. They have innumerable choices, innumerable gadgets which are all of the same sort and keep them occupied and divert their attention from the real issue — which is the awareness that they could both work less and determine their own needs and satisfactions.

The ideology of today lies in that production and consumption reproduce and justify domination. But their ideological character does not change the fact that their benefits are real. The repressiveness of the whole lies to a high degree in its efficacy: it enhances the scope of material culture, facilitates the procurement of the necessities of life, makes comfort and luxury cheaper, draws ever-larger areas into the orbit of industry — while at the same time sustaining toil and destruction. The individual pays by sacrificing his time, his consciousness, his dreams; civilization pays by sacrificing its own promises of liberty, justice, and peace for all.

The discrepancy between potential liberation and actual repression has come to maturity: it permeates all spheres of life the world over. The rationality of progress heightens the irrationality of its organization and direction. Social cohesion and administrative power are sufficiently strong to protect the whole from direct aggression, but not strong enough to eliminate the accumulated aggressiveness. It turns against those who do not belong to the whole, whose existence is its denial. This foe appears as the archenemy and Antichrist himself: he is everywhere at all times; he represents hidden and sinister forces, and his omnipresence requires total mobilization. The difference between war and peace, between civilian and military populations, between truth and propaganda, is blotted out. There is regression to historical stages that had been passed long ago, and this regression reactivates the sado-masochistic phase on a national and international scale. But the impulses of this phase are reactivated in a new, " civilized " manner: practically without sublimation, they become socially " useful " activities in concentration and labor camps, colonial and civil wars, in punitive expeditions, and so on.

Under these circumstances, the question whether the present stage of civilization is demonstrably more destructive than the preceding ones does not seem to be very relevant. In any case, the question cannot be avoided by pointing to the destructiveness prevalent throughout history. The destructiveness of the present stage reveals its full significance only if the present is measured, not in terms of past stages, but in terms of its own potentialities. There is more than a quantitative difference in whether wars are waged by professional armies in confined spaces, or against entire populations on a global scale; whether technical inventions that could make the world free from misery are used for the conquest or for the creation of suffering; whether thousands are slain in combat or millions scientifically exterminated with the help of doctors and engineers; whether exiles can find refuge across the frontiers or are chased around the earth; whether people are naturally ignorant or are being *made* ignorant by their daily intake of information and entertainment. It is with a new ease that terror is assimilated with normality, and destructiveness with construction. Still, progress continues, and continues to narrow the basis of repression. At the height of its progressive achievements, domination not only undermines its own foundations, but also corrupts and liquidates the opposition against domination. What remains is the negativity of reason, which impels wealth and power and generates a climate in which the instinctual roots of the performance principle are drying up.

The alienation of labor is almost complete. The mechanics of the assembly line, the routine of the office, the ritual of buying and selling are freed from any connection with human potentialities. Work relations have become to a great extent relations between persons as exchangeable objects of scientific management and efficiency experts. To be sure, the still prevailing competitiveness requires a certain degree of individuality and spontaneity; but these features have become just as superficial and illusory as the competitiveness to which they belong. Individuality is literally in name only, in the specific representation of types [27] (such as vamp, housewife, Ondine, he-man, career woman, struggling young couple), just as competition tends to be reduced to prearranged varieties in the production of gadgets, wrappings, flavors, colors, and so on. Beneath this illusory surface, the whole work-world and its recreation have become a system of animate and inanimate things — all equally subject to administration. The human existence in this world is mere stuff, matter, material, which does not have the principle of its movement in itself. This state of ossification also affects the instincts, their inhibitions and modifications. Their original dynamic becomes static: the interactions between ego, superego, and id congeal into automatic reactions. Corporealization of the super-ego is accompanied by corporealization of the ego, manifest in the frozen traits and gestures, produced at the appropriate occasions and hours. Consciousness, increasingly less burdened by autonomy, tends to be reduced to the task of regulating the co-ordination of the individual with the whole.

This co-ordination is effective to such a degree that the general unhappiness has decreased rather than increased. We have suggested [28] that the individual's awareness of the prevailing repression is blunted by the manipulated restriction of his consciousness. This process alters the contents of happiness. The concept denotes a more-than-private,

[27] See Leo Lowenthal, "International Who's Who 1937," in *Studies in Philosophy and Social Science* (formerly *Zeitschrift für Sozialforschung*), VIII (1939), 262ff.; and "Historical Perspectives of Popular Culture," in *American Journal of Sociology*, LV (1950), 323ff.

[28] See page 94 above.

more-than-subjective condition; [29] happiness is not in the mere feeling of satisfaction but in the reality of freedom and satisfaction. Happiness involves knowledge: it is the prerogative of the *animal rationale*. With the decline in consciousness, with the control of information, with the absorption of individual into mass communication, knowledge is administered and confined. The individual does not really know what is going on; the overpowering machine of education and entertainment unites him with all the others in a state of anaesthesia from which all detrimental ideas tend to be excluded. And since knowledge of the whole truth is hardly conducive to happiness, such general anaesthesia makes individuals happy. If anxiety is more than a general malaise, if it is an existential condition, then this so-called " age of anxiety " is distinguished by the extent to which anxiety has disappeared from expression.

These trends seem to suggest that the expenditure of energy and effort for developing one's own inhibitions is greatly diminished. *The living links between the individual and his culture are loosened.* This culture was, in and for the individual, the system of inhibitions that generated and regenerated the predominant values and institutions. Now, the repressive force of the reality principle seems no longer renewed and rejuvenated by the repressed individuals. The less they function as the agents and victims of their own life, the less is the reality principle strengthened through " creative " identifications and sublimations, which enrich and at the same time protect the household of culture.

---

[29] See Herbert Marcuse, "Zur Kritik des Hedonismus," in *Zeitschrift für Sozialforschung,* VII (1938), 55ff.

The groups and group ideals, the philosophies, the works of art and literature that still express without compromise the fears and hopes of humanity stand against the prevailing reality principle: they are its absolute denunciation.

The positive aspects of progressive alienation show forth. The human energies which sustained the performance principle are becoming increasingly dispensable. The automatization of necessity and waste, of labor and entertainment, precludes the realization of individual potentialities in this realm. It repels libidinal cathexis. The ideology of scarcity, of the productivity of toil, domination, and renunciation, is dislodged from its instinctual as well as rational ground. The theory of alienation demonstrated the fact that man does not realize himself in his labor, that his life has become an instrument of labor, that his work and its products have assumed a form and power independent of him as an individual. But the liberation from this state seems to require, not the arrest of alienation, but its consummation, not the reactivation of the repressed and productive personality but its abolition. The elimination of human potentialities from the world of (alienated) labor creates the preconditions for the elimination of labor from the world of human potentialities.

CHAPTER FIVE

Philosophical Interlude

Freud's theory of civilization grows out of his psychological theory: its insights into the historical process are derived from the analysis of the mental apparatus of the individuals who are the living substance of history. This approach penetrates the protective ideology in so far as it views the cultural institutions in terms of what they have made of the individuals through whom they function. But the psychological approach seems to fail at a decisive point: history has progressed "behind the back" and over the individuals, and the laws of the historical process have been those governing the reified institutions rather than the individuals.[1] Against this criticism we have argued that Freud's psychology reaches into a dimension of the mental apparatus where the individual is still the genus, the present still the past. Freud's theory reveals the biological de-individualization beneath the sociological one — the former proceeding under the pleasure and Nirvana principles, the latter under the reality principle. By virtue of this generic conception, Freud's psychology of the individual is *per se* psychology of the genus. And his generic psychology un-

[1] See Theodor W. Adorno, "Psychoanalyse und Soziologie," in *Sociologica* (Frankfurt: Europäische Verlagsantalt, 1955). Frankfurter Beiträge zur Soziologie, Vol. I.

folds the vicissitudes of the instincts as historical vicissitudes: the recurrent dynamic of the struggle between Eros and death instinct, of the building and destruction of culture, of repression and the return of the repressed, is released and organized by the historical conditions under which mankind develops.

But the metapsychological implications of Freud's theory go even beyond the framework of sociology. The primary instincts pertain to life and death — that is to say, to organic matter as such. And they link organic matter back with unorganic matter, and forward with its higher mental manifestations. In other words, Freud's theory contains certain assumptions on the structure of the principal modes of being: it contains *onto*logical implications. This chapter attempts to show that these implications are more than formal — that they pertain to the basic context of Western philosophy.

According to Freud, civilization begins with the methodical inhibition of the primary instincts. Two chief modes of instinctual organization may be distinguished: (a) the inhibition of sexuality, ensuing in durable and expanding group relations, and (b) the inhibition of the destructive instincts, leading to the mastery of man and nature, to individual and social morality. As the combination of these two forces sustains ever more effectively the life of ever larger groups, Eros gains over his adversary: social utilization presses the death instinct into the service of the life instincts. But the very progress of civilization increases the scope of sublimation and of controlled aggression; on both accounts, Eros is weakened and destructiveness is released.

This would suggest that progress remains committed to a regressive trend in the instinctual structure (in the last analysis, to the death instinct), that the growth of civilization is counteracted by the persistent (though repressed) impulse to come to rest in final gratification. Domination, and the enhancement of power and productivity, proceed through destruction beyond rational necessity. The quest for liberation is darkened by the quest for Nirvana.

The sinister hypothesis that culture, via the socially utilized impulses, stands under the rule of the Nirvana principle has often haunted psychoanalysis. Progress " contains " regression. From his notion of the *trauma of birth,* Otto Rank came to the conclusion that culture establishes on an ever larger scale " protective shells " which reproduce the intra-uterine state:

> Every " comfort " that civilization and technical knowledge continually strive to increase only tries to replace by durable substitutes the primal goal from which . . . it becomes ever further removed.[2]

Ferenczi's theory, especially his idea of a " genito-fugal " libido,[3] tends to the same conclusion, and Géza Róheim considered the danger of " object-loss, of being left in the dark," as one of the decisive instinctual motives in the evolution of culture.[4]

The persistent strength of the Nirvana principle in civilization illuminates the scope of the constraints placed upon the culture-building power of Eros. Eros creates culture in his struggle against the death instinct: he strives to pre-

[2] *The Trauma of Birth* (New York: Harcourt, Brace, 1929), p. 99; see also p. 103.

[3] See Chapter 10 below.

[4] *The Origin and Function of Culture* (New York: Nervous and Mental Disease Monograph No. 69, 1943), p. 77.

serve being on an ever larger and richer scale in order to satisfy the life instincts, to protect them from the threat of non-fulfillment, extinction. It is the *failure* of Eros, lack of fulfillment in life, which enhances the instinctual value of death. The manifold forms of regression are unconscious protest against the insufficiency of civilization: against the prevalence of toil over pleasure, performance over gratification. An innermost tendency in the organism militates against the principle which has governed civilization and insists on return from alienation. The derivatives of the death instinct join the neurotic and perverted manifestations of Eros in this rebellion. Time and again, Freud's theory of civilization points up these countertrends. Destructive as they appear in the light of the established culture, they testify to the destructiveness of what they strive to destroy: repression. They aim not only against the reality principle, at non-being, but also beyond the reality principle — at another mode of being. They betoken the historical character of the reality principle, the limits of its validity and necessity.

At this point, Freud's metapsychology meets a mainstream of Western philosophy.

As the scientific rationality of Western civilization began to bear its full fruit, it became increasingly conscious of its psychical implications. The ego which undertook the rational transformation of the human and natural environment revealed itself as an essentially aggressive, offensive subject, whose thoughts and actions were designed for mastering objects. It was a subject *against* an object. This *a priori* antagonistic experience defined the *ego cogitans* as well as the *ego agens*. Nature (its own as well as the external world) were " given " to the ego as something that had to be fought, conquered, and even violated — such was the precondition for self-preservation and self-development.

The struggle begins with the perpetual internal conquest of the "lower" faculties of the individual: his sensuous and appetitive faculties. Their subjugation is, at least since Plato, regarded as a constitutive element of human reason, which is thus in its very function repressive. The struggle culminates in the conquest of external nature, which must be perpetually attacked, curbed, and exploited in order to yield to human needs. The ego experiences being as "provocation,[5] as " project ";[6] it experiences each existential condition as a restraint that has to be overcome, transformed into another one. The ego becomes preconditioned for mastering action and productivity even prior to any specific occasion that calls for such an attitude. Max Scheler has pointed out that the " conscious or unconscious impulse or will to power over nature is the *primum movens* " in the relation of the modern individual to being, and that it structurally precedes modern science and technology — a " pre- and a-logical " antecedent before scientific thought and intuition.[7] Nature is *a priori* experienced by an organism bent to domination and therefore experienced as susceptible to mastery and control.[8] And consequently work is *a priori*

[5] Gaston Bachelard, *L'Eau et les Rêves* (Paris: José Corti, 1942), p. 214.
[6] J. P. Sartre, *L'Etre et le Néant* (Paris: Gallimard, 1946), *passim*.
[7] *Die Wissensformen und die Gesellschaft* (Leipzig, 1926), pp. 234–235.
[8] *Ibid.*, pp. 298–299. Scheler refers to " herrschaftswilliges Lebewesen."

power and provocation in the struggle with nature; it is over-coming of resistance. In such work-attitude, the images of the objective world appear as " symbols for points of *aggression* "; action appears as domination, and reality *per se* as " resistance." [9] Scheler calls this mode of thought " knowledge geared to domination and achievement " and sees in it the specific mode of knowledge which has guided the development of modern civilization.[10] It has shaped the predominant notion not only of the ego, the thinking and acting subject, but also of its objective world — the notion of being as such.

Whatever the implications of the original Greek conception of Logos as the essence of being, since the canonization of the Aristotelian logic the term merges with the idea of ordering, classifying, mastering reason. And this idea of reason becomes increasingly antagonistic to those faculties and attitudes which are receptive rather than productive, which tend toward gratification rather than transcendence — which remain strongly committed to the pleasure principle. They appear as the unreasonable and irrational that must be conquered and contained in order to serve the progress of reason. Reason is to insure, through the ever more effective transformation and exploitation of nature, the fulfillment of the human potentialties. But in the process the end seems to recede before the means: the time devoted to alienated labor absorbs the time for individual needs — and defines the needs themselves. The Logos shows forth as the logic of domination. When logic then reduces the units of thought to signs and symbols, the laws

[9] *Ibid.*, pp. 459, 461.
[10] *Die Formen des Wissens und die Bildung* (Bonn, 1925), p. 33. Scheler's phrase is " Herrschafts- und Leistungswissen."

of thought have finally become techniques of calculation and manipulation.

But the logic of domination does not triumph unchallenged. The philosophy which epitomizes the antagonistic relation between subject and object also retains the image of their reconciliation. The restless labor of the transcending subject terminates in the ultimate unity of subject and object: the idea of " being-in-and-for-itself," existing in its own fulfillment. The Logos of gratification contradicts the Logos of alienation: the effort to harmonize the two animates the inner history of Western metaphysics. It obtains its classical formulation in the Aristotelian hierarchy of the modes of being, which culminates in the *nous theos:* its existence is no longer defined and confined by anything other than itself but is entirely itself in all states and conditions. The ascending curve of becoming is bent in the circle which moves in itself; past, present, and future are enclosed in the ring. According to Aristotle, this mode of being is reserved to the god; and the movement of thought, pure thinking, is its sole " empirical " approximation. Otherwise the empirical world does not partake of such fulfillment; only a yearning, " Eros-like," connects this world with its end-in-itself. The Aristotelian conception is not a religious one. The *nous theos* is, as it were, *part* of the universe, neither its creator nor its lord nor its savior, but a mode of being in which all potentiality is actuality, in which the " project " of being has been fulfilled.

The Aristotelian conception remains alive through all subsequent transformations. When, at the end of the Age of Reason, with Hegel, Western thought makes its last and greatest attempt to demonstrate the validity of its categories and of the principles which govern its world, it concludes again with the *nous theos*. Again, fulfillment is relegated to the absolute idea and to absolute knowledge. Again, the movement of the circle ends the painful process of destructive and productive transcendence. Now the circle comprises the whole: all alienation is justified and at the same time canceled in the universal ring of reason which is the world. But now philosophy comprehends the concrete historical ground on which the edifice of reason is erected.

The *Phenomenology of the Spirit* unfolds the structure of reason as the structure of domination — and as the overcoming of domination. Reason develops through the developing self-consciousness of man who conquers the natural and historical world and makes it the material of his self-realization. When mere consciousness reaches the stage of self-consciousness, it finds itself as *ego*, and the ego is first *desire*: it can become conscious of itself only through satisfying itself in and by an " other." But such satisfaction involves the " negation " of the other, for the ego has to prove itself by truly " being-for-itself " *against* all " otherness." [11] This is the notion of the individual which must constantly assert and affirm himself in order to be real, which is set off against the world as his " negativity," as *denying* his freedom, so that he can exist only by incessantly winning and testing his existence *against* some-thing or some-one which contests it. The ego must become *free*, but if the world has the " character of negativity," then the ego's free-

[11] This and the following according to the *Phenomenology* (B, IV, A).

dom depends on being "recognized," "acknowledged" as master — and such recognition can only be tendered by another ego, another self-conscious subject. Objects are not alive; the overcoming of their resistance cannot satisfy or "test" the power of the ego: "Self-consciousness can attain its satisfaction only in another self-consciousness." The aggressive attitude toward the object-world, the domination of nature, thus ultimately aims at the domination of man by man. It is aggressiveness toward the other subjects: satisfaction of the ego is conditioned upon its "negative relation" to another ego:

> The relation of both self-consciousnesses is in this way so constituted that they prove themselves and each other through a life-and-death struggle. . . . And it is solely by risking life, that freedom is obtained . . .[12]

Freedom involves the risk of life, not because it involves liberation from servitude, but because the very content of human freedom is defined by the mutual "negative relation" to the other. And since this negative relation affects the totality of life, freedom can be "tested" only by staking life itself. Death and anxiety — not as "fear for this element or that, not for this or that moment of time," but as fear for one's 'entire being'"[13] — are the essential terms of human freedom *and* satisfaction. From the negative structure of self-consciousness results the relation of master and servant, domination and servitude. This relation is the consequence of the specific nature of self-consciousness and the consequence of its specific attitude toward the other (object and subject).

[12] *The Philosophy of Hegel*, ed. Carl J. Friedrich (New York: Modern Library, 1953), p. 402.
[13] *Ibid.*, p. 407.

But the *Phenomenology of the Spirit* would not be the self-interpretation of Western civilization if it were nothing more than the development of the logic of domination. The *Phenomenology of the Spirit* leads to the overcoming of that form of freedom which derives from the antagonistic relation to the other. And the true mode of freedom is, not the incessant activity of conquest, but its coming to rest in the transparent knowledge and gratification of being. The ontological climate which prevails at the end of the *Phenomenology* is the very opposite of the Promethean dynamic:

> The wounds of the Spirit heal without leaving scars; the deed is not everlasting; the Spirit takes it back into itself, and the aspect of particularity (individuality) present in it . . . immediately passes away.[14]

Mutual acknowledgment and recognition are still the test for the reality of freedom, but the terms are now forgiveness and reconciliation:

> The word of reconciliation is the (objectively) existent Spirit which apprehends in its opposite the pure knowledge of itself *qua* universal essence . . . a mutual recognition which is Absolute Spirit.[15]

These formulations occur at the decisive place where Hegel's analysis of the manifestations of the spirit has reached the position of the " self-conscious spirit " — its be-

---

[14] " Die Wunden des Geistes heilen, ohne dass Narben bleiben; die Tat ist nicht das Unvergängliche, sondern wird von dem Geiste in sich zurückgenommen, und die Seite der Einzelheit . . . ist das unmittelbar Verschwindende." *The Phenomenology of the Mind*, transl. J. B. Baillie (London: Sven Sonnenschein, 1910), II, 679. (Translation changed.)

[15] " Das Wort der Versöhnung ist der daseiende Geist, der das reine Wissen seiner selbst als allgemeines Wesen in seinem Gegenteile . . . anschaut, — ein gegenseitiges Anerkennen, welches der absolute Geist ist." *Ibid.*, p. 680 (with a minor change in translation).

ing-in-and-for-itself. Here, the "negative relation to the other" is ultimately, in the existence of the spirit as *nous*, transformed into productivity which is receptivity, activity which is fulfillment. Hegel's presentation of his system in his *Encyclopedia* ends on the word "enjoys." The philosophy of Western civilization culminates in the idea that the truth lies in the negation of the principle that governs this civilization — negation in the twofold sense that freedom appears as real only in the idea, and that the endlessly projecting and transcending productivity of being comes to fruition in the perpetual peace of self-conscious receptivity.

The *Phenomenology of the Spirit* throughout preserves the tension between the ontological and the historical content: the manifestations of the spirit *are* the main stages of Western civilization, but these historical manifestations remain affected with negativity; the spirit comes to itself only in and as absolute knowledge. It is at the same time the true form of thought and the true form of being. Being is in its very essence reason. But the highest form of reason is, to Hegel, almost the opposite of the prevailing form: it is attained and sustained fulfillment, the transparent unity of subject and object, of the universal and the individual — a dynamic rather than static unity in which all becoming is free self-externalization (*Entäusserung*), release and "enjoyment" of potentialities. The labor of history comes to rest in history: alienation is canceled, and with it transcendence and the flux of time. The spirit "overcomes its temporal form; negates Time." [16] But the "end" of history recaptures its content: the force which accomplishes the

16 ". . . hebt seine Zeitform auf; tilgt die Zeit." *Ibid.*, p. 821.

conquest of time is remembrance (re-collection). Absolute knowledge, in which the spirit attains its truth, is the spirit " entering into its real self, whereby it abandons its (extraneous) existence and entrusts its Gestalt to remembrance." [17] Being is no longer the painful transcendence toward the future but the peaceful recapture of the past. Remembrance, which has preserved everything that was, is " the inner and the actually higher form of the substance." [18]

The fact that remembrance here appears as the decisive existential category for the highest form of being indicates the inner trend of Hegel's philosophy. Hegel replaces the idea of progress by that of a cyclical development which moves, self-sufficient, in the reproduction and consummation of what *is*. This development presupposes the entire history of man (his subjective and objective world) and the comprehension of his history — the remembrance of his past. The past remains present; it is the very life of the spirit; what has been decides on what is. Freedom implies reconciliation — redemption of the past. If the past is just left behind and forgotten, there will be no end to destructive transgression. Somehow the progress of transgression must be arrested. Hegel thought that " the wounds of the spirit heal without leaving scars." He believed that, on the attained level of civilization, with the triumph of reason, freedom had become a reality. But neither the state nor society embodies the ultimate form of freedom. No matter

---

[17] ". . . sein Insichgehen, in welchem er sein Dasein verlässt und seine Gestalt der Erinnerung übergibt." *Ibid*. No English translation can render the connotation of the German term which takes *Er-innerung* as " turning into oneself," *re-turn* from externalization.

[18] ". . . das Innere und die in der Tat höhere Form der Substanz."

how rationally they are organized, they are still afflicted with unfreedom. True freedom is only in the idea. Liberation thus is a spiritual event. Hegel's dialectic remains within the framework set by the established reality principle.

Western philosophy ends with the idea with which it began. At the beginning and at the end, in Aristotle and in Hegel, the supreme mode of being, the ultimate form of reason and freedom, appear as *nous*, spirit, *Geist*. At the end and at the beginning, the empirical world remains in negativity — the stuff and the tools of the spirit, or of its representatives on earth. In reality, neither remembrance nor absolute knowledge redeems that which was and is. Still, this philosophy testifies not only to the reality principle which governs the empirical world, but also to its negation. The consummation of being is, not the ascending curve, but the closing of the circle: the *re-turn* from alienation. Philosophy could conceive of such a state only as that of pure thought. Between the beginning and the end is the development of reason as the logic of domination — progress through alienation. The repressed liberation is upheld: in the idea and in the ideal.

After Hegel, the mainstream of Western philosophy is exhausted. The Logos of domination has built its system, and what follows is epilogue: philosophy survives as a special (and not very vital) function in the academic establishment. The new principles of thought develop outside this establishment: they are qualitatively novel and committed to a different form of reason, to a different reality principle. In metaphysical terms, the change is expressed by the fact that the essence of being is no longer conceived as Logos. And, with this change in the basic experience of being, the logic of domination is challenged. When Schopenhauer defines the essence of being as *will*, it shows forth as unsatiable want and aggression which must be redeemed at all cost. To Schopenhauer, they are redeemable only in their absolute negation; will itself must come to rest — to an end. But the ideal of Nirvana contains the affirmation: the end is fulfillment, gratification. Nirvana is the image of the pleasure principle. As such it emerges, still in a repressive form, in Richard Wagner's music drama: repressive because (as in any good theology and morality) fulfillment here demands the sacrifice of earthly happiness. The *principium individuationis* itself is said to be at fault — fulfillment is only beyond its realm; the most orgastic *Liebestod* still celebrates the most orgastic renunciation.

Only Nietzsche's philosophy surmounts the ontological tradition, but his indictment of the Logos as repression and perversion of the will-to-power is so highly ambiguous that it has often blocked the understanding. First the indictment itself is ambiguous. Historically, the Logos of domination released rather than repressed the will-to-power; it was the *direction* of this will that was repressive — toward productive renunciation which made man the slave of his labor and the enemy of his own gratification. Moreover, the will-to-power is not Nietzsche's last word: " Will — this is the liberator and joybringer: thus I taught you, my friends!

But now this also learn: the Will itself is still a prisoner." [19]
Will is still a prisoner because it has no power over time:
the past not only remains unliberated but, unliberated, continues to mar all liberation. Unless the power of time over
life is broken, there can be no freedom: the fact that
time does not " recur" sustains the wound of bad conscience: it breeds vengeance and the need for punishment,
which in turn perpetuate the past and the sickness to
death. With the triumph of Christian morality, the life instincts were perverted and constrained; bad conscience was
linked with a " guilt against God."   In the human instincts
were implanted " hostility, rebellion, insurrection against
the ' master,' ' father,' the primal ancestor and origin of the
world." [20]   Repression and deprivation were thus justified
and affirmed; they were made into the masterful and aggressive forces which determined the human existence. With
their growing social utilization, progress became of necessity
progressive repression. On this road, there is no alternative,
and no spiritual and transcendental freedom can compensate for the repressive foundations of culture. The " wounds
of the spirit," if they heal at all, do leave scars. The past
becomes master over the present, and life a tribute to death:

And now cloud upon cloud rolled over the Spirit, until at last
madness preached: " all things pass away, therefore all things deserve to pass away! And this is justice itself, this law of Time, that
it must devour its children: thus preached madness." [21]

[19] *Thus Spake Zarathustra*, Part II ("On Redemption"), in *The
Portable Nietzsche*, transl. Walter Kaufmann (New York: Viking Press,
1954), p. 251. (Translation here and in the following quotations changed
in part.)
[20] *The Genealogy of Morals*, Section II:22.
[21] *Thus Spake Zarathustra*, p. 25.

Nietzsche exposes the gigantic fallacy on which Western philosophy and morality were built — namely, the transformation of facts into essences, of historical into metaphysical conditions. The weakness and despondency of man, the inequality of power and wealth, injustice and suffering were attributed to some transcendental crime and guilt; rebellion became the original sin, disobedience against God; and the striving for gratification was concupiscence. Moreover, this whole series of fallacies culminated in the deification of time: because everything in the empirical world is passing, man is in his very essence a finite being, and death is in the very essence of life. Only the higher values are eternal, and therefore really real: the inner man, faith, and love which does not ask and does not desire. Nietzsche's attempt to uncover the historical roots of these transformations elucidates their twofold function: to pacify, compensate, and justify the underprivileged of the earth, and to protect those who made and left them underprivileged. The achievment snowballed and enveloped the masters and the slaves, the rulers and the ruled, in that upsurge of productive repression which advanced Western civilization to ever higher levels of efficacy. However, growing efficacy involved growing degeneration of the life instincts — the decline of man.

Nietzsche's critique is distinguished from all academic social psychology by the position from which it is undertaken: Nietzsche speaks in the name of a reality principle fundamentally antagonistic to that of Western civilization. The traditional form of reason is rejected on the basis of the experience of being-as-end-in-itself — as joy (*Lust*) and enjoyment. The struggle against time is waged from this position: the tyranny of becoming over being must be broken if man is to come to himself in a world which is truly his own. As long as there is the uncomprehended and unconquered flux of time — senseless loss, the painful " it was " that will never be again — being contains the seed of destruction which perverts good to evil and vice versa. Man comes to himself only when the transcendence has been conquered — when eternity has become present in the here and now. Nietzsche's conception terminates in the vision of the closed circle — not progress, but the " eternal return ":

All things pass, all things return; eternally turns the wheel of Being. All things die, all things blossom again, eternal is the year of Being. All things break, all things are joined anew; eternally the house of Being builds itself the same. All things part, all things welcome each other again; eternally the ring of Being abides by itself. In each Now, Being begins; round each Here turns the sphere of There. The center is everywhere. Bent is the path of eternity.[22]

The closed circle has appeared before: in Aristotle and Hegel, as the symbol of being-as-end-in-itself. But while Aristotle reserved it to the *nous theos*, while Hegel identified it with the absolute idea, Nietzsche envisages the eternal return of the finite exactly as it is — in its full concreteness and finiteness. This is the total affirmation of the life instincts, repelling all escape and negation. The eternal return is the will and vision of an *erotic* attitude toward being for which necessity and fulfillment coincide.

> Shield of necessity!
> Star-summit of Being!

[22] *Ibid.*, Part III (" The Convalescent "), pp. 329–330.

> Not reached by any wish,
> not soiled by any No,
> eternal Yes of Being:
> I affirm you eternally,
> for I love you, eternity.[23]

Eternity, long since the ultimate consolation of an alienated existence, had been made into an instrument of repression by its relegation to a transcendental world — unreal reward for real suffering. Here, eternity is reclaimed for the fair earth — as the eternal return of its children, of the lily and the rose, of the sun on the mountains and lakes, of the lover and the beloved, of the fear for their life, of pain and happiness. Death *is*; it is conquered only if it is followed by the real rebirth of everything that was before death here on earth — not as a mere repetition but as willed and wanted re-creation. The eternal return thus includes the return of suffering, but suffering as a means for more gratification, for the aggrandizement of joy.[24] The horror of pain derives from the "instinct of weakness," from the fact that pain overwhelms and becomes final and fatal. Suffering can be affirmed if man's " power is sufficiently strong " [25] to make pain a stimulus for affirmation — a link in the chain of joy. The doctrine of the eternal return obtains all its meaning from the central proposition that "joy wants eternity " — wants itself and all things to be everlasting.

Nietzsche's philosophy contains enough elements of the terrible past: his celebration of pain and power perpetuates features of the morality which he strives to overcome.

[23] " Ruhm und Ewigkeit," in *Werke* (Leipzig: Alfred Kröner, 1919), VIII, 436 (my translation).

[24] *Ibid.*, XIV, 301.

[25] *Ibid.*, p. 295.

However, the image of a new reality principle breaks the repressive context and anticipates the liberation from the archaic heritage. " The earth has all too long been a mad-house! " [26] For Nietzsche, the liberation depends on the reversal of the sense of guilt; mankind must come to associate the bad conscience not with the affirmation but with the denial of the life instincts, not with the rebellion but with the acceptance of the repressive ideals.[27]

We have suggested certain nodal points in the development of Western philosophy which reveal the historical limitations of its system of reason — and the effort to surpass this system. The struggle appears in the antagonism between becoming and being, between the ascending curve and the closed circle, progress and eternal return, transcendence and rest in fulfillment.[28] It is the struggle between the logic of domination and the will to gratification. Both assert their claims for defining the reality principle. The traditional ontology is contested: against the conception of being in terms of Logos rises the conception of being in a-logical terms: will and joy. This countertrend strives to formulate its own Logos: the logic of gratification.

In its most advanced positions, Freud's theory partakes of this philosophical dynamic. His metapsychology, attempting to define the essence of being, defines it as Eros

---

[26] *The Genealogy of Morals*, Section II, 22.

[27] *Ibid.*, 24.

[28] The two antagonistic conceptions of time outlined here are discussed by Mircea Eliade in his book *The Myth of the Eternal Return* (London: Routledge and Kegan Paul, 1955). He contrasts the " cyclical " with the " linear " notion of time, the former characteristic of " traditional " (predominantly primitive) civilizations, the latter of " modern man."

— in contrast to its traditional definition as Logos. The death instinct affirms the principle of non-being (the negation of being) against Eros (the principle of being). The ubiquitous fusion of the two principles in Freud's conception corresponds to the traditional metaphical fusion of being and non-being. To be sure, Freud's conception of Eros refers only to organic life. However, inorganic matter is, as the " end " of the death instinct, so inherently linked to organic matter that (as suggested above) it seems permissable to give his conception a general ontological meaning. Being is essentially the striving for pleasure. This striving becomes an " aim " in the human existence: the erotic impulse to combine living substance into ever larger and more durable, units is the instinctual source of civilization. The sex instincts are *life* instincts: the impulse to preserve and enrich life by mastering nature in accordance with the developing vital needs is originally an erotic impulse. Ananke is experienced as the barrier against the satisfaction of the life instincts, which seek pleasure, not security. And the "struggle for existence " is originally a struggle for pleasure: culture begins with the collective implementation of this aim. Later, however, the struggle for existence is organized in the interest of domination: the erotic basis of culture is transformed. When philosophy conceives the essence of being as Logos, it is already the Logos of domination — commanding, mastering, directing reason, to which man and nature are to be subjected

Freud's interpretation of being in terms of Eros recaptures the early stage of Plato's philosophy, which conceived of culture not as the repressive sublimation but as the free self-development of Eros. As early as Plato, this conception appears as an archaic-mythical residue. Eros is being absorbed into Logos, and Logos is reason which subdues the instincts. The history of ontology reflects the reality principle which governs the world ever more exclusively: The insights contained in the metaphysical notion of Eros were driven underground. They survived, in eschatological distortion, in many heretic movements, in the hedonistic philosophy. Their history has still to be written — as has the history of the transformation of Eros in Agape.[29]   Freud's own theory follows the general trend: in his work, the rationality of the predominant reality principle supersedes the metaphysical speculations on Eros.

We shall presently try to recapture the full content of his speculations.

[29] See Anders Nygren, *Agape and Eros* (Philadelphia: Westminster Press, 1953).

PART TWO

BEYOND THE REALITY PRINCIPLE

"What time has been wasted during man's destiny in the struggle to decide what man's next world will be like! The keener the effort to find out, the less he knew about the present one he lived in. The one lovely world he knew, lived in, that gave him all he had, was, according to preacher and prelate, the one to be least in his thoughts. He was recommended, ordered, from the day of his birth to bid goodbye to it. Oh, we have had enough of the abuse of this fair earth! It is no sad truth that this should be our home. Were it but to give us simple shelter, simple clothing, simple food, adding the lily and the rose, the apple and the pear, it would be a fit home for mortal or immortal man."

Sean O'Casey, *Sunset and Evening Star*

CHAPTER SIX

The Historical Limits of the Established Reality Principle

The preceding analysis tried to identify certain basic trends in the instinctual structure of civilization and, particularly, to define the specific reality principle which has governed the progress of Western civilization. We designated this reality principle as the performance principle; and we attempted to show that domination and alienation, derived from the prevalent social organization of labor, determined to a large extent the demands imposed upon the instincts by this reality principle. The question was raised whether the continued rule of the performance principle as *the* reality principle must be taken for granted (so that the trend of civilization must be viewed in the light of the same principle), or whether the performance principle has perhaps created the preconditions for a qualitatively different, non-repressive reality principle. This question suggested itself when we confronted the psychoanalytical theory of man with some basic historical tendencies:

(1) The very progress of civilization under the performance principle has attained a level of productivity at which the social demands upon instinctual energy to be spent in alienated labor could be considerably reduced. Conse-

quently, the continued repressive organization of the instincts seems to be necessitated less by the "struggle for existence" than by the interest in prolonging this struggle — by the interest in domination.

(2) The representative philosophy of Western civilization has developed a concept of reason which contains the domineering features of the performance principle. However, the same philosophy ends in the vision of a higher form of reason which is the very negation of these features — namely, receptivity, contemplation, enjoyment. Behind the definition of the subject in terms of the ever transcending and productive activity of the ego lies the image of the redemption of the ego: the coming to rest of all transcendence in a mode of being that has absorbed all becoming, that is for and with itself in all otherness.

The problem of the historical character and limitation of the performance principle is of decisive importance for Freud's theory. We have seen that he practically identifies the established reality principle (i.e., the performance principle) with the reality principle as such. Consequently, his dialectic of civilization would lose its finality if the performance principle revealed itself as only one specific historical form of the reality principle. Moreover, since Freud also identifies the historical character of the instincts with their "nature," the relativity of the performance principle would even affect his basic conception of the instinctual dynamic between Eros and Thanatos: their relation and its development would be different under a different reality principle. Conversely, Freud's instinct theory provides one of the strongest arguments *against* the relative (historical) character of the reality principle. If sexuality is in its very essence antisocial and asocial, and if destructiveness is the manifestation of a primary instinct, then the idea of a non-repressive reality principle would be nothing but idle speculation.

Freud's instinct theory indicates the direction in which the problem must be examined. The performance principle enforces an integrated repressive organization of sexuality and of the destruction instinct. Therefore, if the historical process tended to make obsolete the institutions of the performance principle, it would also tend to make obsolete the organization of the instincts — that is to say, to release the instincts from the constraints and diversions required by the performance principle. This would imply the real possibility of a gradual elimination of surplus-repression, whereby an expanding area of destructiveness could be absorbed or neutralized by strengthened libido. Evidently, Freud's theory precludes the construction of any psychoanalytical utopia. If we accept his theory and still maintain that there is historical substance in the idea of a non-repressive civilization, then it must be derivable from Freud's instinct theory itself. His concepts must be examined to discover whether or not they contain elements that require reinterpretation. This approach would parallel the one used in the preceding sociological discussion. There, the attempt was made to "read off" the ossification of the performance principle from the historical conditions which it has created; presently, we shall try to "read off" from the historical vicissitudes of the instincts the possibility of their non-repressive development. Such an approach implies a critique of the established reality principle in the name of the pleasure principle — a re-evalution of the antagonistic relation that has prevailed between the two dimensions of the human existence.

Freud maintains that an essential conflict between the two principles is inevitable; however, in the elaboration of his theory, this inevitability seems to be opened to question. The conflict, in the form it assumes in civilization, is said to be caused and perpetuated by the prevalence of Ananke, *Lebensnot*, the struggle for existence. (The later stage of the instinct theory, with the concepts of Eros and death instinct, does not cancel this thesis: *Lebensnot* now appears as the want and deficiency inherent in organic life itself.) The struggle for existence necessitates the repressive modification of the instincts chiefly because of the lack of sufficient means and resources for integral, painless and toilless gratification of instinctual needs. If this is true, the repressive organization of the instincts in the struggle for existence would be due to *exogenous* factors — exogenous in the sense that they are not inherent in the "nature" of the instincts but emerge from the specific historical conditions under which the instincts develop. According to Freud, this distinction is meaningless, for the instincts themselves are "historical"; [1] there is no instinctual structure "outside" the historical structure. However, this does not dispense with the necessity of making the distinction — except that it must be made *within* the historical structure itself. The latter appears as stratified on

[1] See, for example, *Beyond the Pleasure Principle* (New York: Liveright Publishing Corp., 1950), pp. 47, 49.

two levels: (a) the phylogenetic-biological level, the development of the animal man in the struggle with nature; and (b) the sociological level, the development of civilized individuals and groups in the struggle among themselves and with their environment. The two levels are in constant and inseparable interaction, but factors generated at the second level are exogenous to the first and have therefore a different weight and validity (although, in the course of the development, they can "sink down" to the first level): they are more relative; they can change faster and without endangering or reversing the development of the genus. This difference in the origin of instinctual modification underlies the distinction we have introduced between repression and surplus-repression; [2] the latter originates and is sustained at the sociological level.

Freud is well aware of the historical element in man's instinctual structure. In discussing religion as a specific historical form of "illusion," he adduces against himself the argument: "Since men are so slightly amenable to reasonable arguments, so completely are they ruled by their instinctual wishes, why should one want to take away from them a means for satisfying their instincts and replace it by reasonable arguments?" And he answers: "Certainly men are like this, but have you asked yourselves whether they need be so, whether their inmost nature necessitates it?" [3] However, in his theory of instincts, Freud does not draw any fundamental conclusions from the historical distinction, but ascribes to both levels equal and general valid-

[2] See page 37 above.
[3] *The Future of an Illusion* (New York: Liveright Publishing Corp., 1949), p. 81.

ity. For his metapsychology, it is not decisive whether the inhibitions are imposed by scarcity or by the hierarchical *distribution* of scarcity, by the struggle for existence or by the interest in domination. And indeed the two factors — the phylogenetic-biological and the sociological — have grown together in the recorded history of civilization. But their union has long since become " unnatural " — and so has the oppressive " modification " of the pleasure principle by the reality principle. Freud's consistent denial of the possibility of an essential liberation of the former implies the assumption that scarcity is as permanent as domination — an assumption that seems to beg the question. By virtue of this assumption, an extraneous fact obtains the theoretical dignity of an inherent element of mental life, inherent even in the primary instincts. In the light of the long-range trend of civilization, and in the light of Freud's own interpretation of the instinctual development, the assumption must be questioned. The historical possibility of a gradual decontrolling of the instinctual development must be taken seriously, perhaps even the historical *necessity* — if civilization is to progress to a higher stage of freedom.

To extrapolate the hypothesis of a non-repressive civilization from Freud's theory of the instincts, one must re-examine his concept of the primary instincts, their objectives and their interrelation. In this conception, it is mainly the death instinct that seems to defy any hypothesis of a non-repressive civilization: the very existence of such an instinct seems to engender "automatically" the whole network of constraints and controls instituted by civilization; innate destructiveness must beget perpetual repression.

Our re-examination must therefore begin with Freud's analysis of the death instinct.

We have seen that, in Freud's late theory of the instincts, the "compulsion inherent in organic life to restore an earlier state of things which the living entity has been obliged to abandon under the pressure of external disturbing forces" [4] is common to both primary instincts: Eros and death instinct. Freud regards this retrogressive tendency as an expression of the "inertia" in organic life, and ventures the following hypothetical explanation: at the time when life originated in inanimate matter, a strong "tension" developed which the young organism strove to relieve by returning to the inanimate condition.[5] At the early stage of organic life, the road to the previous state of inorganic existence was probably very short, and dying very easy; but gradually "external influences" lengthened this road and compelled the organism to take ever longer and more complicated "detours to death." The longer and more complicated the "detour," the more differentiated and powerful the organism becomes: it finally conquers the globe as its dominion. Still, the original goal of the instincts remains — return to inorganic life, "dead" matter. Precisely here, in developing his most far-reaching hypothesis, Freud repeatedly states that exogenous factors determined the primary instinctual development: The organism was forced to abandon the earlier state of things "under the pressure of *external* disturbing forces"; the phenomena of organic life must be "attributed to *external* disturbing and diverting influences"; decisive "*external* influences altered in such

---

[4] *Beyond the Pleasure Principle*, p. 47.   [5] *Ibid.*, p. 50.

a way as to oblige the still surviving substance to diverge
ever more widely from its original course of life." [6] If the
organism dies " for *internal* reasons," [7] then the detour to
death must have been caused by external factors. Freud
assumes that these factors must be sought in " the history
of the earth we live in and of its relation to the sun." [8]
However, the development of the animal man does not remain enclosed in geological history; man becomes, on the
basis of natural history, the subject and object of his own
history. If, originally, the actual difference between life
instinct and death instinct was very small, in the history of
the animal man it grows to become an essential characteristic of the historical process itself.

The diagram on the facing page may illustrate Freud's
construction of the basic instinctual dynamic.

The diagram sketches a historical sequence from the beginning of organic life (stages 2 and 3), through the formative stage of the two primary instincts (5), to their " modified " development as human instincts in civilization (6-7).
The turning points are at stages 3 and 6. They are both
caused by exogenous factors by virtue of which the definite formation as well as the subsequent dynamic of the
instincts become "historically acquired." At stage 3, the
exogenous factor is the " unrelieved tension " created by
the birth of organic life; the " experience " that life is less
" satisfactory," more painful, than the preceding stage generates the death instinct as the drive for relieving this tension through regression. The working of the death instinct

---

[6] *Ibid.*, pp. 47, 49, 50. Italics added.   [8] *Ibid.*, p. 49.
[7] *Ibid.*, p. 50.

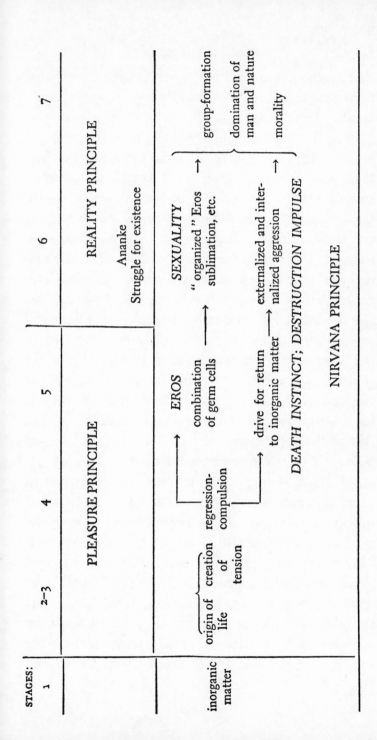

thus appears as the result of the trauma of primary frustration: want and pain, here caused by a geological-biological event.

The other turning point, however, is no longer a geological-biological one: it occurs at the threshold of civilization. The exogenous factor here is Ananke, the conscious struggle for existence. It enforces the repressive controls of the sex instincts (first through the brute violence of the primal father, then through institutionalization and internalization), as well as the transformation of the death instinct into socially useful aggression and morality. This organization of the instincts (actually a long process) creates the civilized division of labor, progress, and " law and order "; but it also starts the chain of events that leads to the progressive weakening of Eros and thereby to the growth of aggressiveness and guilt feeling. We have seen that this development is not " inherent " in the struggle for existence but only in its oppressive organization, and that at the present stage the possible conquest of want makes this struggle ever more irrational.

But are there not, in the instincts themselves, asocial forces that necessitate repressive constraints regardless of scarcity or abundance in the external world? Again, we recall Freud's statement that the nature of the instincts is " historically acquired." Therefore, this nature is subject to change if the fundamental conditions that caused the instincts to acquire this nature have changed. True, these conditions are still the same in so far as the struggle for existence still takes place within the framework of scarcity and domination. But they tend to become obsolete and

" artificial" in view of the real possibility of their elimination. The extent to which the *basis* of civilization has
changed (while its *principle* has been retained) can be illustrated by the fact that the difference between the beginnings of civilization and its present stage seems infinitely
greater than the difference between the beginnings of civilization and the preceding stage, where the " nature " of the
instincts was acquired. To be sure, the change in the conditions of civilization would directly affect only the formed
human instincts (the sex and aggression instincts). In the
biological-geological conditions which Freud assumed for
the living substance as such, no such change can be envisaged; the birth of life continues to be a trauma, and thus the
reign of the Nirvana principle seems to be unshakable.
However, the derivatives of the death instinct operate only
in fusion with the sex instincts; as long as life grows, the
former remain subordinate to the latter; the fate of the
destrudo (the " energy " of the destruction instincts) depends on that of the libido. Consequently, a qualitative
change in the development of sexuality must necessarily
alter the manifestations of the death instinct.

Thus, the hypothesis of a non-repressive civilization must
be theoretically validated first by demonstrating the possibility of a non-repressive development of the libido under
the conditions of mature civilization. The direction of such
a development is indicated by those mental forces which,
according to Freud, remain essentially free from the reality
principle and carry over this freedom into the world of mature consciousness. Their re-examination must be the
next step.

CHAPTER SEVEN

Phantasy and Utopia

In Freud's theory, the mental forces opposed to the reality principle appear chiefly as relegated to and operating from the unconscious. The rule of the "unmodified" pleasure principle obtains only over the deepest and most "archaic" unconscious processes: they can provide no standards for the construction of the non-repressive mentality, nor for the truth value of such a construction. But Freud singles out phantasy as one mental activity that retains a high degree of freedom from the reality principle even in the sphere of the developed consciousness. We recall his description in the "Two Principles of Mental Functioning."

> With the introduction of the reality principle one mode of thought-activity was split off: it was kept free from reality-testing and remained subordinated to the pleasure principle alone. This is the act of *phantasy-making* (*das Phantasieren*), which begins already with the game of children, and later, continued as *daydreaming*, abandons its dependence on real objects.[1]

Phantasy plays a most decisive function in the total mental structure: it links the deepest layers of the unconscious with the highest products of consciousness (art), the dream with the reality; it preserves the archetypes of the genus, the

[1] *Collected Papers* (London: Hogarth Press, 1950), IV, 16–17. See pages 14–15 above.

perpetual but repressed ideas of the collective and individual memory, the tabooed images of freedom. Freud establishes a twofold connection, " between the sexual instincts and phantasy " on the one side, and " between the ego instincts and the activities of consciousness " on the other. This dichotomy is untenable, not only in view of the later formulation of the instinct theory (which abandons the independent ego instincts) but also because of the incorporation of phantasy into artistic (and even normal) consciousness. However, the affinity between phantasy and sexuality remains decisive for the function of the former.

The recognition of phantasy (imagination) as a thought process with its own laws and truth values was not new in psychology and philosophy; Freud's original contribution lay in the attempt to show the genesis of this mode of thought and its essential connection with the pleasure principle. The establishment of the reality principle causes a division and mutilation of the mind which fatefully determines its entire development. The mental process formerly unified in the pleasure ego is now split: its main stream is channeled into the domain of the reality principle and brought into line with its requirements. Thus conditioned, this part of the mind obtains the monopoly of interpreting, manipulating, and altering reality — of governing remembrance and oblivion, even of defining what reality is and how it should be used and altered. The other part of the mental apparatus remains free from the control of the reality principle — at the price of becoming powerless, inconsequential, unrealistic. Whereas the ego was formerly guided and driven by the *whole* of its mental energy, it is now to be guided only by that part of it which conforms to the reality principle. This part and this part alone is to set the objectives, norms, and values of the ego; as *reason* it becomes the sole repository of judgment, truth, rationality; it decides what is useful and useless, good and evil.[2] *Phantasy* as a separate mental process is born and at the same time left behind by the organization of the pleasure ego into the reality ego. Reason prevails: it becomes unpleasant but useful and correct; phantasy remains pleasant but becomes useless, untrue — a mere play, daydreaming. As such, it continues to speak the language of the pleasure principle, of freedom from repression, of uninhibited desire and gratification — but reality proceeds according to the laws of reason, no longer committed to the dream language.

However, phantasy (imagination) retains the structure and the tendencies of the psyche prior to its organization by the reality, prior to its becoming an "individual" set off against other individuals. And by the same token, like the id to which it remains committed, imagination preserves the "memory" of the subhistorical past when the life of the individual was the life of the genus, the image of the immediate unity between the universal and the particular under the rule of the pleasure principle. In contrast, the entire subsequent history of man is characterized by the destruction of this original unity: the position of the ego

---

[2] *Reason* in this sense is not identical with the *rational faculty* (intellect) of traditional theoretical psychology. The term here designates that part of the mind which is brought under the control of the reality principle and includes the organized part of the "vegetative," "sensitive," and "appetitive" faculties.

" in its capacity of independent individual organism " comes into conflict with " itself in its other capacity as a member of a series of generations.[8] The genus now lives in the conscious and ever renewed conflict among the individuals and between them and their world. Progress under the performance principle proceeds through these conflicts. The *principium individuationis* as implemented by this reality principle gives rise to the repressive utilization of the primary instincts, which continue to strive, each in its own way, to cancel the *principium individuationis*, while they are constantly diverted from their objective by the very progress which their energy sustains. In this effort, both instincts are subdued. In and against the world of the antagonistic *principium individuationis*, imagination sustains the claim of the whole individual, in union with the genus and with the " archaic " past.

Freud's metapsychology here restores imagination to its rights. As a fundamental, independent mental process, phantasy has a truth value of its own, which corresponds to an experience of its own — namely, the surmounting of the antagonistic human reality. Imagination envisions the reconciliation of the individual with the whole, of desire with realization, of happiness with reason. While this harmony has been removed into utopia by the established reality principle, phantasy insists that it must and can become real, that behind the illusion lies *knowledge*. The truths of imagination are first realized when phantasy itself takes form, when it creates a universe of perception and compre-

[8] *A General Introduction to Psychoanalysis* (New York: Garden City Publishing Co., 1943), p. 359.

hension — a subjective and at the same time objective universe. This occurs in *art*. The analysis of the cognitive function of phantasy is thus led to aesthetics as the " science of beauty ": behind the aesthetic form lies the repressed harmony of sensuousness and reason — the eternal protest against the organization of life by the logic of domination, the critique of the performance principle.

Art is perhaps the most visible " return of the repressed," not only on the individual but also on the generic-historical level. The artistic imagination shapes the " unconscious memory " of the liberation that failed, of the promise that was betrayed. Under the rule of the performance principle, art opposes to institutionalized repression the " image of man as a free subject; but in a state of unfreedom art can sustain the image of freedom only in the negation of unfreedom." [4] Since the awakening of the consciousness of freedom, there is no genuine work of art that does not reveal the archetypal content: the negation of unfreedom. We shall see later how this content came to assume the aesthetic form, governed by aesthetic principles.[5] As aesthetic phenomenon, the critical function of art is self-defeating. The very commitment of art to form vitiates the negation of unfreedom in art. In order to be negated, unfreedom must be represented in the work of art with the semblance of reality. This element of semblance (show, *Schein*) necessarily subjects the represented reality to aesthetic standards and thus deprives it of its terror. Moreover, the form of the work of art invests the content with the qualities of

[4] Theodor W. Adorno, "Die gegängelte Musik," in *Der Monat*, V (1953), 182.
[5] See Chapter 9 below.

enjoyment. Style, rhythm, meter introduce an aesthetic order which is itself pleasurable: it reconciles with the content. The aesthetic quality of enjoyment, even entertainment, has been inseparable from the essence of art, no matter how tragic, how uncompromising the work of art is. Aristotle's proposition on the cathartic effect of art epitomizes the dual function of art: both to oppose and to reconcile; both to indict and to acquit; both to recall the repressed and to repress it again — " purified." People can elevate themselves with the classics: they read and see and hear their own archetypes rebel, triumph, give up, or perish. And since all this is aesthetically formed, they can enjoy it — and forget it.

Still, within the limits of the aesthetic form, art expressed, although in an ambivalent manner, the return of the repressed image of liberation; art was opposition. At the present stage, in the period of total mobilization, even this highly ambivalent opposition seems no longer viable. Art survives only where it cancels itself, where it saves its substance by denying its traditional form and thereby denying reconciliation: where it becomes surrealistic and atonal.[6] Otherwise, art shares the fate of all genuine human communication: it dies off. What Karl Kraus wrote at the beginning of the Fascist period is still true:

" Das Wort entschlief, als jene Welt erwachte."

In a less sublimated form, the opposition of phantasy to the reality principle is more at home in such sub-real and surreal processes as dreaming, daydreaming, play, the

---

[6] Theodor W. Adorno, *Philosophie der neuen Musik* (Tübingen: J. C. B. Mohr, 1949).

" stream of consciousness." In its most extreme claim for a gratification beyond the reality principle, phantasy cancels the established *principium individuationis* itself. Here perhaps are the roots of phantasy's commitment to the primary Eros: sexuality is " the only function of a living organism which extends beyond the individual and secures its connection with its species." [7] In so far as sexuality is organized and controlled by the reality principle, phantasy asserts itself chiefly against normal sexuality. (We have previously discussed the affinity between phantasy and the perversions.[8]) However, the erotic element in phantasy goes beyond the perverted expressions. It aims at an " erotic reality " where the life instincts would come to rest in fulfillment without repression. This is the ultimate content of the phantasy-process in its opposition to the reality principle; by virtue of this content, phantasy plays a unique role in the mental dynamic.

Freud recognized this role, but at this point his metapsychology reaches a fateful turn. The image of a different form of reality has appeared as the truth of one of the basic mental processes; this image contains the lost unity between the universal and the particular and the integral gratification of the life instincts by the reconciliation between the pleasure and reality principles. Its truth value is enhanced by the fact that the image belongs to mankind over and above the *principium individuationis*. However, according to Freud, the image conjures only the *subhistorical past* of the genus (and of the individual) prior to all civil-

[7] Freud, *A General Introduction to Psychoanalysis*, p. 358.
[8] See Chapter 2 above.

ization. Because the latter can develop only through the destruction of the subhistorical unity between pleasure principle and reality principle, the image must remain buried in the unconscious, and imagination must become mere fantasy, child's play, daydreaming. The long road of consciousness which led from the primal horde to ever higher forms of civilization cannot be reversed. Freud's conclusions preclude the notion of an " ideal " state of nature; but they also hypostatize a specific historical *form* of civilization as the *nature* of civilization. His own theory does not justify this conclusion. From the historical necessity of the performance principle, and from its perpetuation beyond historical necessity, it does not follow that another form of civilization under another reality principle is impossible. In Freud's theory, freedom from repression is a matter of the unconscious, of the subhistorical and even subhuman *past*, of primal biological and mental processes; consequently, the idea of a non-repressive reality principle is a matter of retrogression. That such a principle could itself become a historical reality, a matter of developing consciousness, that the images of phantasy could refer to the unconquered *future* of mankind rather than to its (badly) conquered past — all this seemed to Freud at best a nice utopia.

[The danger of abusing the discovery of the truth value of imagination for retrogressive tendencies is exemplified by the work of Carl Jung. More emphatically than Freud, he has insisted on the *cognitive* force of imagination. According to Jung, phantasy is " undistinguishably " united with all other mental func-

tions; it appears "now as primeval, now as the ultimate and most audacious synthesis of all capabilities."
Phantasy is above all the "creative activity out of
which flow the answers to all answerable questions";
it is "the mother of all possibilities, in which all mental opposites as well as the conflict between internal
and external world are united." Phantasy has always
built the bridge between the irreconcilable demands of
object and subject, extroversion and introversion.[9]
The simultaneously retrospective and expectant character of imagination is thus clearly stated: it looks not
only back to an aboriginal golden past, but also forward
to all still unrealized but realizable possibilities.   But
already in Jung's earlier work the emphasis is on the
retrospective and consequently "phantastic" qualities
of imagination: dream thinking "moves in a retrograde
manner toward the raw material of memory"; it is a
"regression to the original perception."[10]   In the development of Jung's psychology, its obscurantistic and
reactionary trends have become predominant and have
eliminated the critical insights of Freud's metapsychology.[11]]

The truth value of imagination relates not only to the
past but also to the future: the forms of freedom and happiness which it invokes claim to deliver the historical *real-*

[9] Jung, *Psychological Types*, transl. H. Godwin Baynes (New York:
Harcourt, Brace, 1926), p. 69 (with minor changes in translation).

[10] *Psychology of the Unconscious*, transl. Beatrice M. Hinkle (London: Routledge and Kegan Paul, 1951), pp. 13–14.

[11] Edward Glover's excellent analysis makes a further discussion of
Jung's work unnecessary. See *Freud or Jung?* (New York: W. W. Norton, 1950).

ity. In its refusal to accept as final the limitations imposed upon freedom and happiness by the reality principle, in its refusal to forget what *can be,* lies the critical function of phantasy:

> Réduire l'imagination à l'esclavage, quand bien même il y irait de ce qu'on appelle grossièrement le bonheur, c'est se dérober à tout ce qu'on trouve, au fond de soi, de justice suprême. La seule imagination me rend compte de ce qui *peut être.*[12]

The surrealists recognized the revolutionary implications of Freud's discoveries: " Imagination is perhaps about to reclaim its rights." [13] But when they asked, " Cannot the dream also be applied to the solution of the fundamental problems of life? " [14] they went beyond psychoanalysis in demanding that the dream be made into reality without compromising its content. Art allied itself with the revolution. Uncompromising adherence to the strict truth value of imagination comprehends reality more fully. That the propositions of the artistic imagination are untrue in terms of the actual organization of the facts belongs to the essence of their truth:

> The truth that some proposition respecting an actual occasion is untrue may express the vital truth as to the aesthetic achievement. It expresses the " great refusal " which is its primary characteristic.[15]

This Great Refusal is the protest against unnecessary repression, the struggle for the ultimate form of freedom —

---

[12] " To reduce imagination to slavery — even if one's so-called happiness is at stake — means to violate all that one finds in one's inmost self of ultimate justice. Imagination alone tells me what *can be.*" André Breton, *Les Manifestes du Surréalisme* (Paris: Editions du Sagittaire, 1946), p. 15. This was the first manifesto (1924).

[13] *Ibid.,* p. 25.

[14] *Ibid.,* p. 26.

[15] A. N. Whitehead, *Science and the Modern World* (New York: Macmillan, 1926), p. 228.

" to live without anxiety." [16]   But this idea could be formulated without punishment only in the language of art. In the more realistic context of political theory and even philosophy, it was almost universally defamed as utopia.

The relegation of real possibilities to the no-man's land of utopia is itself an essential element of the ideology of the performance principle. If the construction of a nonrepressive instinctual development is oriented, not on the subhistorical past, but on the historical present and mature civilization, the very notion of utopia loses its meaning. The negation of the performance principle emerges not against but *with* the progress of conscious rationality; it presupposes the highest maturity of civilization. The very achievements of the performance principle have intensified the discrepancy between the archaic unconscious and conscious processes of man, on the one hand, and his actual potentialities, on the other. The history of mankind seems to tend toward another turning point in the vicissitudes of the instincts. And, just as at the preceding turning points, the adaptation of the archaic mental structure to the new environment would mean another " castrophe " — an explosive change in the environment itself. However, while the first turning point was, according to the Freudian hypothesis, an event in geological history, and while the second occurred at the beginning of civilization, the third turning point would be located at the highest attained level of civilization. The actor in this event would be no longer the historical animal man but the conscious, rational subject

[16] ". . . Ohne Angst Leben." T. W. Adorno, *Versuch über Wagner* (Berlin-Frankfurt: Suhrkamp, 1952), p. 198.

that has mastered and appropriated the objective world as the arena of his realization. The historical factor contained in Freud's theory of instincts has come to fruition in history when the basis of Ananke (*Lebensnot*) — which, for Freud, provided the rationale for the repressive reality principle — is undermined by the progress of civilization.

Still, there is some validity in the argument that, despite all progress, scarcity and immaturity remain great enough to prevent the realization of the principle " to each according to his needs." The material as well as mental resources of civilization are still so limited that there must be a vastly lower standard of living if social productivity were redirected toward the universal gratification of individual needs: many would have to give up manipulated comforts if all were to live a human life. Moreover, the prevailing international structure of industrial civilization seems to condemn such an idea to ridicule. This does not invalidate the theoretical insistence that the performance principle has become obsolescent. The reconciliation between pleasure and reality principle does not depend on the existence of abundance for all. The only pertinent question is whether a state of civilization can be reasonably envisaged in which human needs are fulfilled in such a manner and to such an extent that surplus-repression can be eliminated.

Such a hypothetical state could be reasonably assumed at two points, which lie at the opposite poles of the vicissitudes of the instincts: one would be located at the primitive beginnings of history, the other at its most mature stage. The first would refer to a non-oppressive distribution of scarcity (as may, for example, have existed in matriarchal phases of ancient society). The second would pertain to a rational organization of fully developed industrial society after the conquest of scarcity. The vicissitudes of the instincts would of course be very different under these two conditions, but one decisive feature must be common to both: the instinctual development would be non-repressive in the sense that at least the surplus-repression necessitated by the interests of domination would not be imposed upon the instincts. This quality would reflect the prevalent satisfaction of the basic human needs (most primitive at the first, vastly extended and refined at the second stage), sexual as well as social: food, housing, clothing, leisure. This satisfaction would be (and this is the important point) *without toil* — that is, without the rule of alienated labor over the human existence. Under primitive conditions, alienation has *not yet* arisen because of the primitive character of the needs themselves, the rudimentary (personal or sexual) character of the division of labor, and the absence of an institutionalized hierarchical specialization of functions. Under the " ideal " conditions of mature industrial civilization, alienation would be completed by general automatization of labor, reduction of labor time to a minimum, and exchangeability of functions.

Since the length of the working day is itself one of the principal repressive factors imposed upon the pleasure principle by the reality principle, the reduction of the working day to a point where the mere quantum of labor time no longer arrests human development is the first prerequisite for freedom. Such reduction by itself would almost certainly mean a considerable decrease in the standard of liv-

ing prevalent today in the most advanced industrial countries. But the regression to a lower standard of living,
which the collapse of the performance principle would
bring about, does not militate against progress in freedom.

The argument that makes liberation conditional upon an
ever higher standard of living all too easily serves to justify
the perpetuation of repression. The definition of the
standard of living in terms of automobiles, television sets,
airplanes, and tractors is that of the performance principle
itself. Beyond the rule of this principle, the level of living
would be measured by other criteria: the universal gratification of the basic human needs, and the freedom from guilt
and fear — internalized as well as external, instinctual as
well as " rational." " La vraie civilization . . . n'est pas
dans le gaz, ni dans la vapeur, ni dans les tables tournantes.
Elle est dans la diminution des traces du péché originel " [17]
— this is the definition of progress beyond the rule of the
performance principle.

Under optimum conditions, the prevalence, in mature
civilization, of material and intellectual wealth would be
such as to allow painless gratification of needs, while domination would no longer systematically forestall such gratification. In this case, the quantum of instinctual energy
still to be diverted into necessary labor (in turn completely
mechanized and rationalized) would be so small that a
large area of repressive constraints and modifications, no
longer sustained by external forces, would collapse. Conse-

---

[17] " True civilization does not lie in gas, nor in steam, nor in turn-
tables. It lies in the reduction of the traces of original sin." Baudelaire,
Mon Coeur Mis à Nu, XXXII, in *Oeuvres Posthumes*, ed. Conard, Vol.
II (Paris, 1952), p. 109.

quently, the antagonistic relation between pleasure principle and reality principle would be altered in favor of the former. Eros, the life instincts, would be released to an unprecedented degree.

Does it follow that civilization would explode and revert to prehistoric savagery, that the individuals would die as a result of the exhaustion of the available means of gratification and of their own energy, that the absence of want and repression would drain all energy which could promote material and intellectual production on a higher level and larger scale? Freud answers in the affirmative. His answer is based on his more or less silent acceptance of a number of assumptions: that free libidinal relations are essentially antagonistic to work relations, that energy has to be withdrawn from the former in order to institute the latter, that only the absence of full gratification sustains the societal organization of work. Even under optimum conditions of a rational organization of society, the gratification of human needs would require labor, and this fact alone would enforce quantitative and qualitative instinctual restraint, and thereby numerous social taboos. No matter how rich, civilization depends on steady and methodical work, and thus on unpleasurable delay in satisfaction. Since the primary instincts rebel " by nature " against such delay, their repressive modification therefore remains a necessity for all civilization.

In order to meet this argument, we would have to show that Freud's correlation " instinctual repression — socially useful labor — civilization " can be meaningfully transformed into the correlation " instinctual liberation — socially useful work — civilization." We have suggested that the prevalent instinctual repression resulted, not so much from the necessity of labor, but from the specific social organization of labor imposed by the interest in domination — that repression was largely surplus-repression. Consequently, the elimination of surplus-repression would *per se* tend to eliminate, not labor, but the organization of the human existence into an instrument of labor. If this is true, the emergence of a non-repressive reality principle would alter rather than destroy the social organization of labor: the liberation of Eros could create new and durable work relations.

Discussion of this hypothesis encounters at the outset one of the most strictly protected values of modern culture — that of *productivity*. This idea expresses perhaps more than any other the existential attitude in industrial civilization; it permeates the philosophical definition of the subject in terms of the ever transcending ego. Man is evaluated according to his ability to make, augment, and improve socially useful things. Productivity thus designates the degree of the mastery and transformation of nature: the progressive replacement of an uncontrolled natural environment by a controlled technological environment. However, the more the division of labor was geared to utility for the established productive apparatus rather than for the individuals — in other words the more the social need deviated from the individual need — the more productivity tended to contradict the pleasure principle and to become an end-in-itself. The very word came to smack of repression or its philistine glorification: it connotes the resentful defamation of rest, indulgence, receptivity — the triumph over the " lower depths " of the mind and body, the taming of the instincts by exploitative reason. Efficiency and repression converge: raising the productivity of labor is the sacrosanct ideal of both capitalist and Stalinist Stakhanovism. This notion of productivity has its historical limits: they are those of the performance principle. Beyond its domain, productivity has another content and another relation to the pleasure principle: they are anticipated in the processes of imagination which preserve freedom from the performance principle while maintaining the claim of a *new* reality principle.

The utopian claims of imagination have become saturated with historical reality. If the achievements of the performance principle surpass its institutions, they also militate against the direction of its productivity — against the subjugation of man to his labor. Freed from this enslavement, productivity loses its repressive power and impels the free development of individual needs. Such a change in the direction of progress goes beyond the fundamental reorganization of social labor which it presupposes. No matter how justly and rationally the material production may be organized, it can never be a realm of freedom and gratification; but it can release time and energy for the free play of human faculties *outside* the realm of alienated labor. The more complete the alienation of labor, the greater the potential of freedom: total automation would be the optimum. It is the sphere outside labor which defines freedom and fulfillment, and it is the definition of the human existence in terms of this sphere which constitutes the negation of the performance principle. This negation cancels the rationality of domination and consciously "de-realizes" the world shaped by this rationality — redefining it by the rationality of gratification. While such a historical turn in the direction of progress is rendered possible only on the basis of the achievements of the performance principle and of its potentialities, it transforms the human existence in its entirety, including the work world and the struggle with nature. Progress beyond the performance principle is not promoted through improving or supplementing the present existence by more contemplation, more leisure, through advertising and practicing the "higher values," through elevating oneself and one's life. Such ideas belong to the cultural household of the performance principle itself. The lamentation about the degrading effect of "total work," the exhortation to appreciate the good and beautiful things in this world and in the world hereafter, is itself repressive in so far as it reconciles man with the work world which it leaves untouched on the side and below. Moreover, it sustains repression by diverting the effort from the very sphere in which repression is rooted and perpetuated.

Beyond the performance principle, its productivity as well as its cultural values become invalid. The struggle for existence then proceeds on new grounds and with new objectives: it turns into the concerted struggle against any constraint on the free play of human faculties, against toil, disease, and death. Moreover, while the rule of the performance principle was accompanied by a corresponding control of the instinctual dynamic, the reorientation of the struggle for existence would involve a decisive change in this dynamic. Indeed, such a change would appear as the prerequisite for sustaining progress. We shall presently try to show that it would affect the very structure of the psyche, alter the balance between Eros and Thanatos, reactivate tabooed realms of gratification, and pacify the conservative tendencies of the instincts. A new basic experience of being would change the human existence in its entirety.

CHAPTER EIGHT

The Images of Orpheus and Narcissus

The attempt to draft a theoretical construct of culture beyond the performance principle is in a strict sense "unreasonable." Reason is the rationality of the performance principle. Even at the beginning of Western civilization, long before this principle was institutionalized, reason was defined as an instrument of constraint, of instinctual suppression; the domain of the instincts, sensuousness, was considered as eternally hostile and detrimental to reason.[1] The categories in which philosophy has comprehended the human existence have retained the connection between reason and suppression: whatever belongs to the sphere of sensuousness, pleasure, impulse has the connotation of being antagonistic to reason — something that has to be subjugated, constrained. Every-day language has preserved this evaluation: the words which apply to this sphere carry the sound of the sermon or of obscenity. From Plato to the "*Schund und Schmutz*" laws of the modern world,[2] the defamation of the pleasure principle has proved its irresisti-

[1] See Chapter 5 above.
[2] A bill proposed by the New York Joint Legislative Committee on Comic Books would prohibit the sale and distribution of books portraying "nudity, sex or lust in a manner which reasonably tends to excite lustful or lecherous desires . . ." (*New York Times,* February 17, 1954).

ble power; opposition to such defamation easily succumbs to ridicule.

Still, the dominion of repressive reason (theoretical and practical) was never complete: its monopoly of cognition was never uncontested. When Freud emphasized the fundamental fact that phantasy (imagination) retains a truth that is incompatible with reason, he was following in a long historical tradition. Phantasy is cognitive in so far as it preserves the truth of the Great Refusal, or, positively, in so far as it protects, against all reason, the aspirations for the integral fulfillment of man and nature which are repressed by reason. In the realm of phantasy, the unreasonable images of freedom become rational, and the "lower depth" of instinctual gratification assumes a new dignity. The culture of the performance principle makes its bow before the strange truths which imagination keeps alive in folklore and fairy tale, in literature and art; they have been aptly interpreted and have found their place in the popular and academic world. However, the effort to derive from these truths the content of a valid reality principle surpassing the prevailing one has been entirely inconsequential. Novalis' statement that "all internal faculties and forces, and all external faculties and forces, must be deduced from productive imagination"[3] has remained a curiosity — as has the surrealist program *de pratiquer la poésie*. The insistence that imagination provide standards for existential attitudes, for practice, and for historical possibilities appears as childish fantasy. Only the archetypes, only the

---

[3] *Schriften*, ed. J. Minor (Jena: Eugen Diederichs, 1923), III, 375. See Gaston Bachelard, *La Terre et les Rêveries de la Volonté* (Paris: José Corti, 1948), pp. 4–5.

symbols have been accepted, and their meaning is usually interpreted in terms of phylogenetic or ontogenetic stages, long since surpassed, rather than in terms of an individual and cultural maturity. We shall now try to identify some of these symbols and examine their historical truth value.

More specifically, we look for the " culture-heroes " who have persisted in imagination as symbolizing the attitude and the deeds that have determined the fate of mankind. And here at the outset we are confronted with the fact that the predominant culture-hero is the trickster and (suffering) rebel against the gods, who creates culture at the price of perpetual pain. He symbolizes productiveness, the unceasing effort to master life; but, in his productivity, blessing and curse, progress and toil are inextricably intertwined. Prometheus is the archetype-hero of the performance principle. And in the world of Prometheus, Pandora, the female principle, sexuality and pleasure, appear as curse — disruptive, destructive. " Why are women such a curse? The denunciation of the sex with which the section [on Prometheus in Hesiod] concludes emphasizes above all else their economic unproductivity; they are useless drones; a luxury item in a poor man's budget." [4] The beauty of the woman, and the happiness she promises are fatal in the work-world of civilization.

If Prometheus is the culture-hero of toil, productivity, and progress through repression, then the symbols of another reality principle must be sought at the opposite pole. Orpheus and Narcissus (like Dionysus to whom they are

[4] See Norman O. Brown, *Hesiod's Theogony* (New York: Liberal Arts Press, 1953), pp. 18–19, 33; and *Hermes the Thief* (University of Wisconsin Press, 1947), pp. 23ff.

akin: the antagonist of the god who sanctions the logic of
domination, the realm of reason) stand for a very different reality.[5] They have not become the culture-heroes of
the Western world: theirs is the image of joy and fulfillment; the voice which does not command but sings; the
gesture which offers and receives; the deed which is peace
and ends the labor of conquest; the liberation from time
which unites man with god, man with nature. Literature
has preserved their image. In the *Sonnets to Orpheus*:

> Und fast ein Mädchen wars und ging hervor
> aus diesem einigen Glück von Sang und Leier
> und glänzte klar durch ihre Frühlingsschleier
> und machte sich ein Bett in meinem Ohr.
>
> Und schlief in mir. Und alles war ihr Schlaf.
> Die Bäume, die ich je bewundert, diese
> fühlbare Ferne, die gefühlte Wiese
> und jedes Staunen, das mich selbst betraf.
>
> Sie schlief die Welt. Singender Gott, wie hast
> du sie vollendet, dass sie nicht begehrte,
> erst wach zu sein? Sieh, sie erstand und schlief.
> Wo ist ihr Tod? [6]

[5] The symbol of Narcissus and the term "Narcissistic" as used here
do not imply the meaning given to them in Freud's theory. See, however, pages 167–168 below.

[6]   "Almost a maid, she came forth shimmering
From the high happiness of song and lyre,
And shining clearly through her veils of spring
She made herself a bed within my ear
And slept in me. All things were in her sleep:
The trees I marvelled at, the enchanting spell
Of farthest distances, the meadows deep,
And all the magic that myself befell.
Within her slept the world. You singing god, o how
Did you perfect her so she did not long
To be awake? She rose and slept.
Where is her death? "

Rainer Maria Rilke, *Sonnets to Orpheus: Duino Elegies*, transl. Jessie
Lemont (New York: Fine Editions Press, 1945), p. 3 (with minor changes
in translation). Reprinted by permission of Columbia University Press.

Or Narcissus, who, in the mirror of the water, tries to grasp his own beauty. Bent over the river of time, in which all forms pass and flee, he dreams:

Narcisse rêve au paradis . . .
Quand donc le temps, cessant sa fuite, laissera-t-il que cet écoulement se repose? Formes, formes divines et pérennelles! qui n'attendez que le repos pour reparaître, oh! quand, dans quelle nuit, dans quel silence, vous recristalliserez-vous?
Le paradis est toujours à refaire; il n'est point en quelque lointaine Thulé. Il demeure sous l'apparence. Chaque chose détient, virtuelle, l'intime harmonie de son être, comme chaque sel, en lui, l'archétype de son cristal; — et vienne un temps de nuit tacite, où les eaux plus denses descendent: dans les abîmes imperturbés fleuriront les trémies secrètes . . .
Tout s'efforce vers sa forme perdue . . .[7]

    Un grand calme m'écoute, où j'écoute l'espoir.
    La voix des sources change et me parle du soir;
    J'entends l'herbe d'argent grandir dans l'ombre sainte,
    Et la lune perfide élève son miroir
    Jusque dans les secrets de la fontaine éteinte.[8]

    Admire dans Narcisse un éternel retour
    Vers l'onde où son image offerte à son amour
    Propose à sa beauté toute sa connaissance:
        Tout mon sort n'est qu'obéissance
        A la force de mon amour.

[7] " Alas, when will Time cease its flight and allow this flow to rest? Forms, divine and perennial forms which only wait for rest in order to reappear! O when, in what night, will you crystallize again?
" Paradise must always be re-created. It is not in some remote Thule; it lingers under the appearance. Everything holds within itself, as potentiality, the intimate harmony of its being — just as every salt holds within itself the archetype of its crystal. And a time of silent night will come when the waters will descend, more dense; then, in the unperturbed abysses, the secret crystals will bloom . . . Everything strives toward its lost form . . ." André Gide, *Le Traité du Narcisse.*

[8] " A great calm hears me, where I hear Hope. The voice of the wells changes and speaks of the night; in the holy shade I hear the silver herb grow, and the treacherous moon raises its mirror deep into the secrets of the extinguished fountain." Paul Valéry, *Narcisse Parle.*

Cher corps, je m'abandonne à ta seule puissance;
L'eau tranquille m'attire où je me tends mes bras:
A ce vertige pur je ne résiste.pas.
Que puis-je, ô ma Beauté, faire que tu ne veuilles? [9]

The climate of this language is that of the " *diminution des traces du péché originel*," — the revolt against culture based on toil, domination, and renunciation. The images of Orpheus and Narcissus reconcile Eros and Thanatos. They recall the experience of a world that is not to be mastered and controlled but to be liberated — a freedom that will release the powers of Eros now bound in the repressed and petrified forms of man and nature. These powers are conceived not as destruction but as peace, not as terror but as beauty. It is sufficient to enumerate the assembled images in order to circumscribe the dimension to which they are committed: the redemption of pleasure, the halt of time, the absorption of death; silence, sleep, night, paradise — the Nirvana principle not as death but as life. Baudelaire gives the image of such a world in two lines:

Là, tout n'est qu'ordre et beauté,
Luxe, calme, et volupté.[10]

This is perhaps the only context in which the word *order* loses its repressive connotation: here, it is the order of gratification which the free Eros creates. Static triumphs over dynamic; but it is a static that moves in its own fullness — a productivity that is sensuousness, play, and song. Any at-

---

[9] " Admire in Narcissus the eternal return toward the mirror of the water which offers his image to his love, and to his beauty all his knowledge. All my fate is obedience to the force of my love. *Body*, I surrender to your sole power; the tranquil water awaits me where I extend my arms: I do not resist this pure madness. What, O my Beauty, can I do that thou dost not will? " Paul Valéry, *Cantate du Narcisse*, Scène II.

[10] " There all is order and beauty, luxury, calm, and sensuousness."

tempt to elaborate the images thus conveyed must be self-defeating, because outside the language of art they change their meaning and merge with the connotations they received under the repressive reality principle. But one must try to trace the road back to the realities to which they refer.

In contrast to the images of the Promethean culture-heroes, those of the Orphic and Narcissistic world are essentially unreal and unrealistic. They designate an "impossible" attitude and existence. The deeds of the culture-heroes also are "impossible," in that they are miraculous, incredible, superhuman. However, their objective and their "meaning" are not alien to the reality; on the contrary, they are useful. They promote and strengthen this reality; they do not explode it. But the Orphic-Narcissistic images do explode it; they do not convey a "mode of living"; they are committed to the underworld and to death. At best, they are poetic, something for the soul and the heart. But they do not teach any "message" — except perhaps the negative one that one cannot defeat death or forget and reject the call of life in the admiration of beauty.

Such moral messages are superimposed upon a very different content. Orpheus and Narcissus symbolize realities just as do Prometheus and Hermes. Trees and animals respond to Orpheus' language; the spring and the forest respond to Narcissus' desire. The Orphic and Narcissistic Eros awakens and liberates potentialities that are real in things animate and inanimate, in organic and inorganic nature — real but in the un-erotic reality suppressed. These potentialities circumscribe the *telos* inherent in them as: "just to be what they are," "being-there," existing.

The Orphic and Narcissistic experience of the world negates that which sustains the world of the performance principle. The opposition between man and nature, subject and object, is overcome. Being is experienced as gratification, which unites man and nature so that the fulfillment of man is at the same time the fulfillment, without violence, of nature. In being spoken to, loved, and cared for, flowers and springs and animals appear as what they are — beautiful, not only for those who address and regard them, but for themselves, " objectively." " Le monde tend à la beauté." [11] In the Orphic and Narcissistic Eros, this tendency is released: the things of nature become free to be what they are. But to be what they are they *depend* on the erotic attitude: they receive their *telos* only in it. The song of Orpheus pacifies the animal world, reconciles the lion with the lamb and the lion with man. The world of nature is a world of oppression, cruelty, and pain, as is the human world; like the latter, it awaits its liberation. This liberation is the work of Eros. The song of Orpheus breaks the petrification, moves the forests and the rocks — but moves them to partake in joy.

The love of Narcissus is answered by the echo of nature. To be sure, Narcissus appears as the *antagonist* of Eros: he spurns love, the love that unites with other human beings, and for that he is punished by Eros.[12] As the antagonist of Eros, Narcissus symbolizes sleep and death, silence and

[11] Gaston Bachelard, *L'Eau et les Rêves* (Paris: José Corti, 1942), p. 38. See also (p. 36) Joachim Gasquet's formulation: " Le monde est un immense Narcisse en train de se penser."

[12] Friedrich Wieseler, *Narkissos: Eine kunstmythologische Abhandlung* (Göttingen, 1856), pp. 90, 94.

rest.[13] In Thracia, he stands in close relation to Dionysus.[14] But it is not coldness, asceticism, and self-love that color the images of Narcissus; it is not these gestures of Narcissus that are preserved in art and literature. His silence is not that of dead rigidity; and when he is contemptuous of the love of hunters and nymphs he rejects one Eros for another. He lives by an Eros of his own,[15] and he does not love only himself. (He does not know that the image he admires is his own.) If his erotic attitude is akin to death and brings death, then rest and sleep and death are not painfully separated and distinguished: the Nirvana principle rules throughout all these stages. And when he dies he continues to live as the flower that bears his name.

In associating Narcissus with Orpheus and interpreting both as symbols of a non-repressive erotic attitude toward reality, we took the image of Narcissus from the mythological-artistic tradition rather than from Freud's libido theory. We may now be able to find some support for our interpretation in Freud's concept of *primary narcissism*. It is significant that the introduction of narcissism into psycho-

---

[13] *Ibid.*, pp. 76, 80–83, 93–94.

[14] *Ibid.*, p. 89. Narcissus and Dionysus are closely assimilated (if not identified) in the Orphic mythology. The Titans seize Zagreus-Dionysus while he contemplates his image in the mirror which they gave him. An ancient tradition (Plotinus, Proclus) interprets the mirror-duplication as the beginning of the god's self-manifestation in the multitude of the phenomena of the world — a process which finds its final symbol in the tearing asunder of the god by the Titans and his rebirth by Zeus. The myth would thus express the reunification of that which was separated, of God and world, man and nature — identity of the one and the many. See Erwin Rhode, *Psyche* (Freiburg, 1898), II, 117 note; Otto Kern, *Orpheus* (Berlin, 1920), pp. 22–23; Ivan M. Linforth, *The Arts of Orpheus* (University of California Press, 1941), pp. 307ff.

[15] In most pictorial representations, Narcissus is in the company of an Amor, who is sad but not hostile. See Wieseler, *Narkissos*, pp. 16–17.

analysis marked a turning point in the development of the instinct theory: the assumption of independent ego instincts (self-preservation instincts) was shaken and replaced by the notion of an undifferentiated, unified libido prior to the division into ego and external objects.[16] Indeed, the discovery of primary narcissism meant more than the addition of just another phase to the development of the libido; with it there came in sight the archetype of another existential relation to *reality*. Primary narcissism is more than autoeroticism; it engulfs the "environment," integrating the narcissistic ego with the objective world. The normal antagonistic relation between ego and external reality is only a later form and stage of the relation between ego and reality:

> Originally the ego includes everything, later it detaches from itself the external world. The ego-feeling we are aware of now is thus only a shrunken vestige of a far more extensive feeling — a feeling which *embraced the universe* and expressed an *inseparable connection of the ego with the external world*.[17]

The concept of primary narcissism implies what is made explicit in the opening chapter of *Civilization and Its Discontents* — that narcissism survives not only as a neurotic symptom but also as a constitutive element in the construction of the reality, coexisting with the mature reality ego. Freud describes the "ideational content" of the surviving primary ego-feeling as "limitless extension and oneness with the universe" (oceanic feeling).[18] And, later in the same chapter, he suggests that the oceanic feeling seeks to rein-

16 See Chapter 2 above.
17 *Civilization and Its Discontents* (London: Hogarth Press, 1949), p. 13. Italics added.
18 *Ibid.*, p. 14.

state "limitless narcissism." [19]   The striking paradox that narcissism, usually understood as egotistic withdrawal from reality, here is connected with oneness with the universe, reveals the new depth of the conception: beyond all immature autoeroticism, narcissism denotes a fundamental relatedness to reality which may generate a comprehensive existential order.[20]   In other words, narcissism may contain the germ of a different reality principle: the libidinal cathexis of the ego (one's own body) may become the source and reservoir for a new libidinal cathexis of the objective world — transforming this world into a new mode of being.   This interpretation is corroborated by the decisive role which narcissistic libido plays, according to Freud, in sublimation.   In *The Ego and the Id*, he asks "whether all sublimation does not take place through the agency of the ego, which begins by changing sexual object-libido into narcissistic libido and then, perhaps, goes on to give it another aim." [21]   If this is the case, then all sublimation would begin with the reactivation of narcissistic libido, which somehow overflows and extends to objects. The hypothesis all but revolutionizes the idea of sublimation: it hints at a non-repressive mode of sublimation which

[19] *Ibid.*, p. 21.

[20] In his paper on "The Delay of the Machine Age," Hanns Sachs made an interesting attempt to demonstrate narcissism as a constitutive element of the reality principle in Greek civilization.   He discussed the problem of why the Greeks did not develop a machine technology although they possessed the skill and knowledge which would have enabled them to do so.   He was not satisfied with the usual explanations on economic and sociological grounds.   Instead, he proposed that the predominant narcissistic element in Greek culture prevented technological progress: the libidinal cathexis of the body was so strong that it militated against mechanization and automatization.   Sachs' paper appeared in the *Psychoanalytic Quarterly*, II (1933), 420ff.

[21] *The Ego and the Id* (London: Hogarth Press, 1950), p. 38.

results from an extension rather than from a constraining deflection of the libido. We shall subsequently resume the discussion of this idea.[22]

The Orphic-Narcissistic images are those of the Great Refusal: refusal to accept separation from the libidinous object (or subject). The refusal aims at liberation — at the reunion of what has become separated. Orpheus is the archetype of the poet as *liberator* and *creator*: [23] he establishes a higher order in the world — an order without repression. In his person, art, freedom, and culture are eternally combined. He is the poet of redemption, the god who brings peace and salvation by pacifying man and nature, not through force but through song:

> Orpheus, the priest, the mouthpiece of the gods,
> Deterred wild men from murders and foul foods,
> And hence was said to tame the raging moods
> Of tigers and of lions . . .
> In times of yore it was the poet's part —
> The part of sapience — to distinguish plain
> Between the public and the private things,
> Between the sacred things and things profane,
> To check the ills that sexual straying brings,
> To show how laws for married people stood,
> To build the towns, to carve the laws in wood.[24]

But the "culture-hero" Orpheus is also credited with the establishment of a very different order — and he pays for it with his life:

[22] See Chapter 10 below.
[23] See Walther Rehm, *Orpheus* (Düsseldorf: L. Schwann, 1950), pp. 63ff. On Orpheus as culture-hero, see Linforth, *The Arts of Orpheus*, p. 69.
[24] Horace, *The Art of Poetry*, transl. Alexander Falconer Murison, in *Horace Rendered in English Verse* (London and New York: Longmans, Green, 1931), p. 426. Reprinted by permission of the publisher.

. . . Orpheus had shunned all love of womankind, whether because of his ill success in love, or whether he had given his troth once for all. Still, many women felt a passion for the bard; many grieved for their love repulsed. He set the example for the people of Thrace of giving his love to tender boys, and enjoying the springtime and first flower of their growth.[25]

He was torn to pieces by the crazed Thracian women.[26]

The classical tradition associates Orpheus with the introduction of homosexuality. Like Narcissus, he rejects the normal Eros, not for an ascetic ideal, but for a fuller Eros. Like Narcissus, he protests against the repressive order of procreative sexuality. The Orphic and Narcissistic Eros is to the end the negation of this order — the Great Refusal. In the world symbolized by the culture-hero Prometheus, it is the negation of *all* order; but in this negation Orpheus and Narcissus reveal a new reality, with an order of its own, governed by different principles. The Orphic Eros transforms being: he masters cruelty and death through liberation. His language is *song*, and his work is *play*. Narcissus' life is that of *beauty*, and his existence is *contemplation*. These images refer to the *aesthetic dimension* as the one in which their reality principle must be sought and validated.

[25] Ovid, *Metamorphoses*, X, 79–85, transl. Frank Justus Miller (Loeb Classical Library), Vol. II, p. 71. See Linforth, *The Arts of Orpheus*, p. 57.
[26] Ovid, *Metamorphoses*, XL, 1ff; Vol. II, pp. 121–122.

CHAPTER NINE

The Aesthetic Dimension

Obviously, the aesthetic dimension cannot validate a reality principle. Like imagination, which is its constitutive mental faculty, the realm of aesthetics is essentially "unrealistic": it has retained its freedom from the reality principle at the price of being ineffective in the reality. Aesthetic values may function in life for cultural adornment and elevation or as private hobbies, but to *live* with these values is the privilege of geniuses or the mark of decadent Bohemians. Before the court of theoretical and practical reason, which have shaped the world of the performance principle, the aesthetic existence stands condemned. However, we shall try to show that this notion of aesthetics results from a "cultural repression" of contents and truths that are inimical to the performance principle. We shall attempt to undo this repression theoretically by recalling the original meaning and function of *aesthetic*. This task involves the demonstration of the inner connection between pleasure, sensuousness, beauty, truth, art, and freedom — a connection revealed in the philosophical history of the term *aesthetic*. There the term aims at a realm which preserves the truth of the senses and reconciles, in the reality of freedom, the "lower" and the "higher" faculties of man, sensuousness and intellect, pleasure and reason. We shall confine the discussion to the period in which the meaning of the term *aesthetic* was fixed: the second half of the eighteenth century.

In Kant's philosophy, the basic antagonism between subject and object is reflected in the dichotomy between the mental faculties: sensuousness and intellect (understanding); desire and cognition; practical and theoretical reason.[1] Practical reason constitutes freedom under self-given moral laws for (moral) ends; theoretical reason constitutes nature under the laws of causality. The realm of nature is totally different from the realm of freedom: no subjective autonomy can break into the laws of causality, and no sense-datum can determine the autonomy of the subject (for otherwise the subject would not be free). Still, the autonomy of the subject is to have an " effect " in the objective reality, and the ends that the subject sets for itself must be real. Thus, the realm of nature must be " susceptible " to the legislation of freedom; an intermediary dimension must exist in which the two meet. A third " faculty " must mediate between theoretical and practical reason — a faculty that brings about a " transition " from the realm of nature to the realm of freedom and links together the lower and higher faculties, those of desire and those of knowledge.[2] This third faculty is that of judgment. A tripartite division of the mind underlies the initial dichotomy. While theoretical reason (understanding) provides

[1] These are not pairs that can be correlated; they designate different conceptual areas (mental faculties in general, cognitive faculties, and their fields of application).

[2] Kant, *Critique of Judgment*, transl. J. H. Bernard (London: Macmillan, 1892), p. 16. Introduction, III.

the *a priori* principles of cognition, and practical reason those of desire (will), the faculty of judgment mediates between these two by virtue of the feeling of pain and pleasure. Combined with the feeling of pleasure, judgment is aesthetic, and its field of application is art.

This, in crude abbreviation, is Kant's classical derivation of the aesthetic function, in his introduction to the *Critique of Judgment*. The obscurity of his exposition is caused largely by the fact that it merges the original meaning of *aesthetic* (pertaining to the senses) with the new connotation (pertaining to beauty, especially in art), which had definitely triumphed during Kant's own period. Although his effort to recapture the unrepressed content exhausts itself within the rigid limits set by his transcendental method, his conception still furnishes the best guidance for understanding the full scope of the aesthetic dimension.

In the *Critique of Judgment*, the aesthetic dimension and the corresponding feeling of pleasure emerge not merely as a third dimension and faculty of the mind, but as its *center*, the medium through which nature becomes susceptible to freedom, necessity to autonomy. In this mediation, the aesthetic function is a " symbolic " one. The famous Paragraph 59 of the *Critique* is entitled " Of Beauty as the Symbol of Morality." In Kant's system, morality is the realm of freedom, in which practical reason realizes itself under self-given laws. Beauty symbolizes this realm in so far as it demonstrates intuitively the reality of freedom. Since freedom is an idea to which no sense-perception can correspond, such demonstration can be only " indirect," symbolical, *per analogiam.* We shall presently try to elucidate the ground for this strange analogy, which is at the same time the ground on which the aesthetic function links the "lower" faculties of sensuousness (*Sinnlichkeit*) to morality. Before doing so, we wish to recall the context in which the problem of aesthetics became acute.

Our definition of the specific historical character of the established reality principle led to a re-examination of what Freud considered to be its universal validity. We questioned this validity in view of the historical possibility of the abolition of the repressive controls imposed by civilization. The very achievements of this civilization seemed to make the performance principle obsolete, to make the repressive utilization of the instincts archaic. But the idea of a non-repressive civilization on the basis of the achievements of the performance principle encountered the argument that instinctual liberation (and consequently total liberation) would explode civilization itself, since the latter is sustained only through renunciation and work (labor) — in other words, through the repressive utilization of instinctual energy. Freed from these constraints, man would exist without work and without order; he would fall back into nature, which would destroy culture. To meet this argument, we recalled certain archetypes of imagination which, in contrast to the culture-heroes of repressive productivity, symbolized creative receptivity. These archetypes envisioned the fulfillment of man and nature, not through domination and exploitation, but through release of inherent libidinal forces. We then set ourselves the task of "verifying" these symbols — that is to say, demonstrating their truth value as symbols of a reality principle *beyond* the performance principle. We thought that the representative content of the Orphic and Narcissistic images was the erotic reconciliation (union) of man and nature in the aesthetic attitude, where order is beauty and work is play. The next step was to eliminate the distortion of the aesthetic attitude into the unreal atmosphere of the museum or of Bohemia. With this purpose in mind, we tried to recapture the full content of the aesthetic dimension by looking for its philosophical legitimation. We found that, in Kant's philosophy, the aesthetic dimension occupies the central position between sensuousness and morality — the two poles of the human existence. If this is the case, then the aesthetic dimension must contain principles valid for both realms.

The basic experience in this dimension is sensuous rather than conceptual; the aesthetic perception is essentially intuition, not notion.[3] The nature of sensuousness is "receptivity," cognition through being affected by given objects. It is by virtue of its intrinsic relation to sensuousness that the aesthetic function assumes its central position. The aesthetic perception is accompanied by pleasure.[4] This pleasure derives from the perception of the pure *form* of an object, regardless of its "matter" and of its (internal

[3] The following discussion is only a condensed summary of the decisive steps in Kant's exposition. The highly complex relation between the assumption of two basic cognitive faculties (sensuousness and understanding) and three such faculties (sensuousness, imagination, apperception) cannot be discussed here. Nor can the relation between the transcendental aesthetic in the *Critique of Pure Reason* and the aesthetic function in the *Critique of Judgment*. Heidegger has for the first time demonstrated the central role of the aesthetic function in Kant's system. See his *Kant und das Problem der Metaphysik* (Bonn: Friedrich Cohen, 1929); for the relation between the basic cognitive faculties, see especially pp. 31ff., 129ff.

[4] The following according to *Critique of Judgment*, Introduction, VII; pp. 29ff.

or external) "purpose." An object represented in its pure form is "beautiful." Such representation is the work (or rather the play) of *imagination*. As imagination, the aesthetic perception is both sensuousness and at the same time more than sensuousness (the "third" basic faculty): it gives pleasure and is therefore essentially subjective; but in so far as this pleasure is constituted by the pure form of the object itself, it accompanies the aesthetic perception universally and necessarily — for *any* perceiving subject. Although sensuous and therefore receptive, the aesthetic imagination is creative: in a free synthesis of its own, it constitutes *beauty*. In the aesthetic imagination, sensuousness generates universally valid principles for an objective order.

The two main categories defining this order are "purposiveness without purpose" and "lawfulness without law." [5] They circumscribe, beyond the Kantian context, the essence of a truly non-repressive order. The first defines the structure of beauty, the second that of freedom; their common character is gratification in the free play of the released potentialities of man and nature. Kant develops these categories only as processes of the mind, but the impact of his theory on his contemporaries went far beyond the frontiers established by his transcendental philosophy; a few years after the publication of the *Critique of Judgment*, Schiller derived from Kant's conception the notion of a new mode of civilization.

To Kant, "purposiveness without purpose" (formal purposiveness) is the form in which the object appears in the

[5] "Zweckmässigkeit ohne Zweck; Gesetzmässigkeit ohne Gesetz." *Ibid.*, §§16–17, 22.

aesthetic representation. Whatever the object may be (thing or flower, animal or man), it is represented and judged not in terms of its usefulness, not according to any purpose it may possibly serve, and also not in view of its "internal" finality and completeness. In the aesthetic imagination, the object is rather represented as free from all such relations and properties, as freely being itself. The experience in which the object is thus "given" is totally different from the every-day as well as scientific experience; all links between the object and the world of theoretical and practical reason are severed, or rather suspended. This experience, which releases the object into its "free" being, is the work of the free play of imagination.[6] Subject and object become free in a new sense. From this radical change in the attitude toward being results a new quality of pleasure, generated by the form in which the object now reveals itself. Its "pure form" suggests a "unity of the manifold," an accord of movements and relations which operates under its own laws — the pure manifestation of its "being-there," its existence. This is the manifestation of beauty. Imagination comes into accord with the cognitive notions of understanding, and this accord establishes a harmony of the mental faculties which is the pleasurable response to the free harmony of the aesthetic object. The order of beauty results from the order which governs the play of imagination. This double order is in conformity with laws, but laws that are themselves free: they are not superimposed and they do not enforce the attainment of

6 See Herman Moerchen, "Die Einbildungskraft bei Kant," in *Jahrbuch für Philosophie und Phaenomenologische Forschung*, ed. Husserl, IX (Halle, 1930), 478–479.

specific ends and purposes; they are the pure form of existence itself. The aesthetic " conformity to law " links Nature and Freedom, Pleasure and Morality. The aesthetic
judgment is,

. . . in respect of the feeling of pleasure or pain, a constitutive
principle. The spontaneity in the play of the cognitive faculties,
the harmony of which contains the ground of this pleasure, makes
the concept [of the purposiveness of nature] the mediating link
between the conceptual realm of nature and that of freedom . . . ,
whilst at the same time this spontaneity promotes the susceptibility
of the mind to moral feeling.[7]

To Kant, the aesthetic dimension is the medium in which
the senses and the intellect meet. The mediation is accomplished by imagination, which is the " third " mental
faculty. Moreover, the aesthetic dimension is also the medium in which nature and freedom meet. This twofold
mediation is necessitated by the pervasive conflict between
the lower and the higher faculties of man generated by the
progress of civilization — progress achieved through the subjugation of the sensuous faculties to reason, and through
their repressive utilization for social needs. The philosophical effort to mediate, in the aesthetic dimension, between
sensuousness and reason thus appears as an attempt to reconcile the two spheres of the human existence which were
torn asunder by a repressive reality principle. The mediating function is performed by the aesthetic faculty, which is
akin to sensuousness, pertaining to the senses. Consequently, the aesthetic reconciliation implies strengthening
sensuousness as against the tyranny of reason and, ulti-

[7] *Critique of Judgment*, Introduction, IX; pp. 40–41 (with changes in
translation).

mately, even calls for the liberation of sensuousness from the repressive domination of reason.

Indeed when, on the basis of Kant's theory, the aesthetic function becomes the central theme of the philosophy of culture, it is used to demonstrate the principles of a non-repressive civilization, in which reason is sensuous and sensuousness rational. Schiller's *Letters on the Aesthetic Education of Man* (1795), written largely under the impact of the *Critique of Judgment*, aim at a remaking of civilization by virtue of the liberating force of the aesthetic function: it is envisaged as containing the possibility of a new reality principle.

The inner logic of the tradition of Western thought impelled Schiller to define the new reality principle, and the new experience corresponding to it, as *aesthetic*. We have emphasized that the term originally designated "pertaining to the senses," with stress on their cognitive function. Under the predominance of rationalism, the cognitive function of sensuousness has been constantly minimized. In line with the repressive concept of reason, cognition became the ultimate concern of the "higher," non-sensuous faculties of the mind; aesthetics were absorbed by logic and metaphysics. Sensuousness, as the "lower" and even "lowest" faculty, furnished at best the mere stuff, the raw material, for cognition, to be organized by the higher faculties of the intellect. The content and validity of the aesthetic function were whittled down. Sensuousness retained a measure of philosophical dignity in a subordinate epistemological position; those of its processes that did not fit into the rationalistic epistemology — that is, those that went beyond the passive perception of data — became homeless. Foremost among these homeless contents and values were those of imagination: free, creative, or reproductive intuition of objects which are not directly " given " — the faculty to represent objects without their being " present." [8] There was no *aesthetics* as the science of sensuousness to correspond to *logic* as the science of conceptual understanding. But around the middle of the eighteenth century, aesthetics appeared as a new philosophical discipline, as the theory of beauty and art: Alexander Baumgarten established the term in its modern usage. The change in meaning, from "pertaining to the senses" to " pertaining to beauty and art " is of far deeper significance than an academic innovation.

The philosophical history of the term *aesthetic* reflects the repressive treatment of the sensuous (and thereby " corporeal ") cognitive processes. In this history, the foundation of aesthetics as an independent discipline counteracts the repressive rule of reason: the efforts to demonstrate the central position of the aesthetic function and to establish it as an existential category invoke the inherent truth values of the senses against their depravation under the prevailing reality principle. The discipline of aesthetics installs the *order of sensuousness* as against the *order of reason*. Introduced into the philosophy of culture, this notion aims at a liberation of the senses which, far from destroying civilization, would give it a firmer basis and would greatly enhance its potentialities. Operating through a basic impulse —

---

[8] Kant's definition in the *Critique of Pure Reason*, " Transcendental Aesthetic," §24.

namely, the play impulse — the aesthetic function would "abolish compulsion, and place man, both morally and physically, in freedom." It would harmonize the feelings and affections with the ideas of reason, deprive the "laws of reason of their moral compulsion," and "reconcile them with the interest of the senses." [9]

It will be objected that this interpretation, which connects the philosophical term *sensuousness* (as a cognitive mental faculty) with liberation of the senses, is a mere play on an etymological ambiguity; the root *sens* in *sensuousness* no longer justifies the connotation of sensuality. In German, *sensuousness* and *sensuality* are still rendered by one and the same term: *Sinnlichkeit*. It connotes instinctual (especially sexual) gratification as well as cognitive sense-perceptiveness and representation (sensation). This double connotation is preserved in every-day as well as philosophical language, and is retained in the use of the term *Sinnlichkeit* for the foundation of aesthetics. Here, the term designates the "lower" ("opaque," "confused") cognitive faculties of man *plus* the "feeling of pain and pleasure," — sensations *plus* affections.[10] In Schiller's *Letters on the Aesthetic Education*, the stress is on the impulsive, instinctual character of the aesthetic function.[11] This content provides the basic material for the new discipline of aesthetics. The latter is conceived as the "science of

[9] Schiller, *The Aesthetic Letters, Essays, and the Philosophical Letters*, transl. J. Weiss (Boston: Little, Brown, 1845), pp. 66–67 (with a minor change in translation).

[10] Alexander Baumgarten, "Meditationes Philosophicae de Nonnullis ad Poema Pertinentibus," §§25–26, in Albert Riemann, *Die Aesthetik A. O. Baumgartens* (Halle: Niemeyer, 1928), p. 114.

[11] Schiller, *The Aesthetic Letters*, fourth and eighth letters, and *passim*.

with their appetitive function (sensuality); they are erotogenic, and they are governed by the pleasure principle.
From this fusion of the cognitive and appetitive functions
derives the confused, inferior, passive character of sense-
cognition which makes it unsuitable for the reality principle
unless subjected to and formed by the conceptual activity
of the intellect, of reason. And in so far as philosophy accepted the rules and values of the reality principle, the
claim of sensuousness free from the dominance of reason
found no place in philosophy; greatly modified, it obtained
refuge in the theory of art. The truth of art is the liberation of sensuousness through its reconciliation with reason:
this is the central notion of classical idealistic aesthetics.
In art,

. . . thought is materialized, and matter is not extraneously determined by thought but is itself free in so far as the natural, sensuous, affectional possess their measure, purpose, and harmony in
themselves. While perception and feeling are raised to the uni-
versality of the spirit, thought not only renounces its hostility
against nature but en-joys itself in nature. Feeling, joy, and pleasure are sanctioned and justified so that nature and freedom, sensuousness and reason, find in their *unity* their right and their gratification.[16]

16 " [Im Kunstschönen ist] der Gedanke verkörpert, und die Materie
von ihm nicht äusserlich bestimmt, sondern existiert selber frei, indem
das Natürliche, Sinnliche, Gemüth u.s.f. in sich selbst Maass, Zweck und
Uebereinstimmung hat, und die Anschauung und Empfindung ebenso in
geistige Allgemeinheit erhoben ist, als der Gedanke seiner Feindschaft
gegen die Natur nicht nur entsagt, sondern sich in ihr erheitert und Empfindung, Lust und Genuss berechtigt und geheiligt ist, so dass Natur und
Freiheit, Sinnlichkeit und Begriff in Einem ihr Recht und Befriedigung
finden." Hegel, *Vorlesungen über die Aesthetik*, Vol. I, Introduction; in
Sämtliche Werke, ed. Herrmann Glockner (Stuttgart, 1927), X, 95. See
The Philosophy of Fine Art, transl. F. P. B. Osmaton (London: G. Bell
and Sons, 1920), I, p. 83.

sensitive cognition " — a " logic of the lower cognitive fac
ulties." [12]   Aesthetics is the " sister " and at the same time
the counterpart to logic. The opposition to the predominance of reason characterizes the new science: ". . . not
reason but sensuousness [*Sinnlichkeit*] is constitutive of aesthetic truth or falsehood. What sensuousness recognizes,
or can recognize, as true, aesthetics can represent as true,
even if reason rejects it as untrue." [13]   And Kant stated in
his lectures on anthropology: ". . . one can establish universal laws of sensuousness [*Sinnlichkeit*] just as one can establish universal laws of understanding; i.e. there is a science of sensuousness, namely, aesthetics, and a science of
understanding, namely, logic." [14]   The principles and truths
of sensuousness supply the content of aesthetics, and " the
objective and purpose of aesthetics is the perfection of sensitive cognition. This perfection is beauty." [15]   Here the
step is made that transforms aesthetics, the science of sensuousness, into the science of *art*, and the order of sensuousness into the order of art.

The etymological fate of a basic term is rarely an accident. What is the reality behind the conceptual development from *sensuality* to *sensuousness* (sensitive cognition)
to *art* (aesthetics)? Sensuousness, the mediating concept,
designates the senses as sources and organs of cognition.
But the senses are not exclusively, and not even primarily,
organs of cognition. Their cognitive function is con-fused

[12] Baumgarten, " Aesthetik," ed. Bernhard Poppe, in A. G. *Baumgarten* (Bonn, Leipzig, 1907), §1; see also p. 44. "Meditationes Philosophicae," §115.
[13] Baumgarten, " Aesthetik," p. 42.
[14] *Ibid.*, p. 57.
[15] Baumgarten, *Aesthetica*, Vol. I (Frankfurt a/O. 1750), §14.

Art challenges the prevailing principle of reason: in representing the order of sensuousness, it invokes a tabooed logic — the logic of gratification as against that of repression. Behind the sublimated aesthetic form, the unsublimated content shows forth: the commitment of art to the pleasure principle.[17] The investigation of the erotic roots of art plays a large role in psychoanalysis; however, these roots are in the work and function of art rather than in the artist. The aesthetic form is sensuous form — constituted by the *order of sensuousness*. If the "perfection" of sense-cognition is defined as beauty, this definition still retains the inner connection with instinctual gratification, and aesthetic pleasure is still pleasure. But the sensual origin is "repressed," and the gratification is in the pure *form* of the object. As aesthetic value, the non-conceptual truth of the senses is sanctioned, and freedom from the reality principle is granted to the "free play" of creative imagination. Here, a reality with quite different standards is recognized. However, since this other, "free" reality is attributed to art, and its experience to the aesthetic attitude, it is non-committing and does not engage the human existence in the ordinary way of life; it is "unreal."

Schiller's attempt to undo the sublimation of the aesthetic function starts from Kant's position: only because imagination is a central faculty of the mind, only because beauty is a "necessary condition of humanity,"[18] can the aesthetic function play a decisive role in reshaping civiliza-

[17] See Otto Rank, "The Play-impulse and Aesthetic Pleasure," in *Art and Artist* (New York: Alfred Knopf, 1932).
[18] Schiller, *The Aesthetic Letters*, p. 46.

tion. When Schiller wrote, the need for such a reshaping seemed obvious; Herder and Schiller, Hegel and Novalis developed in almost identical terms the concept of alienation. As industrial society begins to take shape under the rule of the performance principle, its inherent negativity permeates the philosophical analysis:

> . . . enjoyment is separated from labor, the means from the end, exertion from recompense. Eternally fettered only to a single little fragment of the whole, man fashions himself only as a fragment; ever hearing only the monotonous whirl of the wheel which he turns, he never develops the harmony of his being, and, instead of shaping the humanity that lies in his nature, he becomes a mere imprint of his occupation, his science.[19]

Since it was civilization itself which " dealt modern man this wound," only a new mode of civilization can heal it. The wound is caused by the antagonistic relation between the two polar dimensions of the human existence. Schiller describes this antagonism in a series of paired concepts: sensuousness and reason, matter and form (spirit), nature and freedom, the particular and the universal. Each of the two dimensions is governed by a basic *impulse*: the "sensuous impulse " and the " form-impulse." [20] The former is essentially passive, receptive, the latter active, mastering, domineering. Culture is built by the combination and interaction of these two impulses. But in the established civilization, their relation has been an antagonistic one: instead of reconciling both impulses by making sensuousness rational and reason sensuous, civilization has subjugated sensuousness to reason in such a manner that the former, if

19 *Ibid.*, p. 22 (with minor changes in translation).
20 *Ibid.*, p. 53.

it reasserts itself, does so in destructive and "savage" forms while the tyranny of reason impoverishes and barbarizes sensuousness. The conflict must be resolved if human potentialities are to realize themselves freely. Since only the impulses have the lasting force that fundamentally affects the human existence, such reconciliation between the two impulses must be the work of a third impulse. Schiller defines this third mediating impulse as the *play impulse*, its objective as beauty, and its goal as freedom. We shall presently try to rescue the full content of Schiller's notion from the benevolent aesthetic treatment to which the traditional interpretation has confined it.

The quest is for the solution of a "political" problem: the liberation of man from inhuman existential conditions. Schiller states that, in order to solve the political problem, "one must pass through the aesthetic, since it is beauty that leads to freedom." The play impulse is the vehicle of this liberation. The impulse does not aim at playing "with" something; rather it is the play of life itself, beyond want and external compulsion — the manifestation of an existence without fear and anxiety, and thus the manifestation of freedom itself. Man is free only where he is free from constraint, external and internal, physical and moral — when he is constrained neither by law nor by need.[21] But such constraint *is* the reality. Freedom is thus, in a strict sense, freedom from the established reality: man is free when the "reality loses its seriousness" and when its necessity "becomes light" (*leicht*).[22] "The greatest stupidity and the greatest intelligence have a certain affinity with

[21] *Ibid.*, pp. 70–71, 96.   [22] *Ibid.*, p. 71.

each other in that they both seek only the *real* "; however, such need for and attachment to the real are " merely the results of want." In contrast, " indifference to reality " and interest in " show " (dis-play, *Schein*) are the tokens of freedom from want and a " true enlargement of humanity." [23] In a genuinely humane civilization, the human existence will be play rather than toil, and man will live in display rather than need.

These ideas represent one of the most advanced positions of thought. It must be understood that the liberation from the reality which is here envisaged is not transcendental, " inner," or merely intellectual freedom (as Schiller explicitly emphasizes [24]) but freedom *in* the reality. The reality that " loses its seriousness " is the inhumane reality of want and need, and it loses its seriousness when wants and needs can be satisfied without alienated labor. Then, man is free to " play " with his faculties and potentialities and with those of nature, and only by " playing " with them is he free. His world is then display (*Schein*), and its order is that of beauty. Because it is the realization of freedom, play is *more* than the constraining physical and moral reality: ". . . man is only *serious* with the agreeable, the good, the perfect; but with beauty he plays." [25] Such formulations would be irresponsible " aestheticism " if the realm of play were one of ornament, luxury, holiday, in an otherwise repressive world. But here the aesthetic function is conceived as a principle governing the entire human existence, and it can do so only if it becomes " universal."

[23] *Ibid.*, pp. 130–131.   [25] *Ibid.*, p. 72.
[24] *Ibid.*, pp. 93, 140, 142.

Aesthetic culture presupposes "a total revolution in the mode of perception and feeling," [26] and such revolution becomes possible only if civilization has reached the highest physical and intellectual maturity. Only when the "constraint of need" is replaced by the "constraint of superfluity" (abundance) will the human existence be impelled to a "free movement which is itself both end and means." [27] Liberated from the pressure of painful purposes and performances necessitated by want, man will be restored into the "freedom to be what he ought to be." [28] But what "ought" to be will be freedom itself: the freedom to play. The mental faculty exercising this freedom is that of *imagination.*[29] It traces and projects the potentialities of all being; liberated from their enslavement by constraining matter, they appear as "pure forms." As such, they constitute an order of their own: they exist "according to the laws of beauty." [30]

Once it has really gained ascendancy as a principle of civilization, the play impulse would literally transform the reality. Nature, the objective world, would then be experienced primarily, neither as dominating man (as in primitive society), nor as being dominated by man (as in the established civilization), but rather as an object of "contemplation." [31] With this change in the basic and formative experience, the object of experience itself changes: released from violent domination and exploitation, and instead shaped by the play impulse, nature would also be liberated

[26] *Ibid.*, p. 138. (Translation changed.)
[27] *Ibid.*, p. 140. (Translation changed.)
[28] *Ibid.*, p. 100.
[29] *Ibid.*, p. 133.
[30] *Ibid.*, p. 111.
[31] *Ibid.*, pp. 115, 123.

from its own brutality and would become free to display the wealth of its purposeless forms which express the "inner life" of its objects.[32]   And a corresponding change would take place in the subjective world.   Here, too, the aesthetic experience would arrest the violent and exploitative productivity which made man into an instrument of labor.   But he would not be returned to a state of suffering passivity. His existence would still be activity, but "what he possesses and produces need bear no longer the traces of servitude, the fearful design of its purpose";[33] beyond want and anxiety, human activity becomes *display* — the free manifestation of potentialities.

At this point, the explosive quality of Schiller's conception comes into focus.   He had diagnosed the disease of civilization as the conflict between the two basic impulses of man (the sensuous and the form impulses), or rather as the violent "solution" of this conflict: the establishment of the repressive tyranny of reason over sensuousness.   Consequently, the reconciliation of the conflicting impulses would involve the removal of this tyranny — that is, the restoration of the right of sensuousness.   Freedom would have to be sought in the liberation of sensuousness rather than reason, and in the limitation of the "higher" faculties in favor of the "lower."   In other words, the salvation of culture would involve abolition of the repressive controls that civilization has imposed on sensuousness.   And this is indeed the idea behind the *Aesthetic Education*.   It aims at basing morality on a sensuous ground;[34] the laws of rea-

[32] *Ibid.*, p. 114.

[33] *Ibid.*, pp. 142–143.   (Translation changed.)

[34] *Ibid.*, p. 10.   Weiss here translates *sinnliche* not as "sensuous" but as "sensible."

son must be reconciled with the interest of the senses; [85] the domineering form impulse must be restrained: " sensuousness must triumphantly maintain its province, and resist the violence which spirit (*Geist*) would fain inflict upon it by its encroaching activity." [36] To be sure, if freedom is to become the governing principle of civilization, not only reason but also the " sensuous impulse " requires a restraining transformation. The additional release of sensuous energy must conform with the universal *order* of freedom. However, whatever order would have to be imposed upon the sensuous impulse must itself be " an operation of freedom." [37] The free individual himself must bring about the harmony between individual and universal gratification. In a truly free civilization, all laws are self-given by the individuals: " to give freedom by freedom is the universal law " of the " aesthetic state "; [38] in a truly free civilization, " the will of the whole " fulfills itself only " through the nature of the individual." [39] Order is freedom only if it is founded on and sustained by the free gratification of the individuals.

But the fatal enemy of lasting gratification is *time*, the inner finiteness, the brevity of all conditions. The idea of integral human liberation therefore necessarily contains the vision of the struggle against time. We have seen that the Orphic and Narcissistic images symbolize the rebellion against passing, the desperate effort to arrest the flow of time — the conservative nature of the pleasure principle. If the " aesthetic state " is really to be the state of freedom, then it must ultimately defeat the destructive course of

---

[85] *Ibid.*, p. 67.
[36] *Ibid.*, p. 63.
[37] *Ibid.*, p. 63.

[38] *Ibid.*, p. 145.
[39] *Ibid.*, p. 145.

time. Only this is the token of a non-repressive civilization. Thus, Schiller attributes to the liberating play impulse the function of "abolishing time in time," of reconciling being and becoming, change and identity.[40] In this task culminates the progress of mankind to a higher form of culture.

The idealistic and aesthetic sublimations which prevail in Schiller's work do not vitiate its radical implications. Jung recognized these implications and was duly frightened by them. He warned that the rule of the play impulse would bring about a "release of repression" which would entail a "depreciation of the hitherto highest values," a "catastrophe of culture" — in a word, "barbarism."[41] Schiller himself was apparently less inclined than Jung to identify repressive culture with culture as such; he seemed to be willing to accept the risk of catastrophe for the former and a debasement of its values if this would lead to a higher culture. He was fully aware that, in its first free manifestations, the play impulse "will be hardly recognized," for the sensuous impulse will incessantly interpose with its "wild desire."[42] However, he thought that such "barbarian" outbreaks would be left behind as the new culture developed, and that only a "leap" could lead from the old to the new one. He did not concern himself with the catastrophic changes in the social structure that this "leap" would involve: they lay beyond the limits of idealistic philosophy. But the direction of the change toward a non-

[40] Ibid., p. 65.
[41] Jung, Psychological Types, transl. H. Godwin Baynes (New York: Harcourt, Brace, 1926), p. 135.
[42] Schiller, The Aesthetic Letters, p. 142.

repressive order is clearly indicated in his aesthetic conception.

If we reassemble its main elements, we find:

(1) The transformation of toil (labor) into play, and of repressive productivity into "display" — a transformation that must be preceded by the conquest of want (scarcity) as the determining factor of civilization.[48]

(2) The self-sublimation of sensuousness (of the sensuous impulse) and the de-sublimation of reason (of the form-impulse) in order to reconcile the two basic antagonistic impulses.

(3) The conquest of time in so far as time is destructive of lasting gratification.

These elements are practically identical with those of a reconciliation between pleasure principle and reality principle. We recall the constitutive role attributed to imagination (phantasy) in play and display: Imagination preserves the objectives of those mental processes which have remained free from the repressive reality principle; in their

[48] An attempt to define, on a biological basis, human freedom in terms of play has been recently made by Gustav Bally, in *Vom Ursprung und den Grenzen der Freiheit* (Basel: Benno Schwabe, 1945), especially pp. 29, 71ff, 74–75. He sees the dimension of freedom in freedom from instinctual determination. Man is not, like the animal, necessarily determined by his instincts; he possesses an *entspanntes Feld* — a *Spielraum* in which he "keeps *distant* from his instinctual objectives," plays with them and thus plays with his world. This attitude of a constant distance from the instinctual objective makes human culture possible.

Bally's conception is close to Schiller's, but it is regressive where Schiller's is progressive. Schiller's playful freedom is the result of instinctual liberation; Bally's is "relative freedom against the instincts" (p. 94), freedom to resist instinctual needs. No wonder, then, that the new interpretation of freedom turns out to be the old freedom to renounce, to deny temptations, the "courage" to bind oneself, the power of self-repression (p. 79). And, quite consistently, the ultimate and true freedom, "freedom from anxiety and death," is denounced as a false and "questionable" liberty (p. 100).

aesthetic function, they can be incorporated into the conscious rationality of mature civilization. The play impulse stands for the common denominator of the two opposed mental processes and principles.

Still another element links the aesthetic philosophy with the Orphic and Narcissistic images: the view of a non-repressive order in which the subjective and objective world, man and nature, are harmonized. The Orphic symbols center on the singing god who lives to defeat death and who liberates nature, so that the constrained and constraining matter releases the beautiful and playful forms of animate and inanimate things. No longer striving and no longer desiring "for something still to be attained," [44] they are free from fear and fetter — and thus free *per se*. The contemplation of Narcissus repels all other activity in the erotic surrender to beauty, inseparably uniting his own existence with nature. Similarly, the aesthetic philosophy conceives of non-repressive order in such a manner that nature in man and outside man becomes freely susceptible to " laws " — the laws of display and beauty.

Non-repressive order is essentially an order of *abundance*: the necessary constraint is brought about by " superfluity " rather than need. Only an order of abundance is compatible with freedom. At this point, the idealistic and the materialistic critiques of culture meet. Both agree that non-repressive order becomes possible only at the highest maturity of civilization, when all basic needs can be satisfied with a minimum expenditure of physical and mental energy in a minimum of time. Rejecting the notion of free-

[44] ". . . um ein endlich noch Erreichtes " (Rilke).

dom which pertains to the rule of the performance principle, they reserve freedom for the new mode of existence
that would emerge on the basis of universally gratified ex-
istence-needs. The realm of freedom is envisioned as ly-
ing *beyond* the realm of necessity: freedom is not within
but outside the " struggle for existence." Possession and
procurement of the necessities of life are the prerequisite,
rather than the content, of a free society. The realm of necessity, of labor, is one of unfreedom because the human
existence in this realm is determined by objectives and
functions that are not its own and that do not allow the
free play of human faculties and desires. The optimum in
this realm is therefore to be defined by standards of rationality rather than freedom — namely, to organize production and distribution in such a manner that the least time
is spent for making all necessities available to all members
of society. Necessary labor is a system of essentially inhuman, mechanical, and routine activities; in such a system,
individuality cannot be a value and end in itself. Reasonably, the system of societal labor would be organized rather
with a view to saving time and space for the development
of individuality *outside* the inevitably repressive work-
world. Play and display, as principles of civilization, imply not the transformation of labor but its complete subordination to the freely evolving potentialities of man and
nature. The ideas of play and display now reveal their full
distance from the values of productiveness and performance: play is *unproductive* and *useless* precisely because it
cancels the repressive and exploitative traits of labor and
leisure; it " just plays " with the reality. But it also can-

cels their sublime traits — the "higher values." The desublimation of reason is just as essential a process in the emergence of a free culture as is the self-sublimation of sensuousness. In the established system of domination, the repressive structure of reason and the repressive organization of the sense-faculties supplement and sustain each other. In Freud's terms: civilized morality *is* the morality of repressed instincts; liberation of the latter implies "debasement" of the former. But this debasement of the higher values may take them back into the organic structure of the human existence from which they were separated, and the reunion may transform this structure itself. If the higher values lose their remoteness, their isolation from and against the lower faculties, the latter may become freely susceptible to culture.

CHAPTER TEN

The Transformation of Sexuality into Eros

The vision of a non-repressive culture, which we have lifted from a marginal trend in mythology and philosophy, aims at a new relation between instincts and reason. The civilized morality is reversed by harmonizing instinctual freedom and order: liberated from the tyranny of repressive reason, the instincts tend toward free and lasting existential relations — they generate a *new* reality principle. In Schiller's idea of an " aesthetic state," the vision of a non-repressive culture is concretized at the level of mature civilization. At this level, the organization of the instincts becomes a social problem (in Schiller's terminology, *political*), as it does in Freud's pyschology. The processes that create the ego and superego also shape and perpetuate specific societal institutions and relations. Such psychoanalytical concepts as sublimation, identification, and introjection have not only a psychical but also a social content: they terminate in a system of institutions, laws, agencies, things, and customs that confront the individual as objective entities. Within this antagonistic system, the mental conflict between ego and superego, between ego and id, is at one and the same time a conflict between the individual and his society. The latter embodies the rationality of the whole, and the individual's struggle against the repressive forces is a struggle against objective reason. Therefore, the emergence of a non-repressive reality principle involving instinctual liberation would *regress* behind the attained level of civilized rationality. This regression would be psychical as well as social: it would reactivate early stages of the libido which were surpassed in the development of the reality ego, and it would dissolve the institutions of society in which the reality ego exists. In terms of these institutions, instinctual liberation is relapse into barbarism. However, occurring at the height of civilization, as a consequence not of defeat but of victory in the struggle for existence, and supported by a free society, such liberation might have very different results. It would still be a reversal of the process of civilization, a subversion of culture — but *after* culture had done its work and created the mankind and the world that could be free. It would still be " regression " — but in the light of mature consciousness and guided by a new rationality. Under these conditions, the possibility of a non-repressive civilization is predicated not upon the arrest, but upon the liberation, of progress — so that man would order his life in accordance with his fully developed knowledge, so that he would ask again what is good and what is evil. If the guilt accumulated in the civilized domination of man by man can ever be redeemed by freedom, then the " original sin " must be committed again: " We must again eat from the tree of knowledge in order to fall back into the state of innocence." [1]

[1] " Wir müssen wieder vom Baum der Erkenntnis essen, um in den Stand der Unschuld zurückzufallen." Heinrich von Kleist, " Ueber das Marionettentheater," conclusion.

The notion of a non-repressive instinctual order must first be tested on the most " disorderly " of all instincts — namely, sexuality. Non-repressive order is possible only if the sex instincts can, by virtue of their own dynamic and under changed existential and societal conditions, generate lasting erotic relations among mature individuals. We have to ask whether the sex instincts, after the elimination of all surplus-repression, can develop a " libidinal rationality " which is not only compatible with but even promotes progress toward higher forms of civilized freedom. This possibility will be examined here in Freud's own terms.

We have reiterated Freud's conclusion that any genuine decrease in the societal controls over the sex instincts would, even under optimum conditions, reverse the organization of sexuality toward precivilized stages. Such regression would break through the central fortifications of the performance principle: it would undo the channeling of sexuality into monogamic reproduction and the taboo on perversions. Under the rule of the performance principle, the libidinal cathexis of the individual body and libidinal relations with others are normally confined to leisure time and directed to the preparation and execution of genital intercourse; only in exceptional cases, and with a high degree of sublimation, are libidinal relations allowed to enter into the sphere of work. These constraints, enforced by the need for sustaining a large quantum of energy and time for non-gratifying labor, perpetuate the desexualization of the body in order to make the organism into a subject-object of socially useful performances. Conversely, if the work day and energy are reduced to a minimum, without a corresponding manipula-

tion of the free time, the ground for these constraints
would be undermined. Libido would be released and would
overflow the institutionalized limits within which it is kept
by the reality principle.

Freud repeatedly emphasized that the lasting interpersonal relations on which civilization depends presuppose
that the sex instinct is inhibited in its aim.[2] Love, and the
enduring and responsible relations which it demands, are
founded on a union of sexuality with " affection," and this
union is the historical result of a long and cruel process of
domestication, in which the instinct's legitimate manifestation is made supreme and its component parts are arrested
in their development.[3] This cultural refinement of sexuality, its sublimation to love, took place within a civilization
which established possessive private relations apart from,
and in a decisive aspect conflicting with, the possessive societal relations. While, outside the privacy of the family,
men's existence was chiefly determined by the exchange
value of their products and performances, their life in home
and bed was to be permeated with the spirit of divine and
moral law. Mankind was supposed to be an end in itself
and never a mere means; but this ideology was effective in
the private rather than in the societal functions of the individuals, in the sphere of libidinal satisfaction rather than
in that of labor. The full force of civilized morality was
mobilized against the use of the body as mere object, means,
instrument of pleasure; such reification was tabooed and

[2] *Collected Papers* (London: Hogarth Press, 1950), IV, 203ff; *Group
Psychology and the Analysis of the Ego* (New York: Liveright Publishing
Corp., 1949), pp. 72, 78.
[3] *Collected Papers*, IV, 215.

remained the ill-reputed privilege of whores, degenerates, and perverts. Precisely in his gratification, and especially in his sexual gratification, man was to be a higher being, committed to higher values; sexuality was to be dignified by love. With the emergence of a non-repressive reality principle, with the abolition of the surplus-repression necessitated by the performance principle, this process would be reversed. In the societal relations, reification would be reduced as the division of labor became reoriented on the gratification of freely developing individual needs; whereas, in the libidinal relations, the taboo on the reification of the body would be lessened. No longer used as a full-time instrument of labor, the body would be resexualized. The regression involved in this spread of the libido would first manifest itself in a reactivation of all erotogenic zones and, consequently, in a resurgence of pregenital polymorphous sexuality and in a decline of genital supremacy. The body in its entirety would become an object of cathexis, a thing to be enjoyed — an instrument of pleasure. This change in the value and scope of libidinal relations would lead to a disintegration of the institutions in which the private interpersonal relations have been organized, particularly the monogamic and patriarchal family.

These prospects seem to confirm the expectation that instinctual liberation can lead only to a society of sex maniacs — that is, to no society. However, the process just outlined involves not simply a release but a *transformation* of the libido: from sexuality constrained under genital supremacy to erotization of the entire personality. It is a spread rather than explosion of libido — a spread over private and societal relations which bridges the gap maintained between them by a repressive reality principle. This transformation of the libido would be the result of a societal transformation that released the free play of individual needs and faculties. By virtue of these conditions, the free development of transformed libido *beyond* the institutions of the performance principle differs essentially from the release of constrained sexuality *within* the dominion of these institutions. The latter process explodes *suppressed* sexuality; the libido continues to bear the mark of suppression and manifests itself in the hideous forms so well known in the history of civilization; in the sadistic and masochistic orgies of desperate masses, of "society elites," of starved bands of mercenaries, of prison and concentration-camp guards. Such release of sexuality provides a periodically necessary outlet for unbearable frustration; it strengthens rather than weakens the roots of instinctual constraint; consequently, it has been used time and again as a prop for suppressive regimes. In contrast, the free development of transformed libido within transformed institutions, while eroticizing previously tabooed zones, time, and relations, would *minimize* the manifestations of *mere* sexuality by integrating them into a far larger order, including the order of work. In this context, sexuality tends to its own sublimation: the libido would not simply reactivate precivilized and infantile stages, but would also transform the perverted content of these stages.

The term *perversions* covers sexual phenomena of essentially different origin. The same taboo is placed on instinctual manifestations incompatible with civilization and on those incompatible with repressive civilization, especially with monogamic genital supremacy. However, within the historical dynamic of the instinct, for example, coprophilia and homosexuality have a very different place and function.[4] A similar difference prevails within one and the same perversion: the function of sadism is not the same in a free libidinal relation and in the activities of SS Troops. The inhuman, compulsive, coercive, and destructive forms of these perversions seem to be linked with the general perversion of the human existence in a repressive culture, but the perversions have an instinctual substance distinct from these forms; and this substance may well express itself in other forms compatible with normality in high civilization. Not all component parts and stages of the instinct that have been suppressed have suffered this fate because they prevented the evolution of man and mankind. The purity, regularity, cleanliness, and reproduction required by the performance principle are not naturally those of any mature civilization. And the reactivation of prehistoric and childhood wishes and attitudes is not necessarily regression; it may well be the opposite — proximity to a happiness that has always been the repressed promise of a better future. In one of his most advanced formulations, Freud once defined happiness as the " subsequent fulfillment of a prehistoric wish. That is why wealth brings so little happiness: money was not a wish in childhood." [5]

But if human happiness depends on the fulfillment of

---

[4] See Chapter 2 above.
[5] Ernest Jones, *The Life and Work of Sigmund Freud*, Vol. I (New York: Basic Books, 1953), p. 330.

childhood wishes, civilization, according to Freud, depends on the suppression of the strongest of all childhood wishes: the Oedipus wish. Does the realization of happiness in a free civilization still necessitate this suppression? Or would the transformation of the libido also engulf the Oedipus situation? In the context of our hypothesis, such speculations are insignificant; the Oedipus complex, although the primary source and model of neurotic conflicts, is certainly not the central cause of the discontents in civilization, and not the central obstacle for their removal. The Oedipus complex " passes " even under the rule of a repressive reality principle. Freud advances two general interpretations of the " passing of the Oedipus complex ": it " becomes extinguished by its lack of success "; or it " must come to an end because the time has come for its dissolution, just as the milk-teeth fall out when the permanent ones begin to press forward." [6] The passing of the complex appears as a " natural " event in both cases.

We have spoken of the *self-sublimation of sexuality*. The term implies that sexuality can, under specific conditions, create highly civilized human relations without being subjected to the repressive organization which the established civilization has imposed upon the instinct. Such self-sublimation presupposes historical progress beyond the institutions of the performance principle, which in turn would release instinctual regression. For the development of the instinct, this means regression from sexuality in the service of reproduction to sexuality in the " function of ob-

[6] *Collected Papers*, II, 269.

taining pleasure from zones of the body." [7]   With this restoration of the primary structure of sexuality, the primacy of the genital function is broken — as is the desexualization of the body which has accompanied this primacy.   The organism in its entirety becomes the substratum of sexuality, while at the same time the instinct's objective is no longer absorbed by a specialized function — namely, that of bringing " one's own genitals into contact with those of someone of the opposite sex." [8]   Thus enlarged, the field and objective of the instinct becomes the life of the organism itself. This process almost naturally, by its inner logic, suggests the conceptual transformation of sexuality into Eros.

The introduction of the term Eros in Freud's later writings was certainly motivated by different reasons: Eros, as life instinct, denotes a larger biological instinct rather than a larger scope of sexuality.[9]   However, it may not be accidental that Freud does not rigidly distinguish between Eros and sexuality, and his usage of the term *Eros* (especially in *The Ego and the Id, Civilization and Its Discontents,* and in *An Outline of Psychoanalysis*) implies an enlargement of the meaning of sexuality itself.   Even without Freud's explicit reference to Plato the change in emphasis is clear: Eros signifies a quantitative and qualitative aggrandizement of sexuality.   And the aggrandized concept seems to demand a correspondingly modified concept of sub-

---

[7] *An Outline of Psychoanalysis* (New York: W. W. Norton, 1949), p. 26.
[8] *Ibid.,* p. 25.
[9] See the papers of Siegfried Bernfeld and Edward Bibring in *Imago,* Vols. XXI, XXII (1935, 1936).   See also page 137 above.

limation. The modifications of sexuality are not the same as the modifications of Eros. Freud's concept of sublima-tion refers to the fate of sexuality under a repressive reality principle. Thus, sublimation means a change in the aim and object of the instinct "with regard to which our social values come into the picture." [10] The term is applied to a group of unconscious processes which have in common that

. . . as the result of inner or outer deprivation, the aim of object-libido undergoes a more or less complete deflection, modification, or inhibition. In the great majority of instances, the new aim is one distinct or remote from sexual satisfaction, i.e., is an asexual or non-sexual aim.[11]

This mode of sublimation is to a high degree dictated by specific societal requirements and cannot be automati-cally extended to other and less repressive forms of civiliza-tion with different "social values." Under the perform-ance principle, the diversion of libido into useful cultural activities takes place after the period of early child-hood. Sublimation then operates on a preconditioned in-stinctual structure, which includes the functional and tem-poral restraints of sexuality, its channeling into monogamic reproduction, and the desexualization of most of the body. Sublimation works with the thus preconditioned libido and its possessive, exploitative, aggressive force. The repressive "modification" of the pleasure principle precedes the ac-tual sublimation, and the latter carries the repressive ele-ments over into the socially useful activities.

[10] Freud, New Introductory Lectures on Psychoanalysis (New York: W. W. Norton, 1933), p. 133.
[11] Edward Glover, "Sublimation, Substitution, and Social Anxiety," in International Journal of Psychoanalysis, Vol. XII, No. 3 (1931), p. 264.

However, there are other modes of sublimation. Freud speaks of aim-inhibited sexual impulses which need not be described as sublimated although they are " closely related " to sublimated impulses. " They have not abandoned their directly sexual aims, but they are held back by internal resistances from attaining them; they rest content with certain approximations to satisfaction." [12] Freud calls them " social instincts " and mentions as examples " the affectionate relations between parents and children, feelings of friendship, and the emotional ties in marriage which had their origin in sexual attraction." Moreover, in *Group Psychology and the Analysis of the Ego*, Freud has emphasized the extent to which societal relations (" community " in civilization) are founded on *un*sublimated as well as sublimated libidinous ties: " sexual love for women " as well as " desexualized, sublimated, homosexual love for other men " here appear as instinctual sources of an enduring and expanding culture. [13] This conception suggests, in Freud's own work, an idea of civilization very different from that derived from repressive sublimation, namely, civilization evolving from and sustained by free libidinal relations. Géza Róheim used Ferenczi's notion of a " genitofugal libido " [14] to support his theory of the libidinous origin of culture. With the relief of extreme tension, libido flows back from the object to the body, and this " recathecting of

[12] Encyclopaedia article " The Libido Theory," reprinted in *Collected Papers*, V, 134.
[13] Page 57.
[14] *Versuch einer Genitaltheorie* (Leipzig: Internationaler Psychoanalytischer Verlag, 1924), pp. 51–52. This book has appeared in English as *Thalassa*, transl. H. A. Bunker (Albany: Psychoanalytic Quarterly, Inc., 1938).

the whole organism with libido results in a feeling of happiness in which the organs find their reward for work and stimulation to further activity." [15]   The concept assumes a genitofugal " libido trend to the development of culture " — in other words, an inherent trend in the libido itself toward " cultural" expression, *without* external repressive modification.   And this " cultural" trend in the libido seems to be *genitofugal*, that is to say, *away* from genital supremacy toward the erotization of the entire organism.

These concepts come close to recognizing the possibility of non-repressive sublimation.   The rest is left to speculation.   And indeed, under the established reality principle, non-repressive sublimation can appear only in marginal and incomplete aspects; its fully developed form would be sublimation without desexualization.   The instinct is not " deflected " from its aim; it is gratified in activities and relations that are not sexual in the sense of " organized " genital sexuality and yet are libidinal and erotic.   Where repressive sublimation prevails and determines the culture, non-repressive sublimation must manifest itself in contradiction to the entire sphere of social usefulness; viewed from this sphere, it is the negation of all accepted productivity and performance.   The Orphic and Narcissistic images are recalled: Plato blames Orpheus for his " softness " (he was only a

[15] Róheim, *The Origin and Function of Culture,* (New York: Nervous and Mental Disease Monograph No. 69, 1943), p. 74.   In his article " Sublimation " in the *Yearbook of Psychoanalysis,* Vol. I (1945), Róheim stresses that in sublimation " id strivings reconquer the ground in a disguised form."   Thus, " in contrast to the prevailing view, . . . in sublimation we have no ground wrested from the id by the super-ego, but quite to the contrary, what we have is super-ego territory inundated by the id" (p. 117).   Here, too, the emphasis is on the *ascendancy* of libido in sublimation.

harp-player), which was duly punished by the gods [16] — as was Narcissus' refusal to " participate." Before the reality as it is, they stand condemned: they rejected the required sublimation. However,

. . . La sublimation n'est pas toujours la négation d'un désir; elle ne se présente pas toujours comme une sublimation *contre* des instincts. Elle peut être une sublimation *pour* un idéal. Alors Narcisse ne dit plus: " Je m'aime tel que je suis," il dit: " Je suis tel que je m'aime." [17]

The Orphic and Narcissistic Eros engulfs the reality in libidinal relations which transform the individual and his environment; but this transformation is the isolated deed of unique individuals, and, as such, it generates death. Even if sublimation does not proceed *against* the instincts but as their affirmation, it must be a supra-individual process on common ground. As an isolated individual phenomenon, the reactivation of narcissistic libido is not culture-building but neurotic:

The difference between a neurosis and a sublimation is evidently the social aspect of the phenomenon. A neurosis isolates; a sublimation unites. In a sublimation something new is created — a house, or a community, or a tool — and it is created in a group or for the use of a group.[18]

Libido can take the road of self-sublimation only as a *social* phenomenon: as an unrepressed force, it can promote the formation of culture only under conditions which relate

---

[16] *Symposium* 179 D.

[17] " Sublimation is not always the negation of a desire; it does not always take the form of sublimation *against* the instincts. It could be sublimation *for* an ideal. Thus Narcissus no longer says: ' I love myself such as I am.' He says: ' I am such that I love myself.' " Gaston Bachelard, *L'Eau et les Rêves* (Paris: José Corti, 1942), pp. 34–35.

[18] Róheim, *The Origin and Function of Culture*, p. 74.

associated individuals to each other in the cultivation of the environment for their developing needs and faculties. Reactivation of polymorphous and narcissistic sexuality ceases to be a threat to culture and can itself lead to culture-building if the organism exists not as an instrument of alienated labor but as a subject of self-realization — in other words, if socially useful work is at the same time the transparent satisfaction of an individual need. In primitive society, this organization of work may be immediate and "natural"; in mature civilization, it can be envisaged only as the result of liberation. Under such conditions, the impulse to " obtain pleasure from the zones of the body " may extend to seek its objective in lasting and expanding libidinal relations because this expansion increases and intensifies the instinct's gratification. Moreover, nothing in the nature of Eros justifies the notion that the " extension " of the impulse is confined to the corporeal sphere. If the antagonistic separation of the physical from the spiritual part of the organism is itself the historical result of repression, the overcoming of this antagonism would open the spiritual sphere to the impulse. The aesthetic idea of a sensuous reason suggests such a tendency. It is essentially different from sublimation in so far as the spiritual sphere becomes the " direct " object of Eros and remains a libidinal object: there is a change neither in energy nor in aim.

The notion that Eros and Agape may after all be one and the same — not that Eros is Agape but that Agape is Eros — may sound strange after almost two thousand years of theology. Nor does it seem justifiable to refer to Plato as a defender of this identification — Plato who himself introduced the repressive definition of Eros into the household of Western culture. Still, the *Symposium* contains the clearest celebration of the sexual origin and substance of the spiritual relations. According to Diotima, Eros drives the desire for one beautiful body to another and finally to all beautiful bodies, for " the beauty of one body is akin to the beauty of another," and it would be foolish " not to recognize that the beauty in every body is one and the same." [19] Out of this truly polymorphous sexuality arises the desire for that which animates the desired body: the psyche and its various manifestations. There is an unbroken ascent in erotic fulfillment from the corporeal love of one to that of the others, to the love of beautiful work and play (ἐπιτηδεύματα), and ultimately to the love of beautiful knowledge (καλὰ μαθήματα). The road to " higher culture " leads through the true love of boys (ὀρθῶς παιδεραστειν).[20] Spiritual "procreation" is just as much the work of Eros as is corporeal procreation, and the right and true order of the Polis is just as much an erotic one as is the right and true order of love. The culture-building power of Eros *is* non-repressive sublimation: sexuality is neither deflected from nor blocked in its objective; rather, in attaining its objective, it transcends it to others, searching for fuller gratification.

In the light of the idea of non-repressive sublimation, Freud's definition of Eros as striving to " form living substance into ever greater unities, so that life may be prolonged and brought to higher development " [21] takes on

[19] 210 B. Jowett translates, not " body," but " form."
[20] 211 B. Jowett translates: ". . . under the influence of true love."
[21] Freud, *Collected Papers*, V, 135.

added significance. The biological drive becomes a cultural drive. The pleasure principle reveals its own dialectic. The erotic aim of sustaining the entire body as subject-object of pleasure calls for the continual refinement of the organism, the intensification of its receptivity, the growth of its sensuousness. The aim generates its own projects of realization: the abolition of toil, the amelioration of the environment, the conquest of disease and decay, the creation of luxury. All these activities flow directly from the pleasure principle, and, at the same time, they constitute *work* which associates individuals to " greater unities "; no longer confined within the mutilating dominion of the performance principle, they modify the impulse without deflecting it from its aim. There is sublimation and, consequently, culture; but this sublimation proceeds in a system of expanding and enduring libidinal relations, which are in themselves work relations.

The idea of an erotic tendency toward work is not foreign to psychoanalysis. Freud himself remarked that work provides an opportunity for a " very considerable discharge of libidinal component impulses, narcissistic, aggressive and even erotic." [22] We have questioned this statement [23] because it makes no distinction between alienated and non-alienated labor (between labor and work): the former is by its very nature repressive of human potentialities and therefore also repressive of the "libidinal component impulses" which may enter into work. But the statement assumes a different significance if it is seen in the context of

[22] *Civilization and Its Discontents* (London: Hogarth Press, 1949), p. 34 note.
[23] See Chapter 4 above.

the social psychology which Freud proposes in *Group Psychology and the Analysis of the Ego*. He suggests that "the libido props itself upon the satisfaction of the great vital needs, and chooses as its first objects the people who have a share in that process."[24] This proposition, if unfolded in its implications, comes close to vitiating Freud's basic assumption that the "struggle for existence" (that is, for the "satisfaction of the great vital needs") is *per se* anti-libidinous in so far as it necessitates the regimentation of the instinct by a constraining reality principle. It must be noted that Freud links the libido not merely to the *satisfaction* of the great vital needs but to the joint human efforts to *obtain* satisfaction, i.e., to the work process:

> . . . experience has shown that in cases of collaboration libidinal ties are regularly formed between the fellow-workers which prolong and solidify the relations between them to a point beyond what is merely profitable.[25]

If this is true, then Ananke is not a sufficient cause for the instinctual constraints of civilization — and not a sufficient reason for denying the possibility of a non-repressive libidinous culture. Freud's suggestions in *Group Psychology and the Analysis of the Ego* do more than reformulate his thesis of Eros as the builder of culture; culture here rather appears as the builder of Eros — that is to say, as the "natural" fulfillment of the innermost trend of Eros. Freud's psychology of civilization was based on the inexorable conflict between Ananke and free instinctual development. But if Ananke itself becomes the primary field of libidinal development, the contradiction evaporates. Not only

<hr>

[24] Page 57.   [25] *Ibid.*

would the struggle for existence not necessarily cancel the possibility of instinctual freedom (as we suggested in Chapter 6); but it would even constitute a " prop " for instinctual gratificaiton. The work relations which form the base of civilization, and thus civilization itself, would be " propped " by non-desexualized instinctual energy. The whole concept of sublimation is at stake.

The problem of work, of socially useful activity, without (repressive) sublimation can now be restated. It emerged as the problem of a change in the character of work by virtue of which the latter would be assimilated to play — the free play of human faculties. What are the instinctual preconditions for such a transformation? The most far-reaching attempt to answer this question is made by Barbara Lantos in her article " Work and the Instincts." [26] She defines work and play in terms of the instinctual stages involved in these activities. Play is entirely subject to the pleasure principle: pleasure is in the movement itself in so far as it activates erotogenic zones. " The fundamental feature of play is, that it is gratifying in itself, without serving any other purpose than that of instinctual gratification." The impulses that determine play are the pregenital ones: play expresses objectless autoeroticism and gratifies those component instincts which are already directed toward the objective world. Work, on the other hand, serves ends outside itself — namely, the ends of self-preservation. " To work is the active effort of the ego . . . to get from the outside world whatever is needed for self-preservation." This

[26] In *International Journal of Psychoanalysis*, Vol. XXIV (1943), Parts 3 and 4, pp. 114ff.

contrast establishes a parallelism between the organization of the instincts and that of human activity:

> Play is an aim in itself, work is the agent of self-preservation. Component instincts and auto-erotic activities seek pleasure with no ulterior consequences; genital activity is the agent of procreation. The genital organization of the sexual instincts has a parallel in the work-organization of the ego-instincts.[27]

Thus it is the purpose and not the content which marks an activity as play or work.[28] A transformation in the instinctual structure (such as that from the pregenital to the genital stage) would entail a change in the instinctual value of the human activity *regardless of its content*. For example, if work were accompanied by a reactivation of pregenital polymorphous eroticism, it would tend to become gratifying in itself without losing its *work* content. Now it is precisely such a reactivation of polymorphous eroticism which appeared as the consequence of the conquest of scarcity and alienation. The altered societal conditions would therefore create an instinctual basis for the transformation of work into play. In Freud's terms, the less the efforts to obtain satisfaction are impeded and directed by the interest in domination, the more freely the libido could prop itself upon the satisfaction of the great vital needs. Sublimation and domination hang together. And the dissolution of the former would, with the transformation of the instinctual structure, also transform the basic attitude toward man and nature which has been characteristic of Western civilization.

In psychoanalytic literature, the development of libidinal

----

[27] *Ibid.*, p. 117.   [28] *Ibid.*, p. 118.

work relations is usually attributed to a "general maternal attitude as the dominant trend of a culture." [29]   Consequently, it is considered as a feature of primitive societies rather than as a possibility of mature civilization.   Margaret Mead's interpretation of Arapesh culture is entirely focused on this attitude:

> To the Arapesh, the world is a garden that must be tilled, not for one's self, not in pride and boasting, not for hoarding and usury, but that the yams and the dogs and the pigs and most of all the children may grow.   From this whole attitude flow many of the other Arapesh traits, the lack of conflict between the old and young, the lack of any expectation of jealousy or envy, the emphasis upon co-operation. [30]

Foremost in this description appears the fundamentally different experience of the world: nature is taken, not as an object of domination and exploitation, but as a "garden" which can grow while making human beings grow.   It is the attitude that experiences man and nature as joined in a non-repressive and still functioning order.   We have seen how the otherwise most divergent traditions of thought converged on this idea: the philosophical opposition against the performance principle; the Orphic and Narcissistic archetypes; the aesthetic conception.   But while the psychoanalytical and anthropological concepts of such an order have been oriented on the prehistorical and precivilized *past*, our discussion of the concept is oriented on the *future*, on the conditions of fully mature civilization.   The transformation of sexuality into Eros, and its extension to lasting libidinal work relations, here presuppose the ra-

[29] Róheim, *The Origin and Function of Culture*, p. 75.
[30] *Sex and Temperament in Three Primitive Societies* (New York: New American Library, 1952), p. 100.

tional reorganization of a huge industrial apparatus, a highly specialized societal division of labor, the use of fantastically destructive energies, and the co-operation of vast masses.

The idea of libidinal work relations in a developed industrial society finds little support in the tradition of thought, and where such support is forthcoming it seems of a dangerous nature. The transformation of labor into pleasure is the central idea in Fourier's giant socialist utopia. If

... l'industrie est la destination qui nous est assignée par le créateur, comment penser qu'il veuille nous y amener par la violence, et qu'il n'ait pas su mettre en jeu quelque ressort plus noble, quelqu'amorce capable de transformer les travaux en plaisirs.[31]

Fourier insists that this transformation requires a complete change in the social institutions: distribution of the social product according to need, assignment of functions according to individual faculties and inclinations, constant mutation of functions, short work periods, and so on. But the possibility of " attractive labor " (*travail attrayant*) derives above all from the release of libidinal forces. Fourier assumes the existence of an *attraction industrielle* which makes for pleasurable co-operation. It is based on the *attraction passionnée* in the nature of man, which persists despite the opposition of reason, duty, prejudice. This *attraction passionnée* tends toward three principal objectives: the creation of " luxury, or the pleasure of the five

[31] If " industry is the fate assigned to us by the Creator, how can one believe that he wishes to force us into it — that he does not know how to bring to bear some nobler means, some enticement capable of transforming work into pleasure." F. Armand and R. Maublanc, *Fourier: Textes Choisis* (Paris: Editions Sociales Internationales, 1937), III, 154.

senses "; the formation of libidinal groups (of friendship and love); and the establishment of a harmonious order, organizing these groups for work in accordance with the development of the individual "passions" (internal and external "play" of faculties).[32] Fourier comes closer than any other utopian socialist to elucidating the dependence of freedom on non-repressive sublimation. However, in his detailed blueprint for the realization of this idea, he hands it over to a giant organization and administration and thus retains the repressive elements. The working communities of the *phalanstère* anticipate "strength through joy" rather than freedom, the beautification of mass culture rather than its abolition. Work as free play cannot be subject to administration; only alienated labor can be organized and administered by rational routine. It is beyond this sphere, but on its basis, that non-repressive sublimation creates its own cultural order.

Once more, we emphasize that non-repressive sublimation is utterly incompatible with the institutions of the performance principle and implies the negation of this principle. This contradiction is the more important since post-Freudian psychoanalytic theory itself shows a marked tendency to obliterate it and to glorify repressive productivity as human self-realization. A striking example is provided by Ives Hendrick in his paper "Work and the Pleasure Principle."[33] He suggests that the "energy and the need to exercise the physiological organs available for work" are not provided by the libido but rather by a spe-

[32] *Ibid.*, II, 240ff.
[33] *Psychoanalytic Quarterly*, Vol. XII, No. 3 (1943).

cial instinct, the "mastery instinct." Its aim is "to control, or alter a piece of the environment . . . by the skillful use of perceptual, intellectual, and motor techniques." This drive for "integration and skillful performance" is "mentally and emotionally experienced as the need to perform work efficiently." [34] Since work is thus supposed to be itself the gratification of an instinct rather than the "temporary negation" of an instinct, work "yields pleasure" in efficient performance. Work pleasure results from the satisfaction of the mastery instinct, but "work pleasure" and libidinal pleasure usually coincide, since the ego organizations which function as work are "generally, and perhaps always, utilized concurrently for the discharge of surplus libidinal tension." [35]

As usual, the revision of Freudian theory means a retrogression. The assumption of any special instinct begs the question, but the assumption of a special "mastery instinct" does even more: it destroys the entire structure and dynamic of the "mental apparatus" which Freud has built. Moreover, it obliterates the most repressive features of the performance principle by interpreting them as gratification of an instinctual need. Work pure and simple is the chief social manifestation of the reality principle. In so far as work is conditional upon delay and diversion of instinctual gratification (and according to Freud it is), it contradicts the pleasure principle. If work pleasure and libidinal pleasure "usually coincide," then the very concept of the reality principle becomes meaningless and superfluous, and the vicissitudes of the instincts as described by Freud would

[34] *Ibid.,* p. 314.   [35] *Ibid.,* p. 317.

at best be an abnormal development. Nor can the reality principle be saved by stipulating (as Hendrick does) a work principle different from the reality principle; for if the latter does not govern work it has practically nothing to govern in the reality.

To be sure, there is work that yields pleasure in skillful performance of the bodily organs "available for work." But what kind of work, and what kind of pleasure? If pleasure is indeed in the act of working and not extraneous to it, such pleasure must be derived from the acting organs of the body and the body itself, activating the erotogenic zones or eroticizing the body as a whole; in other words, it must be libidinal pleasure. In a reality governed by the performance principle, such "libidinal" work is a rare exception and can occur only outside or at the margin of the work world — as "hobby," play, or in a directly erotic situation. The normal kind of work (socially useful occupational activity) in the prevailing division of labor is such that the individual, in working, does *not* satisfy *his* own impulses, needs, and faculties but performs a pre-established function. Hendrick, however, takes no notice of the fact of *alienated* labor, which is the predominant mode of work under the given reality principle. Certainly there can be "pleasure" in alienated labor too. The typist who hands in a perfect transcript, the tailor who delivers a perfectly fitting suit, the beauty-parlor attendant who fixes the perfect hairdo, the laborer who fulfills his quota — all may feel pleasure in a "job well done." However, either this pleasure is extraneous (anticipation of reward), or it is the satisfaction (itself a token of repression) of being well occupied, in the right place, of contributing one's part to the functioning of the apparatus. In either case, such pleasure has nothing to do with primary instinctual gratification. To link performances on assembly lines, in offices and shops with instinctual needs is to glorify dehumanization as pleasure. It is no wonder that Hendrick considers as the " sublime test of men's will to perform their work effectively" the efficient functioning of an army which has no longer any "fantasies of victory and a pleasant future," which keeps on fighting for no other reason than because it is the soldier's job to fight, and " to do the job was the only motivation that was still meaningful." [86] To say that the job must be done because it is a " job " is truly the apex of alienation, the total loss of instinctual and intellectual freedom — repression which has become, not the second, but the first nature of man.

In contrast to such aberrations, the true spirit of psychoanalytic theory lives in the uncompromising efforts to reveal the anti-humanistic forces behind the philosophy of productiveness:

Of all things, hard work has become a virtue instead of the curse it was always advertised to be by our remote ancestors. . . . Our children should be prepared to bring their children up so they won't have to work as a neurotic necessity. The necessity to work is a neurotic symptom. It is a crutch. It is an attempt to make oneself feel valuable even though there is no particular need for one's working.[87]

[86] *Ibid.*, p. 324.
[87] C. B. Chisholm in the panel discussion " The Psychiatry of Enduring Peace and Social Progress," in *Psychiatry*, Vol. IX, No. 1 (1946), p. 31.

CHAPTER ELEVEN

Eros and Thanatos

Under non-repressive conditions, sexuality tends to "grow into" Eros — that is to say, toward self-sublimation in lasting and expanding relations (including work relations) which serve to intensify and enlarge instinctual gratification. Eros strives for "eternalizing" itself in a permanent *order*. This striving finds its first resistance in the realm of necessity. To be sure, the scarcity and poverty prevalent in the world could be sufficiently mastered to permit the ascendancy of universal freedom, but this mastery seems to be self-propelling — perpetual labor. All the technological progress, the conquest of nature, the rationalization of man and society have not eliminated and cannot eliminate the necessity of alienated labor, the necessity of working mechanically, unpleasurably, in a manner that does not represent individual self-realization.

However, progressive alienation itself increases the potential of freedom: the more external to the individual the necessary labor becomes, the less does it involve him in the realm of necessity. Relieved from the requirements of domination, the quantitative reduction in labor time and energy leads to a qualitative change in the human existence: the free rather than the labor time determines its content. The expanding realm of freedom becomes truly a realm of play — of the free play of individual faculties. Thus liberated, they will generate new forms of realization and of discovering the world, which in turn will reshape the realm of necessity, the struggle for existence. The altered relation between the two realms of the human reality alters the relation between what is desirable and what is reasonable, between instinct and reason. With the transformation from sexuality into Eros, the life instincts evolve their sensuous order, while reason becomes sensuous to the degree to which it comprehends and organizes necessity in terms of protecting and enriching the life instincts. The roots of the aesthetic experience re-emerge — not merely in an artistic culture but in the struggle for existence itself. It assumes a new rationality. The repressiveness of reason that characterizes the rule of the performance principle does not belong to the realm of necessity *per se*. Under the performance principle, the gratification of the sex instinct depends largely on the " suspension " of reason and even of consciousness: on the brief (legitimate or furtive) oblivion of the private and the universal unhappiness, on the interruption of the reasonable routine of life, of the duty and dignity of status and office. Happiness is almost by definition unreasonable if it is unrepressed and uncontrolled. In contrast, beyond the performance principle, the gratification of the instinct requires the more conscious effort of free rationality, the less it is the by-product of the superimposed rationality of oppression. The more freely the instinct develops, the more freely will its " conservative nature " assert itself. The striving for *lasting* gratification makes not only for an enlarged order of libidinal relations ("community") but also for the perpetuation of this order on a higher scale. The pleasure principle extends to consciousness. Eros redefines reason in his own terms. Reasonable is what sustains the order of gratification.

To the degree to which the struggle for existence becomes co-operation for the free development and fulfillment of individual needs, repressive reason gives way to a new *rationality of gratification* in which reason and happiness converge. It creates its own division of labor, its own priorities, its own hierarchy. The historical heritage of the performance principle is administration, not of men, but of things: mature civilization depends for its functioning on a multitude of co-ordinated arrangements. These arrangements in turn must carry recognized and recognizable authority. Hierarchical relationships are not unfree *per se*; civilization relies to a great extent on rational authority, based on knowledge and necessity, and aiming at the protection and preservation of life. Such is the authority of the engineer, of the traffic policeman, of the airplane pilot in flight. Once again, the distinction between repression and surplus-repression must be recalled. If a child feels the "need" to cross the street any time at its will, repression of this "need" is not repressive of human potentialities. It may be the opposite. The need to "relax" in the entertainments furnished by the culture industry is itself repressive, and its repression is a step toward freedom. Where repression has become so effective that, for the repressed, it assumes the (illusory) form of freedom, the abolition of such freedom readily appears as a totalitarian act. Here, the old conflict arises again: human freedom is not only a private affair — but it is nothing at all unless it is *also* a private affair. Once privacy must no longer be maintained apart from and against the public existence, the liberty of the individual and that of the whole may perhaps be reconciled by a " general will " taking shape in institutions which are directed toward the individual needs. The renunciations and delays demanded by the general will must not be opaque and inhuman; nor must their reason be authoritarian. However, the question remains: how can civilization freely generate freedom, when unfreedom has become part and parcel of the mental apparatus? And if not, who is entitled to establish and enforce the objective standards?

From Plato to Rousseau, the only honest answer is the idea of an educational dictatorship, exercised by those who are supposed to have acquired knowledge of the real Good. The answer has since become obsolete: knowledge of the available means for creating a humane existence for all is no longer confined to a privileged elite. The facts are all too open, and the individual consciousness would safely arrive at them if it were not methodically arrested and diverted. The distinction between rational and irrational authority, between repression and surplus-repression, can be made and verified by the individuals themselves. That they cannot make this distinction now does not mean that they cannot learn to make it once they are given the opportunity to do so. Then the course of trial and error becomes a rational course in freedom. Utopias are susceptible to unrealistic blueprints; the conditions for a free society are not. They are a matter of reason.

It is not the conflict between instinct and reason that provides the strongest argument against the idea of a free civilization, but rather the conflict which instinct creates in itself. Even if the destructive forms of its polymorphous perversity and license are due to surplus-repression and become susceptible to libidinal order once surplus-repression is removed, instinct itself is beyond good and evil, and no free civilization can dispense with this distinction. The mere fact that, in the choice of its objects, the sex instinct is not guided by reciprocity constitutes a source of unavoidable conflict among individuals — and a strong argument against the possibility of its self-sublimation. But is there perhaps in the instinct itself an inner barrier which " contains " its driving power? Is there perhaps a " natural " self-restraint in Eros so that its genuine gratification would call for delay, detour, and arrest? Then there would be obstructions and limitations imposed not from outside, by a repressive reality principle, but set and accepted by the instinct itself because they have inherent libidinal value. Freud indeed suggested this notion. He thought that " unrestrained sexual liberty from the beginning " results in lack of full satisfaction:

It is easy to show that the value the mind sets on erotic needs instantly sinks as soon as satisfaction becomes readily obtainable. Some obstacle is necessary to swell the tide of the libido to its height.[1]

Moreover, he considered the " strange " possibility that " something in the nature of the sexual instinct is unfavorable to the achievement of absolute gratification." [2] The

[1] " The Most Prevalent Form of Degradation in Erotic Life," in Collected Papers (London: Hogarth Press, 1950), IV, 213.
[2] Ibid., p. 214.

idea is ambiguous and lends itself easily to ideological justifications: the unfavorable consequences of readily available satisfaction have probably been one of the strongest props for repressive morality. Still, in the context of Freud's theory, it would follow that the " natural obstacles " in the instinct, far from denying pleasure, may function as a premium on pleasure if they are divorced from archaic taboos and exogenous constraints. Pleasure contains an element of self-determination which is the token of human triumph over blind necessity:

> Nature does not know real pleasure but only satisfaction of want. All pleasure is societal — in the unsublimated no less than in the sublimated impulses. Pleasure originates in alienation.[3]

What distinguishes pleasure from the blind satisfaction of want is the instinct's refusal to exhaust itself in immediate satisfaction, its ability to build up and use barriers for intensifying fulfillment. Though this instinctual refusal has done the work of domination, it can also serve the opposite function: eroticize non-libidinal relations, transform biological tension and relief into free happiness. No longer employed as instruments for retaining men in alienated performances, the barriers against absolute gratification would become elements of human freedom; they would protect that other alienation in which pleasure originates — man's alienation not from himself but from mere nature: his free self-realization. Men would really exist as individuals, each shaping his own life; they would face each other with truly

---

[3] " Natur kennt nicht eigentlich Genuss: sie bringt es nicht weiter als zur Stillung des Bedürfnisses. Alle Lust ist gesellschaftlich in den unsublimierten Affckten nicht weniger als in den sublimierten." Max Horkheimer and Theodor W. Adorno, *Dialektik der Aufklärung* (Amsterdam: Querido Verlag, 1947), p. 127.

different needs and truly different modes of satisfaction — with their own refusals and their own selections. The ascendancy of the pleasure principle would thus engender antagonisms, pains, and frustrations — individual conflicts in the striving for gratification. But these conflicts would themselves have libidinal value: they would be permeated with the rationality of gratification. This *sensuous* rationality contains its own moral laws.

The idea of a libidinal morality is suggested not only by Freud's notion of instinctual barriers to absolute gratification, but also by psychoanalytic interpretations of the superego. It has been pointed out that the superego, as the mental representative of morality, is not unambiguously the representative of the reality principle, especially of the forbidding and punishing father. In many cases, the superego seems to be in secret alliance with the id, defending the claims of the id against the ego and the external world. Charles Odier therefore proposed that a part of the superego is " in the last analysis the representative of a primitive phase, during which morality had not yet freed itself from the pleasure principle." [4] He speaks of a pregenital, prehistoric, pre-oedipal " pseudo-morality " prior to the acceptance of the reality principle, and calls the mental representative of this " pseudo-morality " the *superid*. The psychical phenomenon which, in the individual, suggests such a pregenital morality is an identification with the mother, expressing itself in a castration-wish rather than castration-threat. It might be the survival of a regressive

[4] "Vom Ueber-Ich," in *Internationale Zeitschrift für Psychoanalyse,* XII (1926), 280–281.

tendency: remembrance of the primal Mother-Right, and at the same time a " symbolic means against losing the then prevailing privileges of the woman." According to Odier, the pregenital and prehistorical morality of the superid is incompatible with the reality principle and therefore a neurotic factor.

One more step in the interpretation, and the strange traces of the " superid " appear as traces of a different, lost reality, or lost relation between ego and reality. The notion of reality which is predominant in Freud and which is condensed in the reality principle is " bound up with the father." It confronts the id and the ego as a hostile, external force, and, accordingly, the father is chiefly a hostile figure, whose power is symbolized in the castration-threat, " directed against the gratification of libidinal urges toward the mother." The growing ego attains maturity by complying with this hostile force: " submission to the castration threat " is the " decisive step in the establishment of the ego as based on the reality principle." [5] However, this reality which the ego faces as an outside antagonistic power is neither the only nor the primary reality. The development of the ego is development " away from primary narcissism "; at this early stage, reality " is not outside, but is contained in the pre-ego of primary narcissism." It is not hostile and alien to the ego, but " intimately connected with, originally not even distinguished from it." [6] This reality is first (and last?) experienced in the child's libidinal relation to the mother — a relation which is at the beginning within

[5] Hans W. Loewald, "Ego and Reality," in *International Journal of Psychoanalysis*, Vol. XXXII (1951), Part I, p. 12.
[6] *Ibid.*

the "pre-ego" and only subsequently divorced from it. And with this division of the original unity, an "urge towards re-establishing the original unity" develops: a "libidinal flow between infant and mother." [7] At this primary stage of the relation between "pre-ego" and reality, the Narcissistic and the maternal Eros seem to be one, and the primary experience of reality is that of a libidinous union. The Narcissistic phase of individual pre-genitality "recalls" the maternal phase of the history of the human race. Both constitute a reality to which the ego responds with an attitude, not of defense and submission, but of integral identification with the "environment." But in the light of the paternal reality principle, the "maternal concept" of reality here emerging is immediately turned into something negative, dreadful. The impulse to re-establish the lost Narcissistic-maternal unity is interpreted as a "threat," namely, the threat of "maternal engulfment" by the overpowering womb. [8] The hostile father is exonerated and reappears as savior who, in punishing the incest wish, protects the ego from its annihilation in the mother. The question does not arise whether the Narcissistic-maternal attitude toward reality cannot "return" in less primordial, less devouring forms under the power of the mature ego and in a mature civilization. Instead, the necessity of suppressing this attitude once and for all is taken for granted. The patriarchal reality principle holds sway over the psychoanalytic interpretation. It is only beyond this reality principle that the "maternal" images of the super ego convey promises rather

[7] *Ibid.*, p. 11.   [8] *Ibid.*, p. 15.

than memory traces — images of a free future rather than of a dark past.

However, even if a maternal libidinal morality is traceable in the instinctual structure, and even if a sensuous rationality could make the Eros freely susceptible to order, one innermost obstacle seems to defy all project of a non-repressive development — namely, the bond that binds Eros to the death instinct. The brute fact of death denies once and for all the reality of a non-repressive existence. For death is the final negativity of time, but "joy wants eternity." Timelessness is the ideal of pleasure. Time has no power over the id, the original domain of the pleasure principle. But the ego, through which alone pleasure becomes real, is in its entirety subject to time. The mere anticipation of the inevitable end, present in every instant, introduces a repressive element into all libidinal relations and renders pleasure itself painful. This primary frustration in the instinctual structure of man becomes the inexhaustible source of all other frustrations — and of their social effectiveness. Man learns that "it cannot last anyway," that every pleasure is short, that for all finite things the hour of their birth is the hour of their death — that it couldn't be otherwise. He is resigned before society forces him to practice resignation methodically. The flux of time is society's most natural ally in maintaining law and order, conformity, and the institutions that relegate freedom to a perpetual utopia; the flux of time helps men to forget what was and what can be: it makes them oblivious to the better past and the better future.

This ability to forget — itself the result of a long and terrible education by experience — is an indispensable requirement of mental and physical hygiene without which civilized life would be unbearable; but it is also the mental faculty which sustains submissiveness and renunciation. To forget is also to forgive what should not be forgiven if justice and freedom are to prevail. Such forgiveness reproduces the conditions which reproduce injustice and enslavement: to forget past suffering is to forgive the forces that caused it — without defeating these forces. The wounds that heal in time are also the wounds that contain the poison. Against this surrender to time, the restoration of remembrance to its rights, as a vehicle of liberation, is one of the noblest tasks of thought. In this function, remembrance (*Erinnerung*) appears at the conclusion of Hegel's *Phenomenology of the Spirit*; in this function, it appears in Freud's theory.[9] Like the ability to forget, the ability to remember is a product of civilization — perhaps its oldest and most fundamental psychological achievement. Nietzsche saw in the training of memory the beginning of civilized morality — especially the memory of obligations, contracts, dues.[10] This context reveals the one-sidedness of memory-training in civilization: the faculty was chiefly directed toward remembering duties rather than pleasures; memory was linked with bad conscience, guilt, and sin. Unhappiness and the threat of punishment, not happiness and the promise of freedom, linger in memory.

Without release of the repressed content of memory, without release of its liberating power, non-repressive sublimation is unimaginable. From the myth of Orpheus to

[9] See Chapter 1 above.   [10] *Genealogy of Morals*, Part II, 1–3.

the novel of Proust, happiness and freedom have been
linked with the idea of the recapture of time: the *temps
retrouvé*. Remembrance retrieves the *temps perdu*, which
was the time of gratification and fulfillment. Eros, penetrating into consciousness, is moved by remembrance; with it
he protests against the order of renunciation; he uses memory in his effort to defeat time in a world dominated by
time. But in so far as time retains its power over Eros,
happiness is essentially a thing of the *past*. The terrible
sentence which states that only the lost paradises are the
true ones judges and at the same time rescues the *temps
perdu*. The lost paradises are the only true ones not because, in retrospect, the past joy seems more beautiful than
it really was, but because remembrance alone provides the
joy without the anxiety over its passing and thus gives it an
otherwise impossible duration. Time loses its power when
remembrance redeems the past.

Still, this defeat of time is artistic and spurious; remembrance is no real weapon unless it is translated into historical action. Then, the struggle against time becomes a decisive moment in the struggle against domination:

> The conscious wish to break the continuum of history belongs
> to the revolutionary classes in the moment of action. This con-
> sciousness asserted itself during the July Revolution. In the eve-
> ning of the first day of the struggle, simultaneously but independ-
> ently at several places, shots were fired at the time pieces on the
> towers of Paris.[11]

It is the alliance between time and the order of repression
that motivates the efforts to halt the flux of time, and it
is this alliance that makes time the deadly enemy of Eros.

[11] Walter Benjamin, "Ueber den Begriff der Geschichte," in *Die Neue
Rundschau* (1950), p. 568.

To be sure, the threat of time, the passing of the moment of fullness, the anxiety over the end, may themselves become erotogenic — obstacles that "swell the tide of the libido." However, the wish of Faust which conjures the pleasure principle demands, not the beautiful moment, but eternity. With its striving for eternity, Eros offends against the decisive taboo that sanctions libidinal pleasure only as a temporal and controlled condition, not as a permanent fountainhead of the human existence. Indeed, if the alliance between time and the established order dissolved, "natural" private unhappiness would no longer support organized societal unhappiness. The relegation of human fulfillment to utopia would no longer find adequate response in the instincts of man, and the drive for liberation would assume that terrifying force which actually it never had. Every sound reason is on the side of law and order in their insistence that the eternity of joy be reserved for the hereafter, and in their endeavor to subordinate the struggle against death and disease to the never-ceasing requirements of national and international security.

The striving for the preservation of time in time, for the arrest of time, for conquest of death, seems unreasonable by any standard, and outright impossible under the hypothesis of the death instinct that we have accepted. Or does this very hypothesis make it more reasonable? The death instinct operates under the Nirvana principle: it tends toward that state of "constant gratification" where no tension is felt — a state without want. This trend of the instinct implies that its *destructive* manifestations would be minimized as it approached such a state. If the instinct's

basic objective is not the termination of life but of pain —
the absence of tension — then paradoxically, in terms of the
instinct, the conflict between life and death is the more reduced, the closer life approximates the state of gratification.
Pleasure principle and Nirvana principle then converge.
At the same time, Eros, freed from surplus-repression,
would be strengthened, and the strengthened Eros would,
as it were, absorb the objective of the death instinct. The
instinctual value of death would have changed: if the instincts pursued and attained their fulfillment in a non-
repressive order, the regressive compulsion would lose much
of its biological rationale. As suffering and want recede,
the Nirvana principle may become reconciled with the
reality principle. The unconscious attraction that draws
the instincts back to an " earlier state " would be effectively
counteracted by the desirability of the attained state of life.
The " conservative nature " of the instincts would come to
rest in a fulfilled present. Death would cease to be an instinctual goal. It remains a fact, perhaps even an ultimate
necessity — but a necessity against which the unrepressed
energy of mankind will protest, against which it will wage
its greatest struggle.

In this struggle, reason and instinct could unite. Under
conditions of a truly human existence, the difference between succumbing to disease at the age of ten, thirty, fifty,
or seventy, and dying a " natural " death after a fulfilled
life, may well be a difference worth fighting for with all instinctual energy. Not those who die, but those who die
before they must and want to die, those who die in agony
and pain, are the great indictment against civilization.

They also testify to the unredeemable guilt of mankind. Their death arouses the painful awareness that it was unnecessary, that it could be otherwise. It takes all the institutions and values of a repressive order to pacify the bad conscience of this guilt. Once again, the deep connection between the death instinct and the sense of guilt becomes apparent. The silent "professional agreement" with the fact of death and disease is perhaps one of the most widespread expressions of the death instinct — or, rather, of its social usefulness. In a repressive civilization, death itself becomes an instrument of repression. Whether death is feared as constant threat, or glorified as supreme sacrifice, or accepted as fate, the education for consent to death introduces an element of surrender into life from the beginning — surrender and submission. It stifles "utopian" efforts. The powers that be have a deep affinity to death; death is a token of unfreedom, of defeat. Theology and philosophy today compete with each other in celebrating death as an existential category: perverting a biological fact into an ontological essence, they bestow transcendental blessing on the guilt of mankind which they help to perpetuate — they betray the promise of utopia. In contrast, a philosophy that does not work as the handmaiden of repression responds to the fact of death with the Great Refusal — the refusal of Orpheus the liberator. Death can become a token of freedom. The necessity of death does not refute the possibility of final liberation. Like the other necessities, it can be made rational — painless. Men can die without anxiety if they know that what they love is protected from misery and oblivion. After a fulfilled life, they may take it upon themselves to die — at a moment of their own choosing. But even the ultimate advent of freedom cannot redeem those who died in pain. It is the remembrance of them, and the accumulated guilt of mankind against its victims, that darken the prospect of a civilization without repression.

Critique of Neo-Freudian Revisionism

Psychoanalysis has changed its function in the culture of our time, in accordance with fundamental social changes that occurred during the first half of the century. The collapse of the liberal era and of its promises, the spreading totalitarian trend and the efforts to counteract this trend, are reflected in the position of psychoanalysis. During the twenty years of its development prior to the First World War, psychoanalysis elaborated the concepts for the psychological critique of the most highly praised achievement of the modern era: the individual. Freud demonstrated that constraint, repression, and renunciation are the stuff from which the " free personality " is made; he recognized the " general unhappiness " of society as the unsurpassable limit of cure and normality. Psychoanalysis was a radically critical theory. Later, when Central and Eastern Europe were in revolutionary upheaval, it became clear to what extent psychoanalysis was still committed to the society whose secrets it revealed. The psychoanalytic conception of man, with its belief in the basic unchangeability of human nature, appeared as " reactionary "; Freudian theory seemed to imply that the humanitarian ideals of socialism were humanly unattainable. Then the revisions of psychoanalysis began to gain momentum.

It might be tempting to speak of a split into a left and right wing. The most serious attempt to develop the critical social theory implicit in Freud was made in Wilhelm Reich's earlier writings. In his *Einbruch der Sexualmoral* (1931), Reich oriented psychoanalysis on the relation between the social and instinctual structures. He emphasized the extent to which sexual repression is enforced by the interests of domination and exploitation, and the extent to which these interests are in turn reinforced and reproduced by sexual repression. However, Reich's notion of sexual repression remains undifferentiated; he neglects the historical dynamic of the sex instincts and of their fusion with the destructive impulses. (Reich rejects Freud's hypothesis of the death instinct and the whole depth dimension revealed in Freud's late metapsychology.) Consequently, sexual liberation *per se* becomes for Reich a panacea for individual and social ills. The problem of sublimation is minimized; no essential distinction is made between repressive and non-repressive sublimation, and progress in freedom appears as a mere release of sexuality. The critical sociological insights contained in Reich's earlier writings are thus arrested; a sweeping primitivism becomes prevalent, foreshadowing the wild and fantastic hobbies of Reich's later years.

On the " right wing " of psychoanalysis, Carl Jung's psychology soon became an obscurantist pseudo-mythology.[1]

[1] See Edward Glover, *Freud or Jung?* (New York: W. W. Norton, 1950).

The "center" of revisionism took shape in the cultural and interpersonal schools — the most popular trend of psychoanalysis today. We shall try to show that, in these schools, psychoanalytic theory turns into ideology: the "personality" and its creative potentialities are resurrected in the face of a reality which has all but eliminated the conditions for the personality and its fulfillment. Freud recognized the work of repression in the highest values of Western civilization — which presuppose and perpetuate unfreedom and suffering. The Neo-Freudian schools promote the very same values as cure against unfreedom and suffering — as the triumph over repression. This intellectual feat is accomplished by expurgating the instinctual dynamic and reducing its part in the mental life. Thus purified, the psyche can again be redeemed by idealistic ethics and religion; and the psychoanalytic theory of the mental apparatus can be rewritten as a philosophy of the soul. In doing so, the revisionists have discarded those of Freud's psychological tools that are incompatible with the anachronistic revival of philosophical idealism — the very tools with which Freud uncovered the explosive instinctual *and* social roots of the personality. Moreover, secondary factors and relationships (of the mature person and its cultural environment) are given the dignity of primary processes — a switch in orientation designed to emphasize the influence of the social reality on the formation of the personality. However, we believe that the exact opposite happens — that the impact of society on the psyche is weakened. Whereas Freud, focusing on the vicissitudes of the primary instincts, discovered society in the most concealed layer of the genus and individual man, the revisionists, aiming at the reified, ready-made form rather than at the origin of the societal institutions and relations, fail to comprehend what these institutions and relations have done to the personality that they are supposed to fulfill.   Confronted with the revisionist schools, Freud's theory now assumes a new significance: it reveals more than ever before the depth of its criticism, and — perhaps for the first time — those of its elements that transcend the prevailing order and link the theory of repression with that of its abolition.

The strengthening of this link was the initial impulse behind the revisionism of the cultural school.   Erich Fromm's early articles attempt to free Freud's theory from its identification with present-day society; to sharpen the psychoanalytic notions that reveal the connection between instinctual and economic structure; and at the same time to indicate the possibility of progress beyond the " patricentric-acquisitive " culture.   Fromm stresses the sociological substance of Freud's theory: psychoanalysis understands the socio-psychological phenomena as

. . . processes of active and passive adjustment of the instinctual apparatus to the socio-economic situation.   The instinctual apparatus itself is — in certain of its foundations — a biological datum, but to a high degree modifiable; the economic conditions are the primary modifying factors.[2]

Underlying the societal organization of the human existence are basic libidinal wants and needs; highly plastic and pliable, they are shaped and utilized to " cement " the given society.   Thus, in what Fromm calls the " patricentric-

[2] " Ueber Methode und Aufgabe einer analytischen Sozialpsychologie," in Zeitschrift für Sozialforschung, I (1932), 39–40.

acquisitive " society (which, in this study, is defined in terms of the rule of the performance principle), the libidinal impulses and their satisfaction (and deflection) are coordinated with the interests of domination and thereby become a stabilizing force which binds the majority to the ruling minority. Anxiety, love, confidence, even the will to freedom and solidarity with the group to which one belongs [3] — all come to serve the economically structured relationships of domination and subordination. By the same token, however, fundamental changes in the social structure will entail corresponding changes in the instinctual structure. With the historical obsolescence of an established society, with the growth of its inner antagonisms, the traditional mental ties are loosening:

Libidinal forces become free for new forms of utilization and thus change their social function. Now they no longer contribute to the preservation of society but lead to the building of new social formations; they cease, as it were, to be cement and instead become dynamite.[4]

Fromm followed up this conception in his article on " The Socio-psychological Significance of the Theory of Matriarchy." [5] Freud's own insights into the historical character of the modifications of the impulses vitiate his equation of the reality principle with the norms of patricentric-acquisitive culture. Fromm emphasizes that the idea of a matricentric culture — regardless of its anthropological merit — envisions a reality principle geared not to the interest of domination, but to gratified libidinal relations among

[3] *Ibid.*, pp. 51, 47.
[4] *Ibid.*, p. 53.
[5] In *Zeitschrift für Sozialforschung*, Vol. III (1934).

men. The instinctual structure demands rather than precludes the rise of a free civilization on the basis of the achievements of patricentric culture, but through the transformation of its institutions:

> Sexuality offers one of the most elemental and strongest possibilities of gratification and happiness. If these possibilities were allowed within the limits set by the need for the productive development of the personality rather than by the need for the domination of the masses, the fulfillment of this one fundamental possibility of happiness would of necessity lead to an increase in the claim for gratification and happiness in other spheres of the human existence. The fulfillment of this claim requires the availability of the material means for its satisfaction and must therefore entail the explosion of the prevailing social order.[6]

The social content of Freudian theory becomes manifest: sharpening the psychoanalytical concepts means sharpening their critical function, their opposition to the prevailing form of society. And this critical sociological function of psychoanalysis derives from the fundamental role of sexuality as a " productive force "; the libidinal claims propel progress toward freedom and universal gratification of human needs beyond the patricentric-acquisitive stage. Conversely, the weakening of the psychoanalytic conception, and especially of the theory of sexuality, must lead to a weakening of the sociological critique and to a reduction of the social substance of psychoanalysis. Contrary to appearance, this is what has happened in the cultural schools. Paradoxically (but only apparently paradoxically), such development was the consequence of the improvements in therapy. Fromm has devoted an admirable paper to " The Social Conditions of Psychoanalytic Therapy," in which he

[6] *Ibid.*, p. 215.

shows that the psychoanalytic situation (between analyst and patient) is a specific expression of liberalist toleration and as such dependent on the existence of such toleration in the society. But behind the tolerant attitude of the " neutral " analyst is concealed " respect for the social taboos of the bourgeoisie." [7] Fromm traces the effectiveness of these taboos at the very core of Freudian theory, in Freud's position toward sexual morality. With this attitude, Fromm contrasts another conception of therapy, first perhaps formulated by Ferenczi, according to which the analyst rejects patricentric-authoritarian taboos and enters into a positive rather than neutral relation with the patient. The new conception is characterized chiefly by an " unconditional affirmation of the patient's claim for happiness " and the " liberation of morality from its tabooistic features." [8]

However, with these demands, psychoanalysis faces a fateful dilemma. The " claim for happiness," if truly affirmed, aggravates the conflict with a society which allows only controlled happiness, and the exposure of the moral taboos extends this conflict to an attack on the vital protective layers of society. This may still be practicable in a social environment where toleration is a constitutive element of personal, economic, and political relationships; but it must endanger the very idea of " cure " and even the very existence of psychoanalysis when society can no longer afford such toleration. The affirmative attitude toward the claim for happiness then becomes practicable only if happiness and the " productive development of the personality "

---

[7] *Zeitschrift für Sozialforschung,* IV (1935), 374–375.
[8] *Ibid.,* p. 395.

are redefined so that they become compatible with the prevailing values, that is to say, if they are internalized and idealized. And this redefinition must in turn entail a weakening of the explosive content of psychoanalytic theory as well as of its explosive social criticism. If this is indeed (as I think) the course that revisionism has taken, then it is because of the objective social dynamic of the period: in a repressive society, individual happiness and productive development are in contradiction to society; if they are defined as values to be realized within this society, they become themselves repressive.

The subsequent discussion is concerned only with the later stages of Neo-Freudian psychology, where the regressive features of the movement appear as predominant. The discussion has no other purpose than to throw into relief, by contrast, the critical implications of psychoanalytic theory emphasized in this study; the *therapeutic* merits of the revisionist schools are entirely outside the scope of this discussion. This limitation is enforced not only by my own lack of competence but also by a discrepancy between theory and therapy inherent in psychoanalysis itself. Freud was fully aware of this discrepancy, which may be formulated (much oversimplified) as follows: while psychoanalytic theory recognizes that the sickness of the individual is ultimately caused and sustained by the sickness of his civilization, psychoanalytic therapy aims at curing the individual so that he can continue to function as part of a sick civilization without surrendering to it altogether. The acceptance of the reality principle, with which psychoanalytic therapy ends, means the individual's acceptance of the civilized regimentation of his instinctual needs, especially sexuality. In Freud's theory, civilization appears as established in contradiction to the primary instincts and to the pleasure principle. But the latter survives in the id, and the civilized ego must permanently fight its own timeless past and forbidden future. Theoretically, the difference between mental health and neurosis lies only in the degree and effectiveness of resignation: mental health is successful, efficient resignation — normally so efficient that it shows forth as moderately happy satisfaction. Normality is a precarious condition. "Neurosis and psychosis are both of them an expression of the rebellion of the id against the outer world, of its 'pain,' unwillingness to adapt itself to necessity — to ananke, or, if one prefers, of its incapacity to do so." [9] This rebellion, although originating in the instinctual "nature" of man, is a disease that has to be cured — not only because it is struggling against a hopelessly superior power, but because it is struggling against "necessity." Repression and unhappiness *must be* if civilization is to prevail. The "goal" of the pleasure principle — namely, to be happy — "is not attainable," [10] although the effort to attain it shall not and cannot be abandoned. In the long run, the question is only how much resignation the individual can bear without breaking up. In this sense, therapy is a course in resignation: a great deal will be gained if we succeed in "transforming your hysterical misery into every-

[9] "The Loss of Reality in Neurosis and Psychosis," in *Collected Papers* (London: Hogarth Press, 1950), II, 279.
[10] *Civilization and Its Discontents* (London: Hogarth Press, 1949), p. 39.

day unhappiness," which is the usual lot of mankind.[11] This aim certainly does not (or should not) imply that the patient becomes capable of adjusting completely to an environment repressive of his mature aspirations and abilities. Still, the analyst, as a physician, must accept the social framework of facts in which the patient has to live and which he cannot alter.[12] This irreducible core of conformity is further strengthened by Freud's conviction that the repressive basis of civilization cannot be changed anyway — not even on the supra-individual, societal scale. Consequently, the critical insights of psychoanalysis gain their full force only in the field of theory, and perhaps particularly where theory is farthest removed from therapy — in Freud's " metapsychology."

The revisionist schools obliterated this discrepancy between theory and therapy by assimilating the former to the latter. This assimilation took place in two ways. First, the most speculative and " metaphysical " concepts not subject to any clinical verification (such as the death instinct, the hypothesis of the primal horde, the killing of the primal father and its consequences) were minimized or discarded altogether. Moreover, in this process some of Freud's most decisive concepts (the relation between id and ego, the function of the unconscious, the scope and significance of sexuality) were redefined in such a way that their explosive connotations were all but eliminated. The depth dimen-

[11] Breuer and Freud, *Studies in Hysteria* (New York: Nervous and Mental Disease Monograph No. 61, 1936), p. 232. See also A *General Introduction to Psychoanalysis* (New York: Garden City Publishing Co., 1943), pp. 397-398.

[12] See *New Introductory Lectures* (New York: W. W. Norton, 1933), p. 206.

sion of the conflict between the individual and his society, between the instinctual structure and the realm of consciousness, was flattened out. Psychoanalysis was reoriented on the traditional consciousness psychology of pre-Freudian texture. The right to such reorientations in the interest of successful therapy and practice is not questioned here; but the revisionists have converted the weakening of Freudian theory into a new theory, and the significance of this theory alone will be discussed presently. The discussion will neglect the differences among the various revisionist groups and concentrate on the theoretical attitude common to all of them. It is distilled from the representative works of Erich Fromm, Karen Horney, and Harry Stack Sullivan. Clara Thompson [13] is taken as a representative historian of the revisionists.

The chief objections of the revisionists to Freud may be summed up as follows: Freud grossly underrated the extent to which the individual and his neurosis are determined by conflicts with his environment. Freud's "biological orientation" led him to concentrate on the phylogenetic and ontogenetic *past* of the individual: he considered the character as essentially fixed with the fifth or sixth year (if not earlier), and he interpreted the fate of the individual in terms of primary instincts and their vicissitudes, especially sexuality. In contrast, the revisionists shift the emphasis "from the past to the present," [14] from the biological to the cultural level, from the "constitution" of the

[13] *Psychoanalysis: Evolution and Development* (New York: Hermitage House, 1951).

[14] Thompson, *Psychoanalysis*, pp. 15, 182.

individual to his environment.[15] " One can understand the biological development better if one discards the concept of libido altogether " and instead interprets the different stages " in terms of growth and of human relations." [16] Then the subject of psychoanalysis becomes the " total personality " in its " relatedness to the world "; and the " constructive aspects of the individual," his " productive and positive potentialities," receive the attention they deserve. Freud was cold, hard, destructive, and pessimistic. He did not see that sickness, treatment, and cure are a matter of " interpersonal relationships " in which total personalities are engaged on both sides. Freud's conception was predominantly relativistic: he assumed that psychology can " help us to understand the motivation of value judgments but cannot help in establishing the validity of the value judgments themselves." [17] Consequently, his psychology contained no ethics or only his personal ethics. Moreover, Freud saw society as " static " and thought that society developed as a " mechanism for controlling man's instincts," whereas the revisionists know " from the study of comparative cultures " that " man is not biologically endowed with dangerous fixed animal drives and that the only function of society is to control these." They insist that society " is not a static set of laws instituted in the past at the time of the murder of the primal father, but is rather a growing, changing, developing network of interpersonal experiences and behavior." To this, the following insights are added:

[15] *Ibid.*, pp. 9, 13, 26–27, 155.
[16] *Ibid.*, p. 42.
[17] Erich Fromm, *Man for Himself* (New York and Toronto: Rinehart, 1947), p. 34.

One cannot become a human being except through cultural experience. Society creates new needs in people. Some of the new needs lead in a constructive direction and stimulate further development. Of such a nature are the ideas of justice, equality and cooperation. Some of the new needs lead in a destructive direction and are not good for man. Wholesale competitiveness and the ruthless exploitation of the helpless are examples of destructive products of culture. When the destructive elements predominate, we have a situation which fosters war.[18]

This passage may serve as a starting point to show the decline of theory in the revisionist schools. There is first the laboring of the obvious, of everyday wisdom. Then there is the adduction of sociological aspects. In Freud they are included in and developed by the basic concepts themselves; here they appear as incomprehended, external factors. There is furthermore the distinction between good and bad, constructive and destructive (according to Fromm: productive and unproductive, positive and negative), which is not derived from any theoretical principle but simply taken from the prevalent ideology. For this reason, the distinction is merely eclectic, extraneous to theory, and tantamount to the conformist slogan "Accentuate the positive." Freud was right; life is bad, repressive, destructive — but it isn't so bad, repressive, destructive. There are also the constructive, productive aspects. Society is not only this, but also that; man is not only against himself but also for himself.

These distinctions are meaningless and — as we shall try to show even wrong unless the task (which Freud took upon himself) is fulfilled: to demonstrate how, under the impact of civilization, the two "aspects" are interrelated

18 Thompson, *Psychoanalysis*, p. 143.

in the instinctual dynamic itself, and how the one inevitably turns into the other by virtue of this dynamic. Short of such demonstration, the revisionist "improvement" of Freud's "one-sidedness" constitutes a blank discarding of his fundamental theoretical conception. However, the term *eclecticism* does not adequately express the substance of the revisionist philosophy. Its consequences for psychoanalytic theory are much graver: the revisionist "supplementation" of Freudian theory, especially the adduction of cultural and environmental factors, consecrates a false picture of civilization and particularly of present-day society. In minimizing the extent and the depth of the conflict, the revisionists proclaim a false but easy solution. We shall give here only a brief illustration.

One of the most cherished demands of the revisionists is that the "total personality" of the individual — rather than his early childhood, or his biological structure, or his psychosomatic condition — must be made the subject of psychoanalysis:

The infinite diversity of personalities is in itself characteristic of human existence. By personality I understand the totality of inherited and acquired psychic qualities which are characteristic of one individual and which make the individual unique.[19]

I think it is clear that Freud's conception of counter-transference is to be distinguished from the present-day conception of analysis as an interpersonal process. In the interpersonal situation, the analyst is seen as relating to his patient not only with his distorted affects but with his healthy personality also. That is, the analytic situation is essentially a human relationship.[20]

[19] Erich Fromm, *Man for Himself*, p. 50.
[20] Clara Thompson, *Psychoanalysis*, p. 108.

The preconception to which I am leading is this: personality tends toward the state that we call mental health or interpersonal adjustive success, handicaps by way of acculturation notwithstanding. The basic direction of the organism is forward.[21]

Again, the obvious ("diversity of personalities"; analysis as an "interpersonal process"), because it is not comprehended but merely stated and used, becomes a half-truth which is false since the missing half changes the content of the obvious fact.

The quoted passages testify to the confusion between ideology and reality prevalent in the revisionist schools. It is true that man appears as an individual who "integrates" a diversity of inherited and acquired qualities into a total personality, and that the latter develops in relating itself to the world (things and people) under manifold and varying conditions. But this personality and its development are *pre*-formed down to the deepest instinctual structure, and this pre-formation, the work of accumulated civilization, means that the diversities and the autonomy of individual "growth" are secondary phenomena. How much reality there is behind individuality depends on the scope, form, and effectiveness of the repressive controls prevalent at the given stage of civilization. The autonomous personality, in the sense of creative "uniqueness" and fullness of its existence, has always been the privilege of a very few. At the present stage, the personality tends toward a standardized reaction pattern established by the hierarchy of power and functions and by its technical, intellectual, and cultural apparatus.

---

[21] Harry Stack Sullivan, *Conceptions of Modern Psychiatry* (Washington: William Alanson White Psychiatric Foundation, 1947), p. 48.

The analyst and his patient share this alienation, and since it does not usually manifest itself in any neurotic symptom but rather as the hallmark of " mental health," it does not appear in the revisionist consciousness. When the process of alienation is discussed, it is usually treated, not as the whole that it is, but as a negative aspect of the whole.[22] To be sure, personality has not disappeared: it continues to flower and is even fostered and educated — but in such a way that the expressions of personality fit and sustain perfectly the socially desired pattern of behavior and thought. They thus tend to cancel individuality. This process, which has been completed in the " mass culture " of late industrial civilization, vitiates the concept of inter-personal relations if it is to denote more than the undeni-able fact that all relations in which the human being finds itself are either relations to other persons or abstractions from them. If, beyond this truism, the concept implies more — namely, that " two or more persons come to de-fine an integrated situation " which is made up of " indi-viduals "[23] — then the implication is fallacious. For the individual situations are the derivatives and appearances of the *general* fate, and, as Freud has shown, it is the latter which contains the clue to the fate of the individual. The general repressiveness shapes the individual and universal-izes even his most personal features. Accordingly, Freud's theory is consistently oriented on early infancy — the forma-

[22] Compare Erich Fromm's discussion of the " marketing orientation," in *Man for Himself*, pp. 67ff.
[23] Ernest Beaglehole, " Interpersonal Theory and Social Psychology," in A *Study in Interpersonal Relations*, ed. Patrick Mullahy (New York: Hermitage Press, 1950), p. 54.

tive period of the universal fate in the individual. The subsequent mature relations "re-create" the formative ones. The decisive relations are thus those which are the *least* interpersonal. In an alienated world, specimens of the genus confront each other: parent and child, male and female, then master and servant, boss and employee; they are interrelated at first in specific modes of the universal alienation. If and when they cease to be so and grow into truly personal relations, they still retain the universal repressiveness which they surmount as their mastered and comprehended negative. Then, they do not require treatment.

Psychoanalysis elucidates the universal in the individual experience. To that extent, and only to that extent, can psychoanalysis break the reification in which human relations are petrified. The revisionists fail to recognize (or fail to draw the consequences from) the actual state of alienation which makes the person into an exchangeable function and the personality into an ideology. In contrast, Freud's basic "biologistic" concepts reach beyond the ideology and its reflexes: his refusal to treat a reified society as a "developing network of interpersonal experiences and behavior" and an alienated individual as a "total personality" corresponds to the reality and contains its true notion. If he refrains from regarding the inhuman existence as a passing negative aspect of forward-moving humanity, he is more humane than the good-natured, tolerant critics who brand his "inhuman" coldness. Freud does not readily believe that the "basic direction of the organism is forward." Even without the hypothesis of the death instinct and of the conservative nature of the instincts, Sullivan's proposition is shallow and questionable. The " basic " direction of the organism appears as a quite different one in the persistent impulses toward relief of tension, toward fulfillment, rest, passivity — the struggle against the progress of time is intrinsic not only to the Narcissistic Eros. The sadomasochistic tendencies can hardly be associated with a forward direction in mental health, unless " forward " and " mental health " are redefined to mean almost the opposite of what they are in our social order — " a social order which is in some ways grossly inadequate for the development of healthy and happy human beings." [24] Sullivan refrains from such a redefinition; he makes his concepts conform with conformity:

The person who believes that he *voluntarily* cut loose from his earlier moorings and *by choice* accepted new dogmata, in which he has diligently indoctrinated himself, is quite certain to be a person who has suffered great insecurity. He is often a person whose self-organization is derogatory and hateful. The new movement has given him group support for the expression of ancient personal hostilities that are now directed against the group from which he has come. The new ideology rationalizes destructive activity to such effect that it seems almost, if not quite, constructive. The new ideology is especially palliative of conflict in its promise of a better world that is to rise from the debris to which the present order must first be reduced. In this Utopia, he and his fellows will be good and kind — for them will be no more injustice, and so forth. If his is one of the more radical groups, the activity of more remote memory in the synthesis of decisions and choice may be suppressed almost completely, and the activity of prospective revery channelled rigidly in the dogmatic pattern. In this case, except for his dealings with his fellow radicals, the man may act as if he had acquired the psychopathic type of personality discussed

[24] Patrick Mullahy, introduction to *A Study of Interpersonal Relations*, page xvii.

in the third lecture. He shows no durable grasp of his own reality or that of others, and his actions are controlled by the most immediate opportunism, without consideration of the probable future.[25]

The passage illuminates the extent to which the interpersonal theory is fashioned by the values of the *status quo*. If a person has " cut loose from his earlier moorings " and " accepted new dogmata," the presumption is that he has " suffered great insecurity," that his " self-organization is hateful and derogatory," that his new creed " rationalizes destructive activity " — in short, that he is the psychopathic type. There is no suggestion that his insecurity is rational and reasonable, that not his self-organization but the others' is derogatory and hateful, that the destructiveness involved in the new dogma might indeed be constructive in so far as it aims at a higher stage of realization. This psychology has no other objective standards of value than the prevailing ones: health, maturity, achievement are taken as they are defined by the given society — in spite of Sullivan's awareness that, in our culture, maturity is " often no particular reflection on anything more than one's socioeconomic status and the like." [26] Deep conformity holds sway over this psychology, which suspects all those who " cut loose from their earlier moorings " and become " radicals " as neurotic (the description fits all of them, from Jesus to Lenin, from Socrates to Giordano Bruno), and which almost automatically identifies the " promise of a better world " with " Utopia," its substance with " revery," and

[25] Sullivan, *Conceptions of Modern Psychiatry*, p. 96. See Helen Merrel Lynd's review in *The Nation*, January 15, 1949.

[26] *The Interpersonal Theory of Psychiatry* (New York: W. W. Norton, 1953), p. 298.

mankind's sacred dream of justice for all with the personal resentment (no more injustice " for them ") of maladjusted types. This " operational " identification of mental health with "adjustive success" and progress eliminates all the reservations with which Freud hedged the therapeutic objective of adjustment to an inhuman society [27] and thus commits psychoanalysis to this society far more than Freud ever did.

Behind all the differences among the historical forms of society, Freud saw the basic inhumanity common to all of them, and the repressive controls which perpetuate, in the instinctual structure itself, the domination of man by man. By virtue of this insight Freud's " static concept of society " is closer to the truth than the dynamic sociological concepts supplied by the revisionists. The notion that " civilization and its discontent " had their roots in the biological constitution of man profoundly influenced his concept of the function and goal of therapy. The personality which the individual is to develop, the potentialities which he is to realize, the happiness which he is to attain — they are regimented from the very beginning, and their content can be defined only in terms of this regimentation. Freud destroys the illusions of idealistic ethics: the " personality " is but a " broken " individual who has internalized and successfully utilized repression and aggression. Considering what civilization has made of man, the difference in the development of personalities is chiefly that between an unproportional and a proportional share of that " everyday unhappiness "

[27] See Freud's statement in A *General Introduction to Psychoanalysis*, pp. 332–333.

which is the common lot of mankind. The latter is all that therapy can achieve.

Over and against such a " minimum program," Fromm and the other revisionists proclaim a higher goal of therapy: " optimal development of a person's potentialities and the realization of his individuality." Now it is precisely this goal which is essentially unattainable — not because of limitations in the psychoanalytic techniques but because the established civilization itself, in its very structure, denies it. Either one defines " personality " and " individuality " in terms of their possibilities *within* the established form of civilization, in which case their realization is for the vast majority tantamount to successful adjustment. Or one defines them in terms of their transcending content, including their socially denied potentialities beyond (and beneath) their actual existence; in this case, their realization would imply transgression, beyond the established form of civilization, to radically new modes of " personality " and " individuality " incompatible with the prevailing ones. Today, this would mean " curing " the patient to become a rebel or (which is saying the same thing) a martyr. The revisionist concept vacillates between the two definitions. Fromm revives all the time-honored values of idealistic ethics as if nobody had ever demonstrated their conformist and repressive features. He speaks of the productive realization of the personality, of care, responsibility, and respect for one's fellow men, of productive love and happiness — as if man could actually practice all this and still remain sane and full of " well-being " in a society which Fromm himself describes as one of total alienation, dominated by the commodity relations of the " market." In such a society, the self-realization of the " personality " can proceed only on the basis of a double repression: first, the " purification " of the pleasure principle and the internalization of happiness and freedom; second, their reasonable restriction until they become compatible with the prevailing unfreedom and unhappiness. As a result, productiveness, love, responsibility become " values " only in so far as they contain manageable resignation and are practiced within the framework of socially useful activities (in other words, after repressive sublimation); and then they involve the effective denial of free productiveness and responsibility — the renunciation of happiness.

For example, productiveness, proclaimed as the goal of the healthy individual under the performance principle, must normally (that is, outside the creative, " neurotic," and " eccentric " exceptions) show forth in good business, administration, service, with the reasonable expectation of recognized success. Love must be semi-sublimated and even inhibited libido, staying in line with the sanctioned conditions imposed on sexuality. This is the accepted, " realistic " meaning of productiveness and love. But the very same terms also denote the *free* realization of man, or the idea of such realization. The revisionist usage of these terms plays on this ambiguity, which designates both the unfree and the free, both the mutilated and the integral faculties of man, thus vesting the established reality principle with the grandeur of promises that can be redeemed only *beyond* this reality principle. This ambiguity makes the revisionist philosophy appear to be critical where it is con-

formist, political where it is moralistic. Often, the *style*
alone betrays the attitude. It would be revealing to make a
comparative analysis of the Freudian and Neo-Freudian
styles. The latter, in the more philosophical writings, fre-
quently comes close to that of the sermon, or of the social
worker; it is elevated and yet clear, permeated with good-
will and tolerance and yet moved by an *esprit de sérieux*
which makes transcendental values into facts of everyday
life. What has become a sham is taken as real. In contrast, there is a strong undertone of irony in Freud's usage
of "freedom," "happiness," "personality"; either these
terms seem to have invisible quotation marks, or their negative content is explicitly stated. Freud refrains from calling
repression by any other name than its own; the Neo-
Freudians sometimes sublimate it into its opposite.

But the revisionist combination of psychoanalysis with
idealistic ethics is not simply a glorification of adjustment.
The Neo-Freudian sociological or cultural orientation provides the other side of the picture — the "not only but also."
The therapy of adjustment is rejected in the strongest
terms; [28] the "deification" of success is denounced.[29] Present-day society and culture are accused of greatly impeding
the realization of the healthy and mature person; the principle of "competitiveness, and the potential hostility that
accompanies it, pervades all human relationships." [30] The
revisionists claim that their psychoanalysis is in itself a
critique of society:

[28] Fromm, *Psychoanalysis and Religion* (New Haven: Yale University
Press, 1950), pp. 73ff.
[29] *Ibid.*, p. 119.
[30] Karen Horney, *The Neurotic Personality of Our Time* (New York:
W. W. Norton, 1937), p. 284.

The aim of the " cultural school " goes beyond merely enabling man to submit to the restrictions of his society; in so far as it is possible it seeks to free him from its irrational demands and make him more able to develop his potentialities and to assume leadership in building a more constructive society.[31]

The tension between health and knowledge, normality and freedom, which animated Freud's entire work, here disappears; a qualifying " in so far as it is possible " is the only trace left of the explosive contradiction in the aim. " Leadership in building a more constructive society " is to be combined with normal functioning in the established society.

This philosophy is achieved by directing the criticism against surface phenomena, while accepting the basic premises of the criticized society. Fromm devotes a large part of his writing to the critique of the " market economy " and its ideology, which place strong barriers in the way of productive development.[32] But here the matters rests. The critical insights do not lead to a transvaluation of the values of productiveness and the " higher self " — which are exactly the values of the criticized culture. The character of the revisionist philosophy shows forth in the assimilation of the positive and the negative, the promise and its betrayal. The affirmation absorbs the critique. The reader may be left with the conviction that the " higher values " can and should be practiced within the very conditions which betray them; and they can be practiced because the revisionist philosopher accepts them in their adjusted and idealized form — on the terms of the established reality principle.

[31] Clara Thompson, *Psychoanalysis*, p. 152.
[32] Fromm, *Man for Himself*, especially pp. 67ff, 127–128.

Fromm, who has demonstrated the repressive features of internalization as few other analysts have done, revives the ideology of internalization. The "adjusted" person is blamed because he has betrayed the "higher self," the "human values"; therefore he is haunted by "inner emptiness and insecurity" in spite of his triumph in the "battle for success." Far better off is the person who has attained "inner strength and integrity"; though he may be less successful than his "unscrupulous neighbor,"

. . . he will have security, judgment, and objectivity which will make him much less vulnerable to changing fortunes and opinions of others and will in many areas enhance his ability for constructive work.[33]

The style suggests the Power of Positive Thinking to which the revisionist critique succumbs. It is not the values that are spurious, but the context in which they are defined and proclaimed: " inner strength " has the connotation of that unconditional freedom which can be practiced even in chains and which Fromm himself once denounced in his analysis of the Reformation.[34]

If the values of " inner strength and integrity " are supposed to be anything more than the character traits that the alienated society expects from any good citizen in his business (in which case they merely serve to sustain alienation), then they must pertain to a consciousness that has broken through the alienation as well as its values. But to such consciousness these values themselves become intolerable because it recognizes them as accessories to the enslavement of man. The " higher self " reigns over the domesticated

[33] Fromm, *Psychoanalysis and Religion*, p. 75.
[34] *Escape from Freedom* (New York: Rinehart, 1941), pp. 74ff.

impulses and aspirations of the individual, who has sacrificed and renounced his " lower self " not only in so far as it is incompatible with civilization but in so far as it is incompatible with repressive civilization. Such renunciation may indeed be an indispensable step on the road of human progress. However, Freud's question — whether the higher values of culture have not been achieved at too great a cost for the individual — should be taken seriously enough to enjoin the psychoanalytic philosopher from preaching these values without revealing their forbidden content, without showing what they have *denied* to the individual. What this omission does to psychoanalytic theory may be illustrated by contrasting Fromm's idea of love with Freud's. Fromm writes:

> Genuine love is rooted in productiveness and may properly be called, therefore, " productive love." Its essence is the same whether it is the mother's love for the child, our love for man, or the erotic love between two individuals . . . certain basic elements may be said to be characteristic of all forms of productive love. These are care, responsibility, respect, and knowledge.[35]

Compare with this ideological formulation Freud's analysis of the instinctual ground and underground of love, of the long and painful process in which sexuality with all its polymorphous perversity is tamed and inhibited until it ultimately becomes susceptible to fusion with tenderness and affection — a fusion which remains precarious and never quite overcomes its destructive elements. Compare with Fromm's sermon on love Freud's almost incidental remarks in " The Most Prevalent Form of Degradation in Erotic Life":

[35] *Man for Himself,* p. 98.

. . . we shall not be able to deny that the behavior in love of
the men of present-day civilization bears in general the character
of the psychically impotent type. In only very few people of culture are the two strains of tenderness and sensuality duly fused
into one: the man almost always feels his sexual activity hampered
by his respect for the woman and only develops full sexual potency
when he finds himself in the presence of a lower type of sexual
object . . .[86]

According to Freud, love, in our culture, can and must be
practiced as "aim-inhibited sexuality," with all the taboos
and constraints placed upon it by a monogamic-patriarchal
society. Beyond its legitimate manifestations, love is destructive and by no means conducive to productiveness and constructive work. Love, taken seriously, is outlawed: "There
is no longer any place in present-day civilized life for a
simple natural love between two human beings."[87] But
to the revisionists, productiveness, love, happiness, and
health merge in grand harmony; civilization has not caused
any conflicts between them which the mature person could
not solve without serious damage.

Once the human aspirations and their fulfillment are internalized and sublimated to the "higher self," the social
issues become primarily spiritual issues, and their solution
becomes a *moral* task. The sociological concreteness of
the revisionists reveals itself as surface: the decisive struggles
are fought out in the "soul" of man. Present-day authori-
tarianism and the "deification of the machine and of success" threaten the "most precious spiritual possessions" of
man.[88] The revisionist minimization of the biological

[86] *Collected Papers*, IV, 210.
[87] *Civilization and Its Discontents*, p. 77 note.
[88] Fromm, *Psychoanalysis and Religion*, p. 119.

sphere, and especially of the role of sexuality, shifts the emphasis not only from the unconscious to consciousness, from the id to the ego, but also from the presublimated to the sublimated expressions of the human existence. As the repression of instinctual gratification recedes into the background and loses its decisive importance for the realization of man, the depth of societal repression is reduced. Consequently, the revisionist emphasis on the influence of "social conditions" in the development of the neurotic personality is sociologically and psychologically far more inconsequential than Freud's "neglect" of these conditions. The revisionist mutilation of the instinct theory leads to the traditional devaluation of the sphere of material needs in favor of spiritual needs. Society's part in the regimentation of man is thus played down; and in spite of the outspoken critique of some social institutions, the revisionist sociology accepts the foundation on which these institutions rest.

Neurosis, too, appears as an essentially *moral* problem, and the individual is held responsible for the failure of his self-realization. Society, to be sure, receives a share of the blame, but, in the long run, it is man himself who is at fault:

> Looking at his creation, he can say, truly, it is good. But looking at himself what can he say? . . . While we have created wonderful things we have failed to make of ourselves beings for whom this tremendous effort would seem worthwhile. Ours is a life not of brotherliness, happiness, contentment but of spiritual chaos and bewilderment.[39]

[39] Fromm, *Psychoanalysis and Religion*, p. 1.

The disharmony between society and the individual is stated and left alone. Whatever society may do to the individual, it prevents neither him nor the analyst from concentrating on the " total personality " and its productive development. According to Horney, society creates certain typical difficulties which, "accumulated, may lead to the formation of neuroses." [40] According to Fromm, the negative impact of society upon the individual is more serious, but this is only a challenge to practice productive love and productive thinking. The decision rests with man's " ability to take himself, his life and happiness seriously; on his willingness to face his and his society's moral problem. It rests upon his courage to be himself and to be for himself." [41] In a period of totalitarianism, when the individual has so entirely become the subject-object of manipulation that, for the " healthy and normal " person, even the idea of a distinction between being " for himself " and " for others " has become meaningless, in a period when the omnipotent apparatus punishes real non-conformity with ridicule and defeat — in such a situation the Neo-Freudian philosopher tells the individual to be himself and for himself. To the revisionist, the brute fact of societal repression has transformed itself into a " moral problem " — as it has done in the conformist philosophy of all ages. And as the clinical fact of neurosis becomes, " in the last analysis, a symptom of moral failure," [42] the " psychoanalytic cure of the soul " becomes education in the attainment of a " religious " attitude.[43]

[40] *The Neurotic Personality*, p. 284.
[41] *Man for Himself*, p. 250.
[42] *Man for Himself*, page viii.
[43] *Psychoanalysis and Religion*, p. 76.

The escape from psychoanalysis to internalized ethics and religion is the consequence of this revision of psychoanalytic theory. If the " wound " in the human existence is not operative in the biological constitution of man, and if it is not caused and sustained by the very structure of civilization, then the depth dimension is removed from psychoanalysis, and the (ontogenetic and phylogenetic) conflict between pre-individual and supra-individual forces appears as a problem of the rational or irrational, the moral or immoral behavior of conscious individuals. The substance of psychoanalytic theory lies not simply in the discovery of the role of the unconscious but in the description of its specific instinctual dynamic, of the vicissitudes of the two basic instincts. Only the history of these vicissitudes reveals the full depth of the oppression which civilization imposes upon man. If sexuality does not play the constitutional role which Freud attributed to it, then there is no fundamental conflict between the pleasure principle and the reality principle; man's instinctual nature is " purified " and qualified to attain, without mutilation, socially useful and recognized happiness. It was precisely because he saw in sexuality the representative of the integral pleasure principle that Freud was able to discover the common roots of the " general " as well as neurotic unhappiness in a depth far below all individual experience, and to recognize a primary " constitutional " repression underlying all consciously experienced and administered repression. He took this discovery very seriously — much too seriously to identify happiness with its efficient sublimation in productive love and other productive activities. Therefore he considered a civilization oriented on the realization of happiness as a catastrophe, as the end of all civilization. For Freud, an enormous gulf separated real freedom and happiness from the pseudo freedom and happiness that are practiced and preached in a repressive civilization. The revisionists see no such difficulty. Since they have spiritualized freedom and happiness, they can say that " the problem of production has been virtually solved": [44]

Never before has man come so close to the fulfillment of his most cherished hopes as today. Our scientific discoveries and technical achievements enable us to visualize the day when the table will be set for all who want to eat . . .[45]

These statements are true — but only in the light of their contradiction: precisely because man has never come so close to the fulfillment of his hopes, he has never been so strictly restrained from fulfilling them; precisely because we can visualize the universal satisfaction of individual needs, the strongest obstacles are placed in the way of such satisfaction. Only if the sociological analysis elucidates this connection does it go beyond Freud; otherwise it is merely an inconsequential adornment, purchased at the expense of mutilating Freud's theory of instincts.

Freud had established a substantive link between human freedom and happiness on the one hand and sexuality on the other: the latter provided the primary source for the former and at the same time the ground for their necessary restriction in civilization. The revisionist solution of the conflict through the spiritualization of freedom and happiness demanded the weakening of this link. Therapeutic findings may have motivated the theoretical reduction in

[44] Fromm, *Man for Himself*, p. 140.
[45] Fromm, *Psychoanalysis and Religion*, p. 1.

the role of sexuality; but such a reduction was in any case indispensable for the revisionist philosophy.

> Sexual problems, although they may sometimes prevail in the symptomatic picture, are no longer considered to be in the dynamic center of neuroses. Sexual difficulties are the effect rather than the cause of the neurotic character structure. Moral problems on the other hand gain in importance.[46]

This conception does far more than minimize the role of the libido; it reverses the inner direction of Freudian theory. Nowhere does this become clearer than in Fromm's reinterpretation of the Oedipus complex, which tries to " translate it from the sphere of sex into that of interpersonal relations." [47] The gist of this " translation " is that the essence of the incest wish is not " sexual craving " but the desire to remain protected, secure — a child. " The foetus lives with and from the mother, and the act of birth is only one step in the direction of freedom and independence." True — but the freedom and independence to be gained are (if at all) afflicted with want, resignation, and pain; and the act of birth is the first and most terrifying step in the direction *away from* satisfaction and security. Fromm's ideological interpretation of the Oedipus complex implies acceptance of the unhappiness of freedom, of its separation from satisfaction; Freud's theory implies that the Oedipus wish is the eternal infantile *protest* against this separation — protest not against freedom but against painful, repressive freedom. Conversely, the Oedipus wish is the eternal infantile desire

---

[46] Horney, *New Ways in Psychoanalysis* (New York: W. W. Norton, 1939), p. 10.

[47] *Psychoanalysis and Religion*, pp. 79ff. See also Fromm's more sophisticated interpretation in *The Forgotten Language* (New York: Rinehart, 1951), pp. 231–235.

for the archetype of freedom: freedom from want. And since the (unrepressed) sex instinct is the biological carrier of this archetype of freedom, the Oedipus wish is essentially "sexual craving." Its natural object is, not simply the mother *qua* mother, but the mother *qua* woman — female principle of gratification. Here the Eros of receptivity, rest, painless and integral satisfaction is nearest to the death instinct (return to the womb), the pleasure principle nearest to the Nirvana principle. Eros here fights its first battle against everything the reality principle stands for: against the father, against domination, sublimation, resignation. Gradually then, freedom and fulfillment are being associated with these paternal principles; freedom from want is sacrificed to moral and spiritual independence. It is first the "sexual craving" for the mother-woman that threatens the psychical basis of civilization; it is the "sexual craving" that makes the Oedipus conflict the prototype of the instinctual conflicts between the individual and his society. If the Oedipus wish were in essence nothing more than the wish for protection and security ("escape from freedom"), if the child desired only impermissible security and not impermissible pleasure, then the Oedipus complex would indeed present an essentially educational problem. As such, it can be treated without exposing the instinctual danger zones of society.

The same beneficial result is obtained by the rejection of the death instinct. Freud's hypothesis of the death instinct and its role in civilized aggression shed light on one of the neglected enigmas of civilization; it revealed the hidden unconscious tie which binds the oppressed to their oppressors, the soldiers to their generals, the individuals to their masters. The wholesale destruction marking the progress of civilization within the framework of domination has been perpetuated, in the face of its possible abolition, by the instinctual agreement with their executioners on the part of the human instruments and victims. Freud wrote, during the First World War:

> Think of the colossal brutality, cruelty and mendacity which is now allowed to spread itself over the civilized world. Do you really believe that a handful of unprincipled placehunters and corrupters of men would have succeeded in letting loose all this latent evil, if the millions of their followers were not also guilty? [48]

But the impulses which this hypothesis assumes are incompatible with the moralistic philosophy of progress espoused by the revisionists. Karen Horney states succinctly the revisionist position:

> Freud's assumption [of a Death Instinct] implies that the ultimate motivation for hostility or destructiveness lies in the impulse to destroy. Thus he turns into its opposite our belief that we destroy in order to live: we live in order to destroy. [49]

This rendering of Freud's conception is incorrect. He did not assume that we live in order to destroy; the destruction instinct operates either against the life instincts or in their service; moreover, the objective of the death instinct is not destruction *per se* but the elimination of the need for destruction. According to Horney, we wish to destroy because we "are or feel endangered, humiliated, abused," because we want to defend "our safety or our happiness or what appears to us as such." No psychoanalytic theory

---

[48] *A General Introduction to Psychoanalysis*, pp. 130–131.
[49] *New Ways in Psychoanalysis*, pp. 130–131.

was necessary to arrive at these conclusions, with which individual and national aggression has been justified since times immemorial. Either our safety is really threatened, in which case our wish to destroy is a sensible and rational reaction; or we only " feel " it is threatened, in which case the individual and supra-individual reasons for this feeling have to be explored.

The revisionist rejection of the death instinct is accompanied by an argument that indeed seems to point up the " reactionary " implications of Freudian theory as contrasted with the progressive sociological orientation of the revisionists. Freud's assumption of a death instinct

. . . paralyzes any effort to search in the specific cultural conditions for reasons which make for destructiveness. It must also paralyze efforts to change anything in these conditions. If man is inherently destructive and consequently unhappy, why strive for a better future? [50]

The revisionist argument minimizes the degree to which, in Freudian theory, impulses are modifiable, subject to the " vicissitudes " of history. The death instinct and its derivatives are no exception. We have suggested that the energy of the death instinct does not necessarily " paralyze " the efforts to obtain a " better future "; on the contrary, such efforts are paralyzed by the systematic constraints which civilization places on the life instincts, and by their consequent inability to " bind " aggression effectively. The realization of a " better future " involves far more than the elimination of the bad features of the " market," of the " ruthlessness " of competition, and so on; it involves a fundamental change in the instinctual as well as cultural

[50] *New Ways in Psychoanalysis*, p. 132.

structure. The striving for a better future is " paralyzed "
not by Freud's awareness of these implications but by the
revisionist " spiritualization " of them, which conceals the
gap that separates the present from the future. Freud did
not believe in prospective social changes that would alter
human nature sufficiently to free man from external and internal oppression; however, his " fatalism " was not without
qualification.

The mutilation of the instinct theory completes the
reversal of Freudian theory. The inner direction of the latter was (in apparent contrast to the " therapeutic program "
from id to ego) that from consciousness to the unconscious, from personality to childhood, from the individual to
the generic processes. Theory moved from the surface
to the depth, from the " finished " and conditioned person
to its sources and resources. This movement was essential
for Freud's critique of civilization: only by means of the
" regression " behind the mystifying forms of the mature
individual and his private and public existence did he discover their basic negativity in the foundations on which
they rest. Moreover, only by pushing his critical regression
back to the deepest biological layer could Freud elucidate
the explosive content of the mystifying forms and, at the
same time, the full scope of civilized repression. Identify-
ing the energy of the life instincts as libido meant defining
their gratification in contradiction to spiritual transcenden-
talism: Freud's notion of happiness and freedom is em-
inently critical in so far as it is materialistic — protesting
against the spiritualization of want.

The Neo-Freudians reverse this inner direction of Freud's

theory, shifting the emphasis from the organism to the personality, from the material foundations to the ideal values. Their various revisions are logically consistent: one entails the next. The whole may be summed up as follows: The " cultural orientation " encounters the societal institutions and relationships as finished products, in the form of objective entities — given rather than made facts. Their acceptance in this form demands the shift in psychological emphasis from infancy to maturity, for only at the level of developed consciousness does the cultural environment become definable as determining character and personality over and above the biological level. Conversely, only with the playing down of biological factors, the mutilation of the instinct theory, is the personality definable in terms of objective cultural values divorced from the repressive ground which denies their realization. In order to present these values as freedom and fulfillment, they have to be purged of the material of which they are made, and the struggle for their realization has to be turned into a spiritual and moral struggle. The revisionists do not insist, as Freud did, on the enduring truth value of the instinctual needs which must be " broken " so that the human being can function in interpersonal relations. In abandoning this insistence, from which psychoanalytic theory drew all its critical insights, the revisionists yield to the negative features of the very reality principle which they so eloquently criticize.

Index